A decade of social development in Latin America, 1990-1999

A decade of social development in Latin America, 1990-1999

UNITED NATIONS

ECLAC

Economic Commission for Latin America and the Caribbean
(ECLAC)

Santiago, Chile, April 2004

Libros de la CEPAL

The work of the editorial staff for this book was coordinated by José Antonio Ocampo, former Executive Secretary of ECLAC; Rolando Franco, Director of the Social Development Division; and Pedro Sáinz, former Director of the Statistics and Economic Projections Division. Also on the editorial staff were Arturo León, Juan Carlos Feres, Adolfo Gurrieri and Ernesto Espíndola. The data were processed by the Statistics and Economic Projections Division and the Social Development Division.

This book takes up some of the issues analysed in various annual editions of the *Social Panorama of Latin America* published in the 1990s. The people who contributed to these analyses are, in alphabetical order: Irma Arriagada, Mariluz Avendaño, Rosa Bravo, Mabel Bullemore, Carlos Daroch, Hubert Escaith, Ernesto Espíndola, Vicente Espinoza, Juan Carlos Feres, Rolando Franco, Alvaro Fuentes, Pascual Gerstenfeld, Adolfo Gurrieri, Martín Hopenhayn, Carlos Howe, Rubén Kaztman, Arturo León, Xavier Mancero, Fernando Medina, José Antonio Ocampo, Enrique Ordaz, Roberto Pizarro, Gert Rosenthal, Pedro Sáinz, José Luis Suárez and Tito Velasco.

Cover design: Mariana Babarovic

United Nations publication
ISBN: 92-1-121434-3
LC/G.2212-P
Original: SPANISH
Sales No. E.03.II.G.143

Contents

Index of tables and figures

Tables

Figures

Preface

One of the basic functions of ECLAC is to monitor the economic and social situation of the countries of the region and to analyse changes in the public policies they implement in these areas. These studies take the form of institutional publications of various kinds, including conference documents and annual reports.

The social aspects of the countries' development and their interrelationship with the economic aspects have been analysed in the various editions of the *Social Panorama of Latin America* prepared by the Social Development Division and the Statistics and Economic Projections Division.

This book takes up some of the issues dealt with most often in the *Social Panorama*, revisiting them on the basis of updated, systematized statistical information that provides an overview of the trends that characterized the 1990s. Most of the statistics come from the Commission's databases, which consist of information from household surveys conducted in the Latin American countries and made available to ECLAC by those countries' governments.

The data used in preparing the chapter on social spending are based on official information provided by 17 countries of the region on the functional classification of public expenditure. This information is systematized in the database on social spending.

It should be mentioned that input for the preparation of the *Social Panorama* was provided on a number of occasions by the United Nations Children's Fund (UNICEF), the United Nations Population Fund (UNFPA) and the World Food Programme (WFP).

José Luis Machinea
Executive Secretary
Economic Commission for
Latin America and the Caribbean (ECLAC)

Summary

The final decade of the twentieth century was a momentous one for Latin America, as it witnessed sweeping changes that represented a turning point with regard to previous trends in the region. The most important of these changes were the revival of economic growth and the reduction of poverty in the initial years of that period. Another significant phenomenon was the impact of international crises on the Latin American countries, especially in the second half of the decade.

This book analyses what happened in the countries between 1990 and 1999 and revisits issues of interest to ECLAC, using the same approach that has characterized the *Social Panorama of Latin America*.

The analysis begins with a look at a number of "objective" dimensions —poverty, income distribution, employment, occupational stratification, the role of education, the intergenerational transmission of opportunities for achieving well-being and the contribution of social spending to the improvement of the population's standard of living— and at the interrelationships between these dimensions and economic growth. It also uses the findings of opinion polls carried out in many of the countries to describe the Latin American population's subjective reactions to the changes that took place in the 1990s.

This interplay between objective dimensions and subjective individual responses is particularly relevant today, given the need to take all these factors into account in tackling the challenges of the social development agenda in the coming years, with a view to building a new commitment to that agenda among the citizenry and rallying support for the public policies implemented to foster growth and increase equity.

Introduction

The final decade of the twentieth century was a momentous one for Latin America. In the first seven years of the decade the region's economy grew at a relatively brisk pace, ending a lengthy stretch of recession and stagnation. The region's vulnerability to sudden changes in the international economy was revealed, however, by the impact of the Asian crisis, which destabilized its economy and dragged down growth in the final years of the decade. The effects of this retreat were felt in many of the Latin American countries, and the persistence of this situation has prompted analysts to assert that the period from 1997 to 2002 represented another lost half-decade for the region.

This book attempts to present a balanced view of what happened in the 1990s in terms of social development, understood as the changes that occur in the social structure and in the processes of social mobility that take place within that structure.

Specifically, the analysis seeks to answer the following questions: How did levels of well-being change, especially in population sectors that are hard put to meet their basic needs? How wide are the inequalities between individuals and groups, especially in terms of income distribution? What has happened with respect to employment, which has traditionally been regarded as a key point of linkage between the economic and social structures? What changes have occurred in labour-market participation, which is a determinant of social stratification? And lastly, to what extent has the State fostered social integration, as measured by the amount of resources allocated to social policies and programmes?

Below is a summary of the analyses presented in this book. The concluding section reviews how Latin Americans perceive the economic and social changes that took place in the region in the 1990s and, finally, enumerates some of the pending tasks on the regional agenda.

1.   Poverty

While the proportion of poor people out of the total population went down in most of the countries in the 1990s, the size of the poor population swelled from 200 million to 211 million. Changes in poverty rates were largely determined by fluctuations in economic growth. There was, however, a sharp disparity between the effects of boom and bust periods, in that the increase in poverty that resulted from episodes of recession was not completely offset during subsequent growth spurts.

Poverty rates fell in 11 countries —which are home to most of the region's poor population—, rose sharply in one country and stayed more or less the same in three countries.

In terms of the spatial distribution of poverty, the relative share of urban poverty continued to expand. Rural poverty is more extreme, however, as most of the rural poor are indigent (46 million people), whereas most of the urban poor are not (91 million). The rural poverty rate is still very high, as 64% of rural residents are poor, compared to 37% of urban residents.

In the first half of the decade most of the countries saw their economies pick up, with the notable exceptions of Argentina, Mexico and Uruguay, owing to the crisis of 1994-1995. The South American countries posted feeble growth (or contraction, in some cases) for several years after 1997. Conversely, the Mexican and Central American economies expanded considerably between 1996 and 2000. Owing in part to these disparities, progress in reducing poverty was very uneven in the different countries, with some of them even experiencing setbacks towards the end of the decade.

Throughout the decade, upturns or downturns in per capita income were closely correlated with decreases or increases in poverty. This pattern was especially evident in extreme cases, notably those of Chile and Venezuela. At the same time, there were significant departures from this general trend, as countries with similar growth rates made very disparate degrees of progress in reducing poverty. In Chile, for example, per capita gross domestic product (GDP) surged by 55% between 1990 and 2000, resulting in a 50% decline (16 percentage points) in poverty, while in Uruguay poverty showed a steeper relative decrease (53%, or

6 percentage points) over the same period, even though the rise in per capita GDP was much smaller (28%).

The growth of labour productivity was uneven across different sectors, segments and firms. Among firms, growth in labour productivity tended to be confined mainly to very big companies linked to the international economy, although these companies generated few new jobs.[1] At the same time, low-productivity employment, mostly in the informal sector, expanded in nearly all the countries. Because of this phenomenon, the open unemployment rate, although it remained high throughout the decade, cannot provide a complete picture of the labour market's effects on poverty.

Labour market conditions differed sharply from one country to another. In Brazil and Mexico, for example, open unemployment was relatively low and employment density was high. In Argentina, meanwhile, unemployment was high and employment density was low among low-income households, but earned income was higher in this country than in Brazil or Mexico.

Since earned income accounts for the bulk of household resources,[2] low earned income is a major determinant of poverty. Be that as it may, changes in relative prices over the course of the decade tended to boost the purchasing power of low-income groups, as the cost of the minimum consumption basket, and particularly of food, went down in most of the countries.[3]

Public transfers played a vital role in reducing the incidence or intensity of poverty. Transfers exceeded 20% of total urban household income in Argentina, Costa Rica, Panama and Uruguay, and represented about 10% in Brazil, Chile, Colombia, Ecuador, Mexico and Venezuela.

The level and distribution of urban and rural poverty were also affected by rural-to-urban migration. As might be expected, the fact that most migrants from the countryside to the cities were young people meant that the proportion of the population represented by this age group shrank in rural areas and expanded in urban areas, changing the population pyramid in both places. In Brazil, for example, 67.5% of the

---

[1]　Most new jobs in big companies went to highly qualified workers, who, as a result, earn relatively high wages.

[2]　Urban households in all economic strata obtain almost 70% of their income from the labour market. In turn, 66% of household income from work consists of wages and salaries.

[3]　In some countries the favourable effect of this trend was partly offset by a jump in utility rates (water, electricity, urban transport), which rose faster than the average consumer price index in those countries.

urban population is between the ages of 15 and 64, whereas the proportion drops to 60.4% in rural areas. In Bolivia only 3.4% of the urban population is 65 or over, as against 5.1% in rural areas.

In short, the region's sluggish economic growth and the trends observed in its labour market were generally not conducive to poverty reduction.

2. Income distribution

The highly unequal income distribution that has long been typical of Latin America stayed the same or worsened in most of the countries in the 1990s. It should be noted that some 75% of the region's households have below-average income levels. In the 1990s the proportion of national income that went to households in the top income decile increased in eight countries, decreased in five —although the decrease was significant in only two (Honduras and Uruguay)— and remained unchanged in one (Mexico). This increase in the share of the richest households was observed even in countries that have historically had better income distribution, such as Argentina, Costa Rica and Venezuela. In Uruguay the share of the top decile was smaller in 1999 than it had been in 1990, but expanded from 26% to 27% between 1997 and 1999.

Various situations were observed with respect to the share of total income that went to households in the bottom 40% of the income distribution: this share contracted in five countries, expanded in eight and held steady in one (Nicaragua). The most dramatic downturns were seen in Ecuador and Venezuela, and coincided in both cases with acute crises, but Costa Rica, El Salvador and Mexico also experienced setbacks. What improvements there were did not amount to significant changes; only in Colombia, between 1994 and 1997, did the improvement exceed two percentage points, although it was followed by a slight deterioration between 1997 and 1999.

Among the 50% of the region's households that fell somewhere between the poorest 40% and the richest 10%, the changes observed were different from the ones that took place in the groups at either end of the spectrum. In at least seven countries this group's share did not increase or decrease by more than two percentage points. Only in El Salvador (between 1995 and 1999), Honduras and Uruguay did the amount of income that went to these households grow appreciably. In Brazil and Ecuador these middle strata lost over three percentage points, to the benefit of households in the high-income bracket, while the loss in Argentina amounted to 2.6 percentage points. Despite these fluctuations, the trends observed in the middle strata's relative income show that in a number of countries, these groups have ways of defending their share of total income.

The countries with the biggest increases in their Gini coefficients were Costa Rica and Venezuela. Argentina (greater Buenos Aires) and Ecuador (urban areas) also suffered setbacks, while the opposite occurred in Colombia (between 1994 and 1999), Honduras and urban areas of Uruguay.

There is no clear correlation between development level and income distribution. This is apparent from the cases of Argentina and Uruguay, both of which have high income levels compared to the rest of the region and historically similar patterns of income distribution. Despite these common features, by the end of the decade there were striking differences between these countries in terms of the structure and trends of income distribution. In some countries income distribution remained largely the same throughout the 1980s and 1990s, while in others it changed substantially. In the 1960s Argentina and Chile had had remarkably well balanced income distribution, but by the late 1990s their distribution patterns were no better than the regional average. In contrast, Costa Rica and Uruguay continue to exhibit more egalitarian income distribution, notwithstanding the economic upheavals of the past few years. In Venezuela, too, inequality is still below the regional average, despite the crisis that broke out in the second half of the 1990s.

The primary factors affecting income distribution include education, property ownership, demographic characteristics and employment density. With respect to the first factor, it may be said in general that the higher the level of education, the higher the income, although the two variables are not directly proportional to one another. It should be borne in mind that education, measured by the number of years of schooling, is highly concentrated in the region and that this concentration has had a negative impact on income distribution.

The distribution of the second factor —property ownership— is also highly concentrated, to the point where the average income derived from it coincides with the observed value in the seventh, eighth or ninth income decile, depending on the country. The concentration of property ownership could become a determining factor in reproducing inequalities and affording different people unequal opportunities for achieving well-being.

With respect to the third factor, demographic characteristics have an enormous impact on income distribution. On average, poor households have more members than non-poor households, as well as low earned income and high demographic dependency ratios owing to the large number of members, with the result that such households' per capita income is low.

Lastly, with respect to employment density, a comparison between the top and bottom deciles of the income distribution in terms of the ratio of income earners to the total number of household members shows that the top decile's capacity to generate earned income is at least twice that of the bottom decile.

3.   Employment

In the 1990s wide disparities were observed between rural and urban areas in terms of the growth of the economically active population (EAP). These differences were largely due to migration: the rural EAP grew by only 0.8%, while the urban EAP expanded by 3.3%.

Demographic trends were also influenced by international emigration, whose impact was especially strong in Mexico and the Central American countries. Were it not for this outflow of workers, the EAP of the countries concerned might have expanded substantially, at least in those countries where large-scale emigration dates back 20 years or more.

The annual growth of the region's economy was 3.2% in the 1990s, while that of the EAP was 2.6% and that of employment, 2.2%. At the same time, average labour productivity increased over the previous decade's level. Some negative developments were also observed, however; for example, despite the slower growth of the EAP, employment expanded at a rate 0.4% lower than the one recorded in the 1980s. Towards the end of the decade employment showed a renewed tendency to grow faster than GDP (1.6% versus 1.3%, respectively), with the result that average labour productivity showed negative growth and spurious labour absorption increased. This was compounded by a widening of the gap between the EAP and the employed EAP (0.8%), even though EAP growth slowed to 2.4%. The upshot was that the region's economic performance in the 1990s did not significantly offset the negative trends of the 1980s.

The labour market's difficulty in adequately absorbing the EAP was particularly evident in urban areas, where the EAP increased by an average of 3.3% a year.

Another notable feature of employment was the increased weight of the tertiary and informal sectors. Slow economic growth was accompanied by sweeping changes in the employment structure. The relative share of employment in the primary and secondary sectors continued to shrink, while employment in commerce and services continued to expand. Productivity increased markedly in a handful of segments and sectors, but rose slowly or stayed the same in all the rest. In other words, the modernization of a few occupations was accompanied by an increase in the proportion of the workforce engaged in informal economic activities.

In fact, two thirds of the new jobs generated in urban areas were in the informal sector. This included an increase in the share of unskilled own-account workers in commerce and services (24.2%), followed by increases in the shares of workers (employers and employees) in microenterprises (18.2%), domestic workers (9.4%), unskilled own-account workers in industry and construction (8.1%) and workers engaged in primary occupations (6%).[4] This pattern was seen in most of the 17 countries studied, especially the most populous ones, such as Brazil, Colombia and Mexico. In Argentina and Chile, however, most new jobs were in the formal sector, although Argentina suffered a sharp rise in open unemployment.

Informal-sector employment in urban areas, which had represented 41% of total urban employment in 1990, accounted for 46.3% in 1999. Over the same period, the proportion of formal private-sector employees other than professionals and technicians fell from 35.9% to 29.1%, while that of public-sector employees dropped from 16% to 12.9%.

The wage gap between the formal and informal sectors widened in all the countries for which information is available. The same was true of the gap in average income between workers in these two sectors, except in Costa Rica, Honduras and Panama. Within each sector, income disparities between workers in higher-skilled and lower-skilled jobs also increased in all the countries except Argentina, although that country's situation is not fully comparable to those of the other countries owing to the upsurge in its open unemployment rate.

In the 1990s labour conditions underwent a number of changes, many of which were detrimental to workers, such as the decline in formal employment contracts; the proliferation of temporary and part-time jobs; the lack of social security coverage; the expansion of permissible grounds

---

[4]   In the formal sector, which generated 34.1% of all new jobs, the biggest increases in employment were for wage- or salary-earning professionals and technicians (20.1%), entrepreneurs and independent professionals and technicians (6.5%), wage or salary earners other than professionals and technicians (5.4%) and public-sector employees (2.1%).

for dismissal; the reduction of severance pay; and restrictions on the right to strike, collective bargaining and union membership. The increased precariousness of employment could also be seen in the lack of social protection and health insurance, primarily among workers in microenterprises, although there were significant differences between countries in this respect.

A fourth major trend was the expansion of unemployment, mainly in the South American countries. Unemployment climbed steadily in Argentina, Brazil and Colombia, although in Brazil it reached levels equivalent to only half the rates recorded in the other two countries. Unemployment also worsened in Bolivia, Chile, Ecuador, Paraguay, Uruguay and Venezuela. In Chile it did not begin to rise until 1998, after having gone down systematically since the beginning of the decade. In contrast, unemployment subsided in Mexico and most of the Central American and Caribbean countries.

4.   Occupational stratification

Latin America's employed population carries out a broad range of activities that vary widely in terms of hierarchy, social prestige and, particularly, the amount of income they generate. Access to these activities depends primarily on the degree to which a given worker possesses or controls productive assets and on his or her professional qualifications. These attributes, together with factors such as the degree of authority in the firm, the size of the firm and the branch of production to which it belongs, determine where people fit into the occupational structure and, accordingly, have a decisive impact on their living conditions and the opportunities available to them. On the basis of these criteria, occupations can be grouped into a nine-layer hierarchy, which can be split into three levels. The top level includes 10.3% of the employed workforce, and the corresponding income levels are considerably higher than those of the other occupations. The middle level encompasses 14.5% of the employed workforce, and the bottom level, the remaining 75% of employed workers, many of whom do not earn enough to keep a typical Latin American family of four above the poverty line.

The top level includes jobs involving non-manual labour that can be performed only by workers with productive assets (employers), high-level professional qualifications (professionals) or a high degree of authority in the workplace (managers). Average income from these jobs is equivalent to 12.5 times the poverty line, and the median number of years of schooling completed by workers in this category is 11.6. The middle level consists of non-manual labour requiring an intermediate degree of professional qualification or authority. These workers are supervisors, mid-level professionals, technicians or administrative workers whose average labour income is equivalent to 4.9 times the poverty line and whose median level of schooling is 11.2 years. The bottom level encompasses a variety of manual and non-manual jobs, and the workers concerned have neither productive assets nor positions of authority nor a very high level of professional qualification. As noted above, these workers make up 75% of the labour force. Their average labour income is 2.4 times the poverty line and the median number of years of schooling is 5.5. This level, in turn, can be divided into two subgroups of about the same size, which are differentiated by their income and educational levels. One group consists of workers in the commerce sector, manual workers, artisans and drivers, who have average income of 3 times the poverty line and a median of 6.5 years of schooling. The other group consists of workers in the areas of personal services and agriculture, whose average income is 1.8 times the poverty line and whose median number of years of schooling is 4.3.

The first notable feature of trends in occupational stratification in the 1990s is that the relative share of the different occupational strata remained almost unchanged, indicating that there was very little upward mobility. In countries where average labour income rose, the proportion of the workforce at the top and middle levels increased, whereas the opposite occurred in countries where average labour income fell.

The basic occupational structure described above predominates, with very few variations, in most of the Latin American countries. There is a fairly close relationship between the countries' level of economic development and the distribution of the three levels of occupational stratification. However, there are also some disparities. Chile, for example, which has the highest median labour income (7.3 times the poverty line), also has the occupational structure with the smallest bottom level, equivalent to 65.5% of its workforce. In Brazil and Mexico the proportion of the workforce at the top level —9.3% and 10%, respectively— is similar to the proportion in Guatemala and just under half the proportion in Chile. Conversely, the proportion represented by the middle level in Brazil and Mexico is similar to the equivalent proportion in Chile and more than double the proportion in Guatemala. At the bottom level, the proportion of own-account or unpaid subsistence farmers is still as high as 16% in Brazil and nearly 10% in Mexico, or three times as high as the equivalent proportion in Chile.

A second observation is that the distribution of labour income is much more unequal in Latin America than in developed countries. It is also important to note, however, that some countries in the region have similar average income levels but different degrees of inequality, while others have very different average income levels but similar degrees of inequality. One way to gauge these disparities is to look at the ratio of the income of medium-sized and large non-agricultural employers to the national average: this ratio is 2 to 1 in Costa Rica and 16 to 1 in Guatemala, as against 6 to 1 in Brazil and 11 to 1 in Mexico.

A comparison between Chile and Costa Rica, which have the highest labour income, is also illustrative. The distribution of labour income is significantly unequal in Chile, in contrast to the considerably more even distribution in Costa Rica. Levels of labour income in different sectors in Costa Rica do not depart dramatically from the national average: for example, agricultural workers in that country receive 74% of the average income, while their counterparts in Chile receive only 48%. Likewise, employers in large and medium-sized firms receive 2.2 times the average income in Costa Rica, compared to 6.8 times in Chile.

With respect to levels of education, in 1999 the combined workforce of 10 countries had a weighted average of 6.9 years of schooling. The average among professionals was 14.6 years, followed by that of directors and managers (11.7), technicians (11.5), administrative workers (10.9), employers (8.9), workers in the commerce sector (7.1), manual workers, artisans, machine operators and drivers (6.2), workers in personal and security services (5.9) and agricultural workers (3.1).

Lastly, when households are classified according to the primary breadwinner's occupation, their average per capita income reflects fairly accurately the median incomes of the different occupational strata. This indicates the importance of the main breadwinner's occupation in determining the stratification of households. However, the fact that nearly half of Latin America's households have more than one income earner influences those households' per capita income by helping to reduce, especially in the case of relatively low-paying occupations, either the intensity or the percentage of poverty, depending on the country's average income and the size of the households concerned. At the top level, the presence of more than one income earner in the household has less of an impact than it does at lower levels, since the primary breadwinner's income is usually quite high. This factor has the strongest influence at the middle level and at the upper end of the bottom level, where the average income of households with more than one income earner is usually significantly higher than that of households with a single income earner.

5.   The intergenerational transmission of opportunities for achieving well-being

Despite the efforts made in the region to provide universal access to the formal educational system, the acquisition of educational capital is still conditioned by intergenerational dynamics. The fact that educational opportunities and, consequently, access to more stable, better-paying jobs are to a large extent inherited is a key reason why current socio-economic inequalities are reproduced indefinitely in successive generations.

An individual's likelihood of receiving at least an adequate minimum level of education is largely determined by the level of education of his or her parents and by the economic capacity of his or her household of origin. Towards the end of the 1990s, some 75% of young people in urban areas came from households in which the parents had insufficient education —fewer than 10 years of schooling— and, on average, more than 45% had not finished secondary school (equivalent to 12 years of schooling in most of the countries), which today is regarded as the minimum level of education needed to achieve well-being in urban areas.

Opportunities are even more limited for young people in rural areas, since about 80% of them fail to reach what is regarded as the minimum educational level needed in rural areas: completion of primary school. Here, too, differences between households in terms of the educational environment they offer mean that young people in rural areas have unequal chances of completing primary school, although their chances of completing secondary school are even more strongly affected by this factor and, as a result, more unequal.

Differences with respect to the number of years of schooling are not the only source of inequality in the acquisition of educational capital. There is a significant gap between public and private schools in terms of the quality of the education they provide. This gap reinforces the inequalities among young people in different social strata, since the ones who complete more years of schooling are also likely to receive a higher-quality education.

Most young people with insufficient educational capital will have trouble finding a job and will have access only to low-paying jobs which, in turn, will not enable them to create the conditions needed to give their own children the minimum required level of educational capital.

Young people who are currently employed and who have completed post-secondary studies (that is, more than 12 years of schooling) can be divided into two groups. The first, which accounts for about 45% of the total, consists of professionals, technicians or managers whose median monthly income is equivalent to 6.5 times the poverty line in the case of professionals and technicians and 10 times the poverty line in the case of managers. The second group, which accounts for the other 55%, consists mainly of individuals who have completed fewer years of post-secondary schooling than the individuals in the first group. People in the second group are more likely to work as administrative employees, accountants, salespeople and dependent employees, with an average monthly income ranging from 3.5 to 5.5 times the poverty line.

In contrast, nearly 80% of urban workers with eight or fewer years of schooling are manual workers, security guards, waiters or domestic workers, whose average monthly income, at two to three times the poverty line, is not enough to guarantee family well-being. This percentage rises as countries broaden their secondary-education coverage because when the supply of qualified workers expands, less qualified workers tend to become concentrated in jobs with lower prestige, quality and pay, which generally involve manual labour. Moreover, the growing predominance, among workers who have not completed secondary school, of jobs that provide an insufficient level of well-being reflects the process of educational devaluation to which younger generations are also exposed, as the coverage and completion of more basic levels of education increase.

The intergenerational transmission of opportunities for achieving well-being is also affected by the social contacts derived from the household of origin. The vast network of contacts enjoyed by some households, along with their greater cultural capital, increase by an average of 40% the income received by young people from these households over the income of young people who lack such advantages, even when they work in the same occupational category and have a similar level of education.

Lastly, the close link between the occupational structure and income distribution, which explains the latter's resistance to change, is evident from the fact that about half of the employed members of households in the top income decile are professionals, technicians or managers whose monthly income is equivalent to about 17 times the poverty line. These workers, who account for some 5% of total employment, receive almost 21% of total income. Among workers from households in the bottom 40% of the income distribution, just under 75% are machine operators, manual workers, security guards, waiters or domestic employees. Workers in this group account for 25% of total employment but receive only 11% of total income. The occupational profile of the workforce that will continue to shape the pay structure in the future, as well as its relationship to income distribution, have already been largely defined in advance by the characteristics of workers' households of origin. This means, for example, that for the next 10 years the occupational distribution of the workforce will look much the same as it does today.

These circumstances lend weight to the argument that educational reform and social policy in general should be aimed essentially at giving children and young people in low-resource social strata more equitable access to quality education through measures such as large-scale scholarship programmes, since this is the only kind of capital they inherit. The recent upturn in the number of jobs for employees with two, three or four years of post-secondary education implies that employment opportunities for individuals with this level of education could well be on the rise. Reducing inequality in education also appears to be feasible because as individuals in the low- and middle-income strata increase their level of education, those in the high-income strata are less likely to stand out because of the number of years of schooling they have completed.

At the same time, a strategy for reducing social inequity cannot rely on education policy alone, since experience has shown that efforts in this area have been insufficient in themselves to stop the intergenerational transmission of unequal opportunity. First, changes in education policy should be closely and strategically coordinated with improvements in housing, nutrition, health and other areas that affect school performance. Second, the reduction of inequity in the short and medium terms depends on income policies, the operation of various public services and the creation of human and social capital outside the formal educational system, since it is through this channel that various kinds of productive assets are redistributed. Third, income gaps —the key factor in the reproduction of unequal opportunity— can be narrowed through measures such as minimum wages and legal reforms that safeguard employees' collective bargaining rights.

6.   Social expenditure in Latin America

The allocation of public resources to social sectors —defined, in the framework of public expenditure, as health, social assistance, social security, housing and other areas— increased considerably in the 1990s. Social spending, measured as the percentage of total public expenditure allocated to social sectors, rose from an average of US$ 360 to US$ 540 a year per capita between the beginning and the end of the decade. This represents a 50% increase.

This expansion, which took place in most of the countries, was made possible by the recovery of economic growth and by the higher fiscal priority given to social spending. Thus, social spending rose from 10.4% to 13.1% of GDP over the period, although most of the increase took place in the first half of the decade.

The 17 countries considered differ widely in terms of the percentages of GDP they have historically allocated to social sectors. Although some of the countries that boosted social spending in the 1990s had previously kept their expenditure low in this area, most of the countries' historical patterns in this regard stayed virtually the same over the course of the decade. In the countries that had traditionally had the highest levels of per capita social spending (Argentina, Brazil, Costa Rica, Panama and Uruguay), the proportion of GDP allocated to social sectors continued to be higher than expected in view of their levels of per capita income, while in countries with a history of low or very low levels of per capita social spending (such as the Dominican Republic, El Salvador, Guatemala, Paraguay and Peru), the percentage of GDP allocated to social sectors remained far below the regional average.

Notwithstanding this pronounced upturn in social spending, current levels are still too low to meet the needs of large sectors of the population. Covering these unmet needs is not an impossible goal, since most of the countries have considerable room to expand the government income base and raise expenditure on social programmes.

Although GDP fell more or less dramatically in 1999 in a number of countries, such as Argentina, Chile, Colombia, Honduras, Uruguay and Venezuela, the resources earmarked for social sectors were not affected by this slump, thanks in part to the inertia that characterizes many items of current expenditure. In 1998-1999 total public expenditure grew in nearly all the countries except Venezuela, and even in that country expenditure rebounded between 1999 and 2000, growing at nearly the same rates observed before the crisis.

It has been said that the countries of the region should better target their social spending so that it provides more direct benefits to vulnerable or poor groups. The sectors with the most progressive patterns of social spending —that is, where such spending benefits the poorest households most— are primary and secondary education, followed by health and nutrition and, in third place, housing and basic services (water and sanitation).

Overall, social spending was redistributive in all the countries, especially if social security is excluded. Not counting social security, the poorest 20% of households received 28% of public resources, while the richest 20% received 12%. This means that the poorest households received a proportion of social spending —excluding social security— which, on average, was six times their share of primary income (28.2% of social spending, compared to 4.8% of total primary income). This ratio was reversed for the richest 20% of households, with the share of social spending representing only one fourth of the share of income (12.4% of social spending versus 50.7% of total primary income).

The net redistributive effect of public social spending resulted from the relative weight of transfers of money and of free or subsidized goods and services as a share of total household income. This share was biggest by far in the poorest groups, where it accounted for 43% of household income. In the richest and second-richest income quintiles, on the other hand, it represented 7% and 13%, respectively. However, the percentage of social spending received by the richest households, though small, represented a considerable volume of resources which, in some countries, exceeded or even doubled the volume allocated to the poorest households, owing to the amount of social security transfers.

Higher social spending had the most pronounced redistributive effect in the countries with the lowest per capita income, owing to the sharp rise in public spending on education and health care. In countries with higher per capita income the redistributive effect was less significant because nearly 50% of the increase in public social spending went to social security, its least progressive component.

7.   Concluding observations

This section presents an analysis of the findings of opinion polls describing the Latin American population's reactions to developments in the 1990s. These findings reveal disappointment with the results achieved by the end of the period; dissatisfaction with the persistence of inequality, which seems to have become the population's main concern, even overtaking poverty; and displeasure with many key institutions of society, especially politics, political parties and politicians themselves. These attitudes must be taken into account in identifying the challenges of the social development agenda in the coming years. Another priority, and perhaps the most important one —because otherwise it will be hard to set these societies on the course they need to take— is to induce the citizenry to make a new commitment to political participation, since it is this participation that will steer decisions on public policies to achieve the objectives of growth with greater equity.

Other pending tasks, apart from those of further reducing poverty and eliminating indigence, include the consolidation of consumer societies and the opening of channels for social mobility.

This is clearly a very broad spectrum of challenges that must be tackled simultaneously, since they are closely intertwined.

Chapter I

Poverty

This chapter describes a number of aspects of poverty in Latin America in the 1990s. It looks at poverty trends, the asymmetrical effects of economic growth on poverty in boom and bust periods, the factors that had the most bearing on poverty, the vulnerability that poverty often entails and the particular features of rural poverty.

1. Magnitude and profile of poverty

(a) Poverty trends in the 1990s

The processes of economic recession, expansion and stagnation that the Latin American countries experienced in the 1980s and 1990s had a significant impact on the levels of poverty and indigence they recorded. Although, as the next section will show, economic performance is not the only factor that impinges on poverty and how it evolves, there is a clear link between general economic trends and the signs of this phenomenon.

Figure I.1 shows how poverty levels changed in the 1980s and 1990s, in keeping with variations in economic growth. In particular, in the 1990s the growth experienced between 1990 and 1997 and the corresponding reduction in poverty contrast with the biennium 1998-1999, when economic growth virtually stood still and poverty increased slightly.

Figure I.1
LATIN AMERICA: ANNUAL GROWTH RATES OF GROSS DOMESTIC PRODUCT (GDP)
AND OF THE POOR POPULATION, 1980-1999
(Percentages)

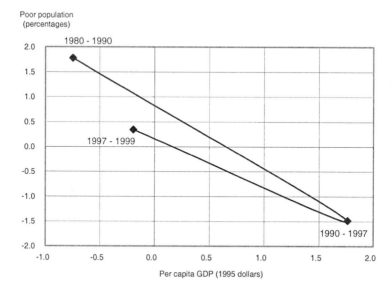

Source: ECLAC, on the basis of special tabulations of data from household surveys conducted in the respective countries.

The link between economic growth and changes in poverty percentages was patently asymmetrical from one decade to the next. In the 1980s per capita output declined by an annual average rate of just under 1%, while poverty moved upward. This increase in poverty was not completely offset in the 1990s, even though output expanded at close to 2%. In fact, the poor population represented 40.5% of the total in 1980, 48.3% in 1990 and 43.5% in 1997, then moved to 43.8% in 1999. Bearing in mind that per capita output at 1995 values dropped from US$ 3,654 in 1980 to US$ 3,342 in 1990, then rose to US$ 3,807 in 1999, the ground lost in the 1980s was only partially made up in the 1990s (see figure I.1 and table I.1).

Despite the developments of the biennium 1998-1999, the balance of the 1990s overall was positive, since poverty declined in at least 11 countries, where the majority of the region's poor live (see table I.2). For further information see tables A.1 and A.2 in the statistical appendix.

Table I.1
LATIN AMERICA: POOR AND INDIGENT HOUSEHOLDS AND INDIVIDUALS, [a] 1980-1999
(Millions of households and individuals and percentages)

	Poor [b]						Indigent [c]					
	Total		Urban		Rural		Total		Urban		Rural	
	Millions	%	Millions	%	Millions	%	Millions	%	Millions	%	Millions	%
Households												
1980	24.2	34.7	11.8	25.3	12.4	53.9	10.4	15.0	4.1	8.8	6.3	27.5
1990	39.1	41.0	24.7	35.0	14.4	58.2	16.9	17.7	8.5	12.0	8.4	34.1
1994	38.5	37.5	25.0	31.8	13.5	56.1	16.4	15.9	8.3	10.5	8.1	33.5
1997	39.4	35.5	25.1	29.7	14.3	54.0	16.0	14.4	8.0	9.5	8.0	30.3
1999	41.3	35.3	27.1	29.8	14.2	54.3	16.3	13.9	8.3	9.1	8.0	30.7
Individuals												
1980	135.9	40.5	62.9	29.8	73.0	59.9	62.4	18.6	22.5	10.6	39.9	32.7
1990	200.2	48.3	121.7	41.4	78.5	65.4	93.4	22.5	45.0	15.3	48.4	40.4
1994	201.5	45.7	125.9	38.7	75.6	65.1	91.6	20.8	44.3	13.6	47.4	40.8
1997	203.8	43.5	125.7	36.5	78.2	63.0	88.8	19.0	42.2	12.3	46.6	37.6
1999	211.4	43.8	134.2	37.1	77.2	63.7	89.4	18.5	43.0	11.9	46.4	38.3

Source: ECLAC, on the basis of special tabulations of data from household surveys conducted in the respective countries.

[a] Estimates corresponding to 19 countries of the region.
[b] Households and population living in poverty. Includes indigent households (population).
[c] Indigent households and population.

Brazil, Chile and Panama made considerable headway, with reductions of over 10 percentage points in poverty levels. Significantly, in the period 1991-2000, those countries' per capita GDP grew at average annual rates of 1.2%, 5% and 2.6%, respectively. Poverty also decreased in Costa Rica, Guatemala and Uruguay, by between 5 and 10 percentage points.

By contrast, in Venezuela the percentage of poor households increased from 22% in 1981 to 34% in 1990. Ecuador, Colombia and Paraguay also failed to make much progress in reducing poverty in the last decade.

Table I.2
LATIN AMERICA (18 COUNTRIES): POVERTY AND INDIGENCE INDICATORS,
1990-1999
(Percentages)

Country	Year	Households and population below the poverty line [a]		Households and population below the indigence line	
		Households	Population	Households	Population
Argentina [b]	1990	16.2	21.2	16.2	21.2
	1999	13.1	19.7	13.1	19.7
Bolivia	1989 [c]	49.4	53.1	49.4	53.1
	1999	54.7	60.6	54.7	60.6
Brazil	1990	41.4	48.0	41.4	48.0
	1999	29.9	37.5	29.9	37.5
Chile	1990	33.3	38.6	33.3	38.6
	2000	16.6	20.6	16.6	20.6
Colombia	1991	50.5	56.1	50.5	56.1
	1999	48.7	54.9	48.7	54.9
Costa Rica	1990	23.7	26.2	23.7	26.2
	1999	18.2	20.3	18.2	20.3
Ecuador [d]	1990	55.8	62.1	55.8	62.1
	1999	58.0	63.6	58.0	63.6
El Salvador	1999	43.5	49.8	43.5	49.8
Guatemala	1989	63.0	69.1	63.0	69.1
	1998	53.5	60.5	53.5	60.5
Honduras	1990	75.2	80.5	75.2	80.5
	1999	74.3	79.7	74.3	79.7
Mexico	1989	39.0	47.8	39.0	47.8
	2000	33.3	41.1	33.3	41.1
Nicaragua	1993	68.1	73.6	68.1	73.6
	1998	65.1	69.9	65.1	69.9
Panama	1991	36.3	42.8	36.3	42.8
	1999	24.2	30.2	24.2	30.2
Paraguay	1990 [e]	36.8	42.2	36.8	42.2
	1999	51.7	60.6	51.7	60.6
Peru	1999	42.3	48.6	42.3	48.6
Dominican Republic	1998	25.7	30.2	25.7	30.2
Uruguay [d]	1990	11.8	17.8	11.8	17.8
	1999	5.6	9.4	5.6	9.4
Venezuela	1990	34.2	40.0	34.2	40.0
	1999	44.0	49.4	44.0	49.4
Latin America [f]	1990	41.0	48.3	41.0	48.3
	1999	35.3	43.8	35.3	43.8

Source: ECLAC, on the basis of special tabulations of data from household surveys conducted in the respective countries. For a definition of each indicator, see ECLAC, *Social panorama of Latin America, 2000-2001* (LC/G.2138-P), Santiago, Chile, October 2001. United Nations publication, Sales No. E.01.II.G.141, box I.1.

[a] Includes households (individuals) living in indigence or extreme poverty.
[b] Greater Buenos Aires.
[c] Eight departmental capitals plus the city of El Alto.
[d] Urban areas.
[e] Asunción metropolitan area.
[f] Estimates for 19 countries of the region.

(b)   Spatial distribution of poverty

A major change has taken place in the spatial distribution of the population, with the result that poverty today is largely an urban phenomenon. Of the region's 211 million poor people in 1999, 134 million lived in urban areas and 77 million in rural areas. The incidence of poverty is much higher in rural areas than in cities, however (64% as against 37%). In addition, as shown in table I.2, poverty is more extreme in rural areas, since most of the rural poor are indigent (46 million), while the urban poor are mainly non-indigent (91 million).

Migration from the country to the city brought about an increase in the urban poor as a proportion of the region's total poor population. As a result of migration, the urban economy faced the challenge of absorbing a larger proportion of the working-age population and of meeting the increased demand for social services. Despite this, the urban economy proved able to absorb rural migrants into jobs that were of higher productivity than those in their places of origin.

Trends in urban poverty have followed trends in total poverty fairly closely. Figure I.2 shows that in the 1980s and 1990s urban poverty, like total poverty, evolved in consonance with the cycles of recession (1980-1989), expansion (1990-1997) and stagnation (1998-1999) described previously. Nevertheless, changes in urban poverty and non-agricultural output were sharper than changes in total poverty and total output. In fact, the coefficient of urban poverty increased by 10 points in the 1980s and dropped by 5 points in the 1990s (see table I.1), which indicates that economic growth affected urban poverty more asymmetrically than total poverty.

The situation in rural areas differed from the one in urban areas. Agricultural output did not follow the same cycle as total output. In fact, agricultural GDP grew in all three periods examined, expanding particularly vigorously in the biennium 1998-1999. In turn, rural poverty rates increased in the period 1980-1990, dropped in 1990-1997 and rose again in 1998-1999 (see figure I.3). This shows that rural poverty patterns were more closely linked to the growth of the economy at large than to variations in agricultural output. A subsequent section of this chapter will analyse in greater detail the particular features of rural poverty and the migration phenomenon, which has helped to accentuate the differences in productivity between different strata in the rural environment.

Figure I.2
LATIN AMERICA: GROWTH RATE OF GDP AND OF THE POOR POPULATION,
URBAN AREAS, 1980-1999
(Percentages)

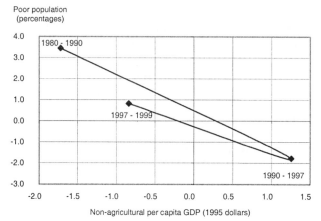

Source: ECLAC, on the basis of special tabulations of data from household surveys conducted in the
respective countries.

Figure I.3
LATIN AMERICA: GROWTH RATE OF GDP AND OF THE POOR POPULATION,
RURAL AREAS, 1980-1999
(Percentages)

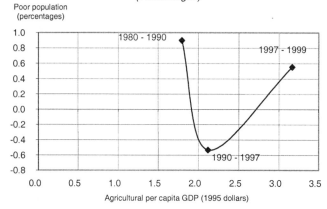

Source: ECLAC, on the basis of special tabulations of data from household surveys conducted in the
respective countries.

(c)   The profile of poor households

Of the 211 million Latin Americans living in poverty in 1999, about 22 million lived in households whose per capita income was not less than 90% of the minimum monetary threshold needed to meet their basic needs. This means that close to 10% of the poor were relatively well placed to rise above the poverty line, since their current income was only just below the level needed to satisfy their minimum consumption needs. Presumably the better position of this subgroup with respect to the rest of the poor population gave them a greater capacity to respond to economic and social policies for poverty reduction. On the other hand, 45 million people were categorized as the non-poor population most at risk of becoming poor, since their income was not more than 25% above the poverty line income level. This population group is highly vulnerable to economic fluctuations, since the slightest negative impact on their income can lead to a significant decline in their living standards (see table I.3).

The vulnerability of poor households is exacerbated by certain features that go hand in hand with the phenomenon of poverty. These tend to occur in contexts of low income and offer a more complete picture of the living standards of the region's poor. An overcrowded dwelling, an unemployed head of household and a poor educational climate in the household are traits that entail a high probability of poverty.

In effect, about 77 million Latin Americans live in overcrowded dwellings (defined as three or more people to a room). Of the features selected for the analysis, this is the characteristic that most clearly differentiates the poor from the non-poor, insofar as overcrowding is a powerful indication that the individuals in question do not receive enough income to cover their basic needs. Of Latin America's poor, 29% live in overcrowded dwellings, while only 6% of the non-poor live in such conditions.

Another dwelling-related indicator that points to a shortage of resources, although it is less likely to indicate poverty, is the lack of access to drinking water, which affects 165 million people, of whom over 109 million are poor (66.7%). While problems of access to drinking water affect 52% of the poor population, they are not unique to this group, since 20% of the region's non-poor share this difficulty.

Table I.3
LATIN AMERICA: SELECTED FEATURES OF THE POVERTY PROFILE, 1999

Population in private households	Number of individuals (thousands)	Proportion of total population [a] (%)		Probability of [b]	
				Poverty	Indigence
Total	482 727	100.0		43.1	18.4
Urban	361 619	74.9		36.6	11.9
Rural	121 108	25.1		62.7	37.8
Poor	211 392	100.0		-	-
Urban	134 229	63.5		-	-
Rural	77 163	36.5		-	-
Indigent	89 368	100.0		-	-
Urban	43 033	48.2		-	-
Rural	46 334	51.8		-	-
With income of 0.9-1.0 poverty lines per capita	21 668	4.5		100.0	-
With income of 1.0-1.25 poverty lines per capita	44 897	9.3		-	-
With less than US$ 1 per capita per day [c]	76 415	15.8		100.0	88.1
With less than US$ 2 per capita per day [c]	175 189	36.3		95.1	50.0
In overcrowded households [d]	76 605	15.9		79.6	46.4
In households without access to drinking water [e]	164 506	34.1		66.7	34.9
In households with a high demographic dependency ratio [f]	68 381	14.2		68.1	41.2
In households with low employment density [g]	109 995	22.8		65.1	35.9
In households where the head of households is:					
Female	90 677	18.8		43.1	17.5
With a low level of education					
- Fewer than 3 years of schooling	130 465	27.0		63.3	31.8
- Fewer than 10 years of schooling	375 636	77.8		51.7	22.3
Unemployed	15 825	3.3		71.2	43.6
Employed in low-productivity sectors [h]	152 615	31.6		48.7	23.4
Employed in agriculture [i]	100 696	20.9		65.1	36.8
Employed in establishments of:					
- Up to 5 workers	37 879	7.8	(17.8)	39.0	12.2
- Between 6 and 10 workers	12 575	2.6	(5.9)	29.1	8.2
Employed without professional or technical skills	165 443	34.3	(86.4)	38.5	14.1
Children not attending school [j]	5 972	1.2	(7.9)	76.5	48.2
Children in households with poor educational climate [k]	83 661	17.3	(56.0)	74.0	39.2
Young people aged 15 to 19 who work	18 655	3.9	(36.6)	46.9	18.6
Young people aged 15 to 24 who neither study nor work	21 823	4.5	(23.2)	58.1	24.7

Source: ECLAC, on the basis of special tabulations of data from household surveys conducted in the respective countries.

[a] Figures in brackets refer to the percentage of individuals with the attribute in question out of the total group (for example, children aged 6 to 12 who do not attend school as a proportion of all children in that age group).
[b] Poor and indigent as percentages of all the individuals in each category.
[c] Calculated on the basis of the current exchange rate in each country.
[d] Households are considered overcrowded when they house three or more individuals per room (excluding kitchen and bathroom).
[e] Households without piped drinking water inside the dwelling.
[f] Households in which the proportion of individuals under the age of 15 and over the age of 64 to those between 15 and 64 is higher than 0.75.
[g] Households in which the proportion of employed to total household members is less than 0.25.
[h] Employers and wage earners in establishments of up to 5 individuals, domestic employees and own-account and unpaid family workers with no professional or technical skills.
[i] Includes those employed in agriculture, forestry, hunting and fishing.
[j] Refers to children between the ages of 6 and 12.
[k] Children under the age of 15 in households whose adult members (aged 25 and over) have an average of 0 to 5.99 years of schooling.

A number of demographic features also display a close correlation with poverty, especially since they are strongly linked to the capacity to generate income. One of these is a high rate of demographic dependency, since the lower the ratio of individuals of working age to the number of children and elderly people in the household, the harder it is for those individuals to obtain enough resources to sustain the whole household. Another relevant feature is low employment density, defined as the existence of not more than one employed person per four members of the household. This is also associated with an above-average probability of poverty. Although both factors are representative of poverty —with a probability of 68.1% and 65.1%, respectively— the second is more extensive in the region, as it affects one third of all poor people.

The likelihood of being poor also depends, among other factors, on the employment and educational status of the head of household, who is usually the main breadwinner. The unemployment of the head of household is therefore one of the most likely indicators of poverty (71%) for the members of the household in question. However, the proportion of poor people in this situation is very low (5.3%), which means that this feature is not particularly significant, quantitatively speaking, in the overall picture of poverty. It can therefore be inferred that job creation programmes, however well targeted at poor population groups, have only a limited capacity to significantly alter overall poverty figures. Instead, the objective of reducing poverty requires measures to help increase wages, be it through wage policies or through training and skills programmes. This last point is further supported by the fact that close to 39% of poor people live in households headed by an individual with fewer than three years of schooling, even though this is also true of 18% of non-poor individuals.

Two other important features with regard to heads of household warrant discussion. One of these is that the probability of poverty among the almost 91 million people who live in households headed by women is similar to the average probability, indicating that this feature is not in itself a conditioning factor of poverty. It has also been observed that the probability of poverty among members of households headed by agricultural workers, whose income is typically precarious, is no greater than the probability deriving from the simple fact of living in a rural area.

Often, poverty seriously affects the preparation of children and young people to join the labour market by increasing rates of school non-attendance and dropping out. Indeed, according to the data considered, children who do not attend school have a high probability of being poor (76.5%). Nevertheless, non-attendance at school is becoming less common among poor and non-poor population groups alike, accounting today for only 1.2% of the population and 7.9% of children between the ages of 6 and 12. By contrast, children under 15 who live in households with a poor educational environment —that is, households whose adult members have fewer than six years of schooling on average— number over 83 million in Latin America (56% of the children in this age group), of whom 74% are poor. The educational environment in the household is a key determinant of the continuity of schooling and the achievement of higher levels of education on the part of children and young people. In addition, the presence in the household of young people who work and young people who neither work nor study is also associated with above-average probabilities of poverty. In the region there are just over 18 million young people between the ages of 15 and 19 who work, and almost 22 million young people between the ages of 15 and 24 who neither work nor study. Together these two segments represent about a quarter of all the individuals in this age group (see table I.3).

In summary, and in very general terms, a review of the living conditions of Latin America's poor reveals that these people often live in dwellings without access to drinking water and, to a lesser extent, in dwellings that are overcrowded (i.e., with more than three people per room); that the households to which they belong have a high ratio of demographic dependency and low employment density; and that the head of household often has fewer than three years of schooling and, in some cases, is unemployed. Among children under the age of 15, low levels of education among the adults in the household is also associated with poverty.

2.   Factors related to poverty reduction

Poverty levels are affected by both economic factors and demographic and social factors. The economic factors include economic growth, public transfers and relative prices. Demographic and social factors include the size, composition and geographical location of the household, as well as the level of education of its members. The labour market forms the bridge between economic growth and the features of the households that supply the labour force.

It should be pointed out, first, that the impact of these factors varies from one country to another within Latin America. This is indicative of structural differences among the countries and of their varying degrees of freedom to implement the relevant public policies in the framework of similar development patterns. Moreover, urban and rural areas are affected differently by these factors. As noted earlier, aggregate economic growth does not have the same impact on urban poverty as it has on rural poverty. Migration also affects the two areas unevenly. The consideration of the labour market in this section refers basically to urban areas, since the specific features of rural Latin America are dealt with in another section. By the same token, the effects of poverty on education will be examined in greater detail in chapter V.

(a)   Economic growth

In general, economic growth in Latin America proceeded at a moderate pace, without recessions, until 1997, except in Argentina, Mexico and Uruguay, which were hit by the crisis of 1994-1995. After 1997 the South American countries moved into a period of slow growth and, in some cases, recession. By contrast, Mexico, the Central American countries and some Caribbean nations enjoyed strong economic expansion in the five-year period 1996-2000. This shows that poverty reduction did not follow the same pattern over time in the different countries and that in some of them the process reversed itself towards the end of the 1990s, as shown in table I.2.

An examination of developments over the whole of the 1990s shows more clearly than ever the strong relationship that exists between poverty reduction and growth. As shown in figure I.4, the largest upturns and downturns in per capita income were associated with reductions and increases, respectively, in poverty levels. This was particularly obvious in the extreme cases —Chile and Venezuela— but there were also significant departures from this linear relationship.

Similar growth rates had different impacts on poverty levels. In Chile, for example, per capita GDP expanded by 55% between 1990 and 2000, which translated into a 50% drop in poverty (16 percentage points). In Uruguay a much smaller increase in per capita GDP (28%) brought about a larger relative decrease in poverty (53%, or 6 percentage points) within a similar period of time. In Bolivia and Panama per capita GDP grew at similar cumulative rates of around 16% and 20% over the period, but the decline in urban poverty was very different in the two countries: 14% and 25%, respectively. By contrast, the 9% expansion of per capita GDP in Brazil brought poverty levels down by 28% (see table I.4 and figure I.4). To a large extent, these differences in poverty reduction rates reflect the varying degrees to which low-income groups were able to benefit from the fruits of economic growth. This ability, in turn, depends not only on the magnitude of economic growth, but also on its quality and on the particular characteristics of economic, social and demographic changes in each country, which are themselves a reflection of the factors discussed below.

Table I.4

LATIN AMERICA (14 COUNTRIES): PER CAPITA GDP AND PERCENTAGE OF THE
POPULATION LIVING IN POVERTY AND INDIGENCE, 1990-1999

Country	Year	Per capita GDP (1995 dollars)	Percentage of the population		Variation over the period (annual average)			Coefficient of elasticity	
			Poor	Indigent	GDP[a]	Coefficient of		(P)/GDP[a]	(I)/GDP[a]
						Poverty (P)	Indigence (I)		
Argentina [b]	1990	5 545	21.2	5.2					
	1999	7 435	19.7	4.8	3.3	-0.8	-0.9	-0.21	-0.23
Brazil	1990	3 859	48.0	23.4					
	1999	4 204	37.5	12.9	1.0	-2.7	-6.4	-2.45	-5.03
Chile	1990	3 425	38.6	12.9					
	2000	5 309	20.6	5.7	4.5	-6.1	-7.8	-0.85	-1.01
Colombia	1991	2 158	56.1	26.1					
	1999	2 271	54.9	26.8	0.6	-0.3	0.3	-0.41	0.51
Costa Rica	1990	2 994	26.2	9.8					
	1999	3 693	20.4	7.8	2.4	-2.7	-2.5	-0.95	-0.87
Ecuador [c]	1990	1 472	62.1	26.2					
	1999	1 404	63.5	31.3	-0.5	0.2	2.0	-0.49	-4.27
El Salvador	1995	1 675	54.2	21.7					
	1999	1 750	49.8	21.9	1.1	-2.1	0.2	-1.81	0.21
Guatemala	1989	1 347	69.1	41.8					
	1998	1 534	60.5	34.1	1.5	-1.5	-2.2	-0.90	-1.33
Honduras	1990	686	80.5	60.6					
	1999	694	79.7	56.8	0.1	-0.1	-0.7	-	-
Mexico	1989	3 925	47.8	18.8					
	1998	4 489	46.9	18.5	1.5	-0.2	-0.2	-0.13	-0.11
Nicaragua	1993	416	73.6	48.4					
	1998	453	69.9	44.6	1.7	-1.0	-1.6	-0.57	-0.89
Panama	1991	2 700	42.8	19.2					
	1999	3 264	30.2	10.7	2.4	-4.3	-7.0	-1.41	-2.12
Uruguay [c]	1990	4 707	17.8	3.4					
	1999	5 982	9.4	1.8	2.7	-6.8	-6.8	-1.74	-1.74
Venezuela	1990	3 030	40.0	14.6					
	1999	3 037	49.4	21.7	0.0	2.4	4.5	-	-
Latin America	1990	3 349	48.3	22.5					
	1999	3 804	43.8	18.5	1.4	-1.1	-2.2	-0.69	-1.31

Source: ECLAC, on the basis of official figures and special tabulations of data from household surveys
conducted in the respective countries.

[a] c/p: at constant 1995 prices.
[b] Greater Buenos Aires.
[c] Total for urban areas.

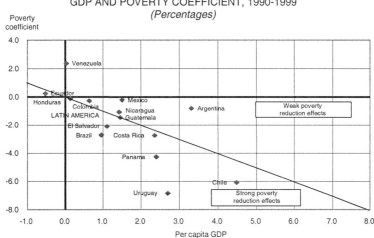

Figure I.4
LATIN AMERICA (14 COUNTRIES): AVERAGE ANNUAL VARIATION IN PER CAPITA
GDP AND POVERTY COEFFICIENT, 1990-1999
(Percentages)

Source: ECLAC, on the basis of special tabulations of data from household surveys conducted in the respective countries.

(b)   Employment and wages

In the 1990s economic growth was accompanied by significant changes in the labour market. In general, the higher rates of economic growth were achieved through uneven increases in labour productivity among sectors, segments and firms of different sizes and through the integration of firms, also to differing degrees, into the international economy. Rises in productivity, especially in urban areas, were concentrated in more highly skilled, better paying types of employment. The effect of economic growth on poverty through the channel of employment was therefore not as strong as might have been expected. The countries also varied in terms of their economic capacity to increase low-productivity employment and in terms of the associated social patterns. Since most low-productivity jobs are in the informal sector, the open unemployment rate, though important, cannot provide a complete picture of the labour market's effects on poverty.

A given household's total number of members, number of employed and unemployed members and level of labour income —measured in multiples of the poverty line— clearly help determine how likely it is to be poor. An important observation in this regard is that the nature of the labour market is very uneven across the Latin American countries. Open unemployment and the employment density of households vary considerably from one country to another. For example, Brazil and Mexico have relatively low rates of open unemployment and high employment density. By contrast, in Argentina rates of unemployment are high and employment density is low in low-income households, but labour income is higher. The combination of these dimensions gives rise to very different profiles with respect to earned income in poor households.

In 1999 employment density in the decile in which the poverty line is situated ranged from 0.24 in Argentina to between 0.27 and 0.28 in Chile, Costa Rica and Uruguay to just over 0.4 in Brazil and Colombia and 0.48 in Honduras. In the 1990s employment density in this decile increased in most of the countries, with Brazil, Ecuador, Honduras, Mexico, Panama and Venezuela posting the biggest upturns (see table I.5). In Chile, where economic growth was much stronger, average employment density in households close to the poverty line increased from 0.24 to 0.27, while in Brazil it rose from 0.38 to 0.43. Real income, however, rose faster in Chile than in Brazil. The regional overview shows that, in most countries, rates of poverty reduction were determined not so much by increases in real income as by increases in average employment density, which rose by between 0.02 and 0.06 in almost all the countries except Colombia, Paraguay and Uruguay, where it virtually stood still. In most of the countries poor households dealt with the situation by sending more of their members to work in low-productivity jobs.

As will be discussed in greater detail in chapter III, open unemployment rose in the 1990s and adversely affected poverty trends. Owing to a decrease in urban unemployment —for just a few years of the decade— in Bolivia, Chile and Costa Rica, urban poverty fell slightly more in those countries than in the rest of the region. In those three countries the number of employed persons in low-income households increased and open unemployment declined among the active population in the poorest quintile. This trend was especially pronounced in urban areas of Bolivia and Costa Rica.

Households obtain a very high proportion of their resources from the earned income of their economically active members.[1] Low earned income accounts for a substantial proportion of cases of poverty. It is therefore useful to examine the kinds of employment in which low pay levels are most common.

---

[1]   Almost 70% of the income of urban households in all strata is generated in the labour market. In turn, two thirds of household income from work consists of wages and salaries (see chapter IV).

Table I.5
LATIN AMERICA (12 COUNTRIES): EMPLOYMENT DENSITY IN SELECTED STRATA
OF THE POPULATION, [a] 1990-1999

Country/Year	Employment density			
	Total	Decile 1	Decile 10	Households close to the poverty line [b]
Argentina (Greater Buenos Aires)				
1990	0.40	0.13	0.71	0.23
1999	0.42	0.19	0.72	0.24
Brazil				
1990	0.45	0.27	0.59	0.38
1999	0.47	0.33	0.55	0.43
Chile				
1990	0.36	0.17	0.52	0.24
2000	0.39	0.20	0.58	0.27
Colombia				
1990 [c]	0.41	0.25	0.59	0.41
1999	0.41	0.24	0.56	0.41
Costa Rica				
1990	0.38	0.16	0.59	0.26
1999	0.41	0.15	0.63	0.27
Ecuador (urban areas)				
1990	0.41	0.21	0.61	0.42
1999	0.43	0.21	0.60	0.46
EL Salvador				
1995	0.39	0.23	0.59	0.37
1999	0.41	0.24	0.60	0.38
Honduras				
1990	0.35	0.27	0.53	0.43
1999	0.41	0.25	0.59	0.48
Mexico				
1989	0.37	0.25	0.52	0.33
2000	0.44	0.32	0.59	0.39
Panama				
1991	0.36	0.15	0.54	0.29
1999	0.42	0.20	0.62	0.33
Uruguay (urban areas)				
1990	0.40	0.25	0.52	0.25
1999	0.41	0.28	0.53	0.28
Venezuela				
1990	0.36	0.12	0.63	0.29
1999	0.41	0.14	0.65	0.39

Source: ECLAC, on the basis of special tabulations of data from household surveys conducted in the respective countries.

[a] Employment density: number of employed persons as a proportion of the total number of household members. Decile 1 and decile 10 refer to the bottom and top 10% of households, respectively, in terms of per capita income.
[b] According to the definition of the poverty line in the country in the final year.
[c] Eight major cities.

It is well known, and confirmed by the figures for the 1990s, that the likelihood of poverty is lower among professionals and technicians than among other workers; among public-sector wage earners than among private-sector wage earners; and among formal-sector workers than among informal-sector workers. As will be discussed in the chapter on employment, in the 1980s and 1990s both private and informal employment increased as a proportion of total employment. Bearing wage differences in mind, this phenomenon alone tended to increase poverty levels. In effect, in the late 1990s in urban areas, poverty levels were lower among public-sector workers than among workers in private firms with over five employees. In turn, the incidence of poverty was higher among those employed in establishments with fewer than five employees than among those employed in firms with more than five. The highest rates were observed among wage earners in small establishments and among individuals employed in domestic service (see table I.6). In most of the countries poverty levels were a little lower among own-account workers.

Poverty levels among wage earners in formal-sector establishments with five or more employees call for some discussion. In most of the countries these levels were very similar to the average for the employed poor population considered in table I.6 (the table does not include employers, professionals or technicians), and the difference in poverty rates between formal- and informal-sector workers was smaller than many qualitative studies have suggested. Furthermore, formal-sector employees living in poor households represent over 25% of the total poor population, on average, and over 50% in Chile, for example.

This explains the fact that, in some countries, a high proportion of the employed poor are formal-sector wage earners. In Brazil, Chile, the Dominican Republic, Mexico and Venezuela, and in representative (though not all) urban areas of Argentina and Colombia, this proportion is over 35%. By the same token, in 10 of the 16 countries considered, between 30% and 60% of private-sector wage earners live in poor households. Patterns vary greatly in this respect, however: the proportion ranges from less than 10% in Uruguay to over 50% in Ecuador, Honduras and Nicaragua. In Argentina, Chile, Costa Rica and Panama it is between 10% and 20%, while in Bolivia, Brazil, Colombia, El Salvador, Mexico, Paraguay and Venezuela it ranges from 30% to 50%[2] (see table I.6).

---

[2]   This study of the relationship between employment and poverty does not take into account groups in which poverty levels are higher than among the employed population, i.e. inactive groups receiving income (retirees and pensioners) and the unemployed. This explains the fact that the percentage of poverty among the employed is lower than among the population at large.

Table I.6
LATIN AMERICA: EMPLOYED POOR BY EMPLOYMENT CATEGORY AND
DISTRIBUTION OF TOTAL POOR [a] [b], URBAN AREAS, 1999
(Percentages)

Country	Total employed [c]	Public sector wage earners [d]	Non-professional and non-technical private sector wage earners			Non-professional and non-technical own-account workers
			In establishments employing		Domestic employees	
			More than 5 workers	Up to 5 workers		
Argentina	10	6	9	17	22	9
(Greater Buenos Aires)	100	7	36	25	12	21
Bolivia	41	23	41	53	27	50
	90	6	15	15	2	52
Brazil	24	14	26	32	39	28
	85	7	28	11	14	25
Chile	14	6	16	22	17	13
	98	7	52	15	9	15
Colombia[d]	38	12	38	...	35	55
(8 major cities)	95	3	38	...	5	49
Costa Rica	10	3	9	14	27	16
	94	6	28	17	15	28
Ecuador	53	30	55	70	61	63
	87	6	23	18	6	34
El Salvador	29	9	26	44	41	37
	88	4	23	21	6	34
Guatemala	40	19	41	53	46	48
	77	4	19	24	8	23
Honduras	64	41	64	81	58	74
	85	6	27	14	4	34
Mexico	25	11	26	44	38	26
	94	6	36	27	5	20
Nicaragua[d]	54	...	54	68	74	53
	83	...	25	18	9	30
Panama	15	5	12	24	20	25
	82	6	26	11	8	31
Paraguay	26	11	27	40	27	33
(Asunción)	91	6	26	21	10	28
Peru	28	14	21	32	23	38
	84	5	12	15	5	47
Dominican Republic	21	21	18	25	26	24
	88	12	27	10	6	32
Uruguay	5	2	5	9	12	10
	98	5	26	15	17	35
Venezuela	35	28	37	52	50	34
	90	12	26	18	3	30

Source: ECLAC, *Social Panorama of Latin America, 2001-2002* (LC/G.2183-P), Santiago, Chile, October 2002. United Nations publication, Sales No. E.02.II.G.65.

[a] The upper line of each entry shows the percentage of employed poor in each category who live in households that receive income below the poverty line.
[b] The lower line of each entry shows the percentage of employed poor with respect to the total employed in the respective category.
[c] The total does not add up to 100 because employers and professionals and technicians are not included.
[d] In Nicaragua public-sector wage earners are included with wage earners in establishments employing more than 5 workers. In Colombia wage earners in microenterprises are also included in this category.

Although poverty among State employees is relatively low, it reaches significant levels in a number of countries. In Bolivia, the Dominican Republic, Ecuador and Venezuela over 20% of public-sector workers are poor, while in most of the countries the poor employed in the public sector represent between 3% and 7% of the total.

Wage earners in microenterprises and domestic service workers together account for between 20% and 35% of the employed poor. In countries with a high proportion of low-skilled own-account workers (see table I.6), poor wage earners in that group represent between 17% and 27% of the total. Clearly, this profile of poverty among the urban employed is closely linked to their low occupational earnings. Non-professional, non-technical wage earners employed in firms with five or more workers received, on average, an income of between 2.5 and 3.6 times the poverty line per capita, which in most of the countries was about 20% lower than the average income of the employed population, and not always higher than the earnings of non-professional, non-technical own-account workers (see ECLAC, 2001a).

Workers in microenterprises received an average monthly income of between 1.6 and 2.7 times the poverty line. In many countries this was below the threshold needed to give them a good chance of remaining above the poverty line. Domestic employees, who accounted for 4% to 7% of urban employment, earned an average income of 1.4 to 2.2 times the poverty line.

From these findings it can be surmised that, for a large proportion of private-sector workers, employment offers no assurance that they will stay above the poverty threshold, even if they work in medium-sized or large firms. Similarly, in a number of the countries, the fact that a significant proportion of public-sector employees are poor constitutes an obstacle to the process of State reform and modernization.

(c)   Reduced inflation

The decline in the rate of inflation also helped to reduce poverty levels, particularly in those countries where it dropped rapidly from very high levels, such as Argentina, Peru, Brazil and, to a lesser extent, Chile, Mexico and Uruguay. Greater consumer price stability lessened or eliminated the erosion of average real wages, especially lower wages, whose purchasing power falls faster in conditions of high inflation or hyperinflation. The slowdown in inflation was accompanied in many cases by a rise in the real minimum wage. Later in the decade the impact of lower inflation on poverty declined, especially when the objective of keeping inflation very low was adopted as part of economic policy.

(d)   Variations in relative prices

In most of the countries changes in the relative prices of goods and services effectively made the basic consumption basket of lower-income sectors cheaper. For a number of reasons, such as changes in the production and trade structure, trade liberalization, exchange-rate policies and the characteristics of the agricultural sector, in some countries the average variation in the retail prices of products that are used to estimate inflation differed appreciably from that of products that make up the consumption basket of poor population groups. In general, the prices of mass consumer products, particularly food, rose more slowly than the prices of other domestically consumed goods and services, which boosted the purchasing power of low-income strata.[3]

This development is evident from a comparison between trends in food prices, which have a stronger impact on the budgets of low-income households, and the variation in the prices of other goods used to estimate the consumer price index. As shown in table I.7, between 1990 and 1999 the price of food rose by a smaller percentage than the prices of other goods in 10 of the 13 countries considered. In five of those countries (Colombia, Ecuador, Paraguay, Uruguay and Venezuela) this percentage was about 80% or even lower. Argentina, Bolivia, Chile, the Dominican Republic and Mexico exhibited a similar (albeit smaller) price gap. Only in Costa Rica, Honduras and Panama did food prices rise faster than the prices of other goods.

(e)   Increased transfers

Public and private transfers, predominantly retirement and other pensions, played a key role in reducing poverty in the 1990s. Although they are usually poorly distributed, these transfers often represent a significant financial contribution to poor households. The relative importance of transfers in household income varied considerably from one country to another within the region. The degree to which they targeted poor households also varied. In a number of countries, including Argentina, Costa Rica, Panama and Uruguay, transfers accounted for over 20% of the total income of urban households, while in Brazil, Chile, Colombia, Mexico and Venezuela, this percentage hovered around 10%. Brazil is a particularly interesting case in this regard, since its policy of massive transfers to low-income sectors in urban and rural areas between 1990 and 1993 made a major contribution to poverty reduction.

---

[3]   In some countries the positive impact of this trend was partially offset by a steep rise in utility rates (water, electricity and urban transport), which rose faster than the average consumer price index in those countries.

Table I.7
LATIN AMERICA: RELATIVE VARIATION IN CONSUMER FOOD PRICES
WITH RESPECT TO OTHER GOODS AND SERVICES, 1990-1999
(Percentages)

Country	Reference date[a]	Food CPI[b]	Other goods and services CPI[b]	Ratio food CPI[b]/CPI[b] other
Argentina	September 1990	100.0	100.0	1.00
	September 1999	270.5	304.5	0.89
Bolivia	August 1990	100.0	100.0	1.00
	October-November 1999	225.6	233.9	0.96
Colombia	August 1990	100.0	100.0	1.00
	August 1999	475.8	587.2	0.81
Costa Rica	June 1990	100.0	100.0	1.00
	June 1999	404.7	392.5	1.03
Chile	November 1990	100.0	100.0	1.00
	November 2000	207.3	233.2	0.89
Ecuador	October 1990	100.0	100.0	1.00
	October 1999	1 506.3	1 901.6	0.79
Honduras	August 1990	100.0	100.0	1.00
	August 1999	489.3	461.2	1.06
Mexico	Third quarter 1990	100.0	100.0	1.00
	Third quarter 2000	503.4	551.7	0.91
Panama	August 1989	100.0	100.0	1.00
	July 1999	114.1	111.7	1.02
Paraguay	June- August 1990	100.0	100.0	1.00
	July-December 1999	265.9	335.4	0.79
Dominican Republic	March 1990	100.0	100.0	1.00
	March 1997	256.7	282.6	0.91
Uruguay	Second semester 1990	100.0	100.0	1.00
	1999	1 222.5	1 837.2	0.67
Venezuela	Second semester 1990	100.0	100.0	1.00
	Second semester 1999	2 559.9	4 164.3	0.61

Source: ECLAC, Statistics and Economic Projections Division.

[a] Corresponds to the reference month for income measurement in the household surveys used to estimate poverty in each country.
[b] Consumer price index.

In Uruguay further reductions in poverty levels were achieved partly through the maintenance of a high rate of transfers and a steep rise in pensions in the early part of the decade. Transfers also rose in Chile, albeit to a lesser degree, in the form of monetary subsidies —welfare pensions and family allowances— and non-monetary assistance provided to low-income households, which helped to reduce poverty from 1990 onward.

(f)   Migration

The findings on rural and urban poverty set out above illustrate the importance of migration in the distribution of poverty between the two sectors and in total poverty.

The effects of migration on nationwide poverty levels are also related to the age structure and educational status of both migrants and those they leave behind. Migration has a major impact on the age and gender structure of the urban and rural population. In urban areas the pyramid is broader in the productive age groups, while the opposite occurs in rural areas. In Brazil, for example, 67.5% of the urban population is between the ages of 15 and 64, while only 60.4% of the rural population is in this age group. In addition, the rural population has a higher proportion of older adults than its fertility and mortality rates would suggest. In Bolivia only 3.4% of the urban population is aged 65 or over, while this age group accounts for 5.1% of the rural population.[4] Both the bulking out of the urban pyramid in the middle age groups and the ageing of the rural population are largely the result of the selective migration —and its cumulative effects over time— of young people moving from the country to the city.

These observations are consistent with the net rural-to-urban migration rate, which is higher in the 15-19 and 20-24 age groups. In addition, in many countries the migration rate for women is higher than the one for men (ECLAC, 2001a). In Brazil the average annual rate of net rural-to-urban migration in the 1990s was 13 per 1,000 for men aged 20 to 24 and 14 per 1,000 for women in the same age group. This means that almost 50% of the expansion of the urban population between the ages of 20 and 24 was due to migration. In the age groups between 40 and 60 the rate was 5 per 1,000 and represented less than 20% of the growth of the urban population in this age group. This reveals two phenomena: first, that the individuals who migrate are usually the ones who are better placed to position themselves in the urban environment and, second, that the rural environment retains the relatively less educated part of its original population.

---

[4]   See www.eclac.cl/celade/proyecciones.

Moreover, processes of international migration are becoming increasingly important. When migration is increased by economic recession, a particular kind of relationship develops between growth and poverty —a relationship that is even more particular when migrants send monetary remittances back to their country of origin. As noted earlier, the age, family and educational composition of households plays a key role in determining the magnitude and frequency of transfers and the variation in the household income of those who remain in their place of origin.

In summary, a number of the determining factors of poverty are difficult to alter in the short term. Basically, economic growth affects poverty through the labour market, the source from which households obtain the bulk of their autonomous income. In this regard, all the findings indicate that the region's employment structure fails to generate enough sufficiently productive and adequately paid jobs, forcing vast sectors of the Latin American population to seek employment in low-productivity, low-paying activities in order to avoid poverty.

In these circumstances, the role of other poverty-reducing instruments is also important. These instruments include public transfers —properly targeted— and policies for reducing inflation or altering relative prices to make them more favourable for lower-income strata.

3.   The nature of rural poverty

(a)   The magnitude of rural poverty and recent trends

Although the majority of the poor live in cities, the incidence of poverty continues to be higher in rural areas. In Brazil, Colombia, Mexico and Venezuela, about half of the rural population is poor, while in Honduras the figure is 80%.

Furthermore, in Bolivia, Costa Rica, El Salvador, Guatemala, Honduras, Nicaragua, Paraguay and Peru poverty remains predominantly a rural phenomenon, while in Colombia, Mexico and the Dominican Republic almost 45% of the poor reside in rural areas (see table I.8). Similarly, about half of the indigent population lives in rural sectors.[5]

---

[5]   In the Latin American countries with the lowest per capita output, where indigence is more widespread, rural indigence is more than twice the level of urban indigence (see tables A.1 and A.2 of the statistical appendix).

Table I.8
LATIN AMERICA: MAGNITUDE AND RELATIVE SHARE OF RURAL POVERTY,
AROUND 1999
(Percentages)

Rural households below the poverty line	Poor rural households in relation to total poor households		
	Less than 35%	Between 35% and 49%	50% or more
Over 65%			Guatemala Honduras Nicaragua
Between 51% and 65%		Colombia Ecuador Mexico	Bolivia El Salvador Paraguay Peru
Between 31% and 50%	Brazil Panama Venezuela	Dominican Republic	
Up to 30%	Argentina Chile Uruguay		Costa Rica

Source: Prepared on the basis of ECLAC, *Social Panorama of Latin America, 1998* (LC/G.2050-P), Santiago, Chile, May 1999. United Nations publication, Sales No. E.99.II.G.4, table 16 of the statistical appendix.

Even where poverty is predominantly urban and progress has been made in reducing it, rural poverty still persists. In most of region, rural poverty declined only very slightly or even increased, although some countries —Brazil, Chile and Panama— made substantial headway in reducing it. Rural poverty is therefore structural in nature: it is deeper than urban poverty and less directly linked to economic growth in the agricultural sector.[6] These features are associated with the low productivity of the population employed in agricultural activities and with the high rate of population growth typical of areas that are still in the early stages of demographic transition.

Rural-to-urban migration is partly responsible for the continued low productivity of the rural poor, since, as already noted, young people with a higher level of education are generally the ones who migrate, while adults with less schooling remain in the rural environment.

In countries where the bulk of the rural population still lives in poverty —Bolivia, Colombia, Honduras and Mexico— most of this population is indigent. By contrast, where rural poverty is less widespread

---

[6]   In the first half of the 1990s the decline in urban poverty followed the growth of per capita GDP more closely than rural poverty. Of course, rural poverty also fluctuates in response to business cycles, natural phenomena and public policies on issues such as agricultural prices and income transfers.

—Chile, Costa Rica and Panama— the non-indigent poor outnumber the indigent poor. These differences between countries appear to reflect trends in structural mobility associated with rural economic development.

Where rural poverty has declined, the decrease in levels of indigence has been proportionally higher. This shows that the improvements were no less beneficial for the indigent poor than for the non-indigent poor. In other words, economic growth and policies to combat rural poverty helped much of the population living in hard-core poverty, not only those households whose income was closest to the indigence threshold. This is also supported by the fact that, as shown in table I.9, the average income of indigent households rose between 1990 and 1997.

Table I.9
LATIN AMERICA: POVERTY AND AVERAGE INCOME [a] IN RURAL AREAS, 1990s
(Percentages)

Country	Period	Percentages			Percentages			Average household income:			
		Indigence initial year	Non-indigent poverty initial year	Total poverty initial year	Indigence final year	Non-indigent poverty final year	Total poverty final year	Indigence initial year	Non-indigent poverty initial year	Indigence final year	Non-indigent poverty final year
Bolivia	1997-1999	53.8	18.2	72.0	59.6	16.0	75.6	0.24	0.75	0.2	0.76
Brazil	1990-1999	37.9	26.0	63.9	20.5	24.7	45.2	0.34	0.74	0.29	0.71
Chile	1990-2000	12.1	21.4	33.5	6.7	12.6	19.3	0.37	0.79	0.37	0.81
Colombia	1991-1999	30.6	24.8	55.4	31.1	24.7	55.8	0.34	0.77	0.32	0.77
Costa Rica	1990-1999	12.3	12.6	24.9	9.4	11.1	20.5	0.31	0.79	0.31	0.79
El Salvador	1995-1999	26.5	31.7	58.2	29.3	29.7	59.0	0.32	0.75	0.27	0.73
Guatemala	1989-1998	45.2	26.9	72.1	39.6	25.1	64.7	0.32	0.76	0.37	0.76
Honduras	1990-1999	66.4	17.1	83.5	63.2	19.1	82.3	0.26	0.75	0.27	0.74
Mexico	1989-1998	22.6	26.1	48.7	23.0	26.0	49.0	0.39	0.78	0.4	0.75
Nicaragua	1993-1998	58.3	20.4	78.7	52.6	20.1	72.7	0.27	0.77	0.26	0.76
Panama	1989-1999	21.1	21.4	42.5	12.6	20.0	32.6	0.35	0.76	0.39	0.78
Venezuela	1990-1994	16.5	21.9	38.4	22.9	24.8	47.7	0.39	0.78	0.38	0.77

Source: ECLAC, on the basis of special tabulations of data from household surveys conducted in the respective countries.

[a] In multiples of the per capita poverty line.

Overall, in the 1990s rural poverty declined in six of the eight countries for which information is available, namely Brazil, Chile, Costa Rica, Guatemala, Honduras and Panama. Some households managed to cross the poverty threshold, while others shed their indigent status to become non-indigent poor households. This indicates that hard-core poverty was also eased by the upturn in income and the other factors mentioned, such as policies to combat rural poverty.

The increase in rural income benefited all income strata, albeit in differing proportions, as a result of the general expansion of agricultural output and the intensification of non-agricultural rural activities (commerce and services). In almost all the cases examined declines in indigence and poverty levels were associated with increases in average real income.[7]

In Chile both the average labour income and the average autonomous income of rural households fell between 1990 and 1998. The maintenance of these households' monetary income and the resulting decline in rural poverty are therefore attributable to income from the monetary subsidies extended by the State (see MIDEPLAN, 1999).

(b)   Factors affecting rural poverty

The persistence of rural poverty is attributable to factors which are comparatively more rigid than the factors affecting urban poverty. Rural areas' demographic and educational profiles are characteristic of stages through which urban areas have already passed, while their geographical features, such as isolation, lack of access to communications and difficulties in obtaining basic services, also leave the rural population at a clear disadvantage with respect to city-dwellers. As well, there are a number of difficulties related to agricultural activity —the mainstay of most rural workers— such as technological backwardness, high risk and low productive potential. In addition, the soils worked by the poor often show the effects of environmental degradation. Another problem is insufficient access to water, credit and, in particular, land, which is a key cause of rural poverty in many countries because of its impact on income generation and the effect of the structure of land ownership on the productive potential of agriculture.

In countries where poverty is mainly a rural phenomenon and where more than half the rural population is poor, the rate of natural population growth is also a key problem. These countries are at an incipient or moderate stage of demographic transition and have high fertility rates. This means that they are caught in a kind of demographic trap: the division of the land among numerous heirs contributes to soil exhaustion and the proliferation of smallholdings, and this, in turn, is associated with an increase in the number of landless poor families and

---

[7]   Had this not been the case, and had the decline in the percentage of indigent households been accompanied by a downturn in their average income, this would have meant that hard-core rural poverty did not benefit from the expansion of output in rural areas.

with the growing need to resort to survival strategies based on family labour.

However, according to projections prepared by the Population Division of ECLAC - Latin American and Caribbean Demographic Centre (CELADE), the number of Latin American countries in which the rural population is growing in absolute terms will have fallen from 14 in the period 1990-1995 to 10 by 2010, owing to the universal phenomenon of gradually declining fertility rates and persistent rural-to-urban migration.[8]

(c)   Rural poverty and the structure of production and employment

Seasonality, multiple employment, production for home consumption and unpaid family work —which characterize agricultural activities in many parts of the region— make trends in rural employment hard to identify. Nevertheless, a number of general features can be noted. First, according to estimates, wage employment varied little as a proportion of total rural employment in the 1990s, since it held steady or declined only slightly in several countries, including Chile, Colombia, Costa Rica, Honduras and Mexico. It dropped sharply, however, in the Dominican Republic and increased in Guatemala, Panama and Venezuela. In turn, the campesino population[9] remained unchanged or shrank slightly in Chile and Venezuela, expanded in Brazil, Colombia and the Dominican Republic and declined in the other countries. In most of the countries own-account non-agricultural work tended to increase, and trends in the proportion of employers were uneven (see table I.10).

In addition, the data available suggest that the incidence of poverty is higher among campesinos than among other occupational groups, although, as shown in table I.10, there are large differences between countries in this respect: poverty among campesinos ranges from 20% in Chile to 89% in Bolivia.

---

[8]   According to estimates, rural population growth will change course by 2010, causing the rural population to shrink in absolute terms in Colombia, the Dominican Republic, Ecuador and Mexico. These countries will thus join the eight other countries in which this phenomenon has already begun (see ECLAC, 1999a).

[9]   In household survey terminology, "campesinos" are own-account workers and unpaid family members employed in agricultural activities.

Table I.10
LATIN AMERICA (16 COUNTRIES): DISTRIBUTION OF ECONOMICALLY ACTIVE
POPULATION BY TYPE OF EMPLOYMENT, RURAL AREAS, 1990-2000
(Percentages)

Country	Year	Total	Employers	Wage earners			Own-account and unpaid family workers	
				Total	Public sector	Private sector [a]	Total	Agriculture
Bolivia	2000	100.0	0.5	8.6	2.8	5.8	90.9	83.0
Brazil	1990	100.0	3.0	44.3	-	44.3	52.7	44.3
	1999	100.0	2.0	34.3	5.2	29.1	63.7	56.4
Chile [b]	1990	100.0	2.8	64.9	-	64.9	32.3	25.0
	2000	100.0	2.5	65.1	4.9	60.2	32.5	24.3
Colombia	1991	100.0	6.3	48.6	-	48.6	45.0	25.5
	1999	100.0	3.7	47.2	3.7	43.5	49.2	27.9
Costa Rica	1990	100.0	5.1	66.2	10.5	55.7	28.7	16.8
	2000	100.0	5.8	66.9	9.6	57.3	27.3	12.3
Ecuador	2000	100.0	3.2	42.4	3.9	38.5	54.3	40.7
El Salvador	2000	99.8	4.6	47.2	3.9	43.3	48.1	26.7
Guatemala	1989	100.0	0.6	38.7	2.9	35.8	60.7	47.5
	1998	100.0	2.0	42.9	1.7	41.2	55.1	34.8
Honduras	1990	100.0	0.6	34.9	4.0	30.9	64.6	47.6
	1999	100.0	3.1	33.4	3.7	29.7	63.5	41.3
Mexico [c]	1989	100.0	2.5	50.2	-	50.2	47.3	34.6
	2000	100.0	5.0	51.0	6.6	44.4	44.0	25.1
Nicaragua	1993	100.0	0.2	38.4	6.6	31.8	61.3	45.8
	1998	100.0	3.3	43.7	-	43.7	53.0	39.7
Panama	1991	100.0	2.9	39.1	12.5	26.6	58.0	45.5
	1999	100.0	3.2	44.9	10.1	34.8	51.9	31.6
Paraguay	1999	100.0	3.4	27.0	3.4	23.6	69.7	54.0
Peru	1999	100.0	6.3	19.9	2.3	17.6	73.9	61.9
Dominican Republic	1992	100.0	4.0	52.4	13.2	39.2	43.7	21.6
	2000	100.0	1.8	40.3	8.1	32.2	57.8	32.6
Venezuela	1990	100.0	6.9	46.6	8.3	38.3	46.5	33.3
	1997	100.0	5.4	49.6	5.4	44.2	44.9	33.1

Source: ECLAC, on the basis of special tabulations of data from household surveys conducted in the respective countries.

[a] Includes domestic employees. In Brazil (1990), Chile (1990), Mexico (1989) and Nicaragua (1998), includes public-sector wage earners.
[b] Data from national socio-economic surveys (CASEN).
[c] Data from national surveys of household income and expenditure (ENIGH).

An increase in wage employment in both agricultural and non-agricultural activities has helped to reduce poverty. In a few cases, however, these changes have raised poverty among workers engaged in wage-earning activities, even in private firms with more than five employees (see table I.11).

Table I.11
LATIN AMERICA (15 COUNTRIES): POVERTY IN SELECTED OCCUPATIONAL
GROUPS, [a] RURAL AREAS, 1990-2000
(Percentages)

Country	Year	Total population	Total employed	Public-sector wage earners	Non-professional, non-technical private-sector wage earners			Non-professional, non-technical own-account workers	
					In establishments employing over 5 workers	In establishments employing up to 5 workers [b]	Domestic employees	Total	In agriculture, forestry and fishing
Bolivia	1999	81	80	14	25	58	37	86	88
Brazil [c]	1990	71	64	-	45	72	61	70	74
	1999	55	49	39	47	40	41	54	55
Chile	1990	40	27	-	28	36	23	22	24
	2000	24	16	9	16	20	10	16	21
Colombia	1991	60	53	-	42[d e]	-	54	67	73
	1999	62	50	12	41[e]	-	45	64	66
Costa Rica	1990	27	17	-	13	23	22	24	27
	1999	22	12	3	7	21	22	17	21
El Salvador	1995	64	53	24	43	56	50	63	72
	1999	65	55	16	42	56	47	71	80
Guatemala	1989	78	70	42	72	76	61	71	76
	1998	70	66	40	63	77	60	69	69
Honduras	1990	88	83	-	71	90	72	88	90
	1999	86	81	38	79	89	75	85	89
Mexico	1989	57	49	-	53[f]	-	50	47	54
	1998	55	46	16	44	59	64	49	61
Nicaragua	1993	83	75	71	64	77	59	82	89
	1998	77	70	-	61	69	49	80	87
Panama	1991	51	40	10	25	43	43	52	57
	1999	42	29	5	19	39	30	37	42
Paraguay	1999	74	65	10	47	57	43	75	79
Peru	1999	73	66	33	42	54	38	73	78
Dominican Republic	1997	39	25	17	14	26	40	30	42
Venezuela	1990	47	31	22	35	36	44	31	36
	1994	56	42	27	50	50	53	42	44

Source: ECLAC, on the basis of special tabulations of data from household surveys conducted in the respective countries.

[a] Refers to the percentage of employed in each category residing in households that have an income below the poverty line.
[b] In Bolivia (1999), Chile (1996), El Salvador, Panama, the Dominican Republic and Venezuela, includes establishments employing up to 4 workers only.
[c] The 1990 figures for establishments employing over 5 workers refer to workers with a contract of employment ("carteira"), and the 1990 figures for establishments employing up to 5 workers refer to workers without such a contract.
[d] Includes public-sector wage earners.
[e] Includes wage earners in establishments employing up to 5 workers.
[f] Includes wage earners in the public sector and in establishments employing up to 5 workers.

Agriculture is the sector of the economy with the largest proportion of precarious employment. The highest proportion of workers without a contract or social security coverage is to be found among agricultural wage earners. In addition, the practice of subcontracting is becoming more and more widespread.

Male non-agricultural rural employment increased in seven of the eight Latin American countries for which recent information is available (see table I.12). In those seven countries the proportion of the male rural population whose main activity was non-agricultural work ranged from 22% to 57%, while the corresponding rate for employed rural women was over 65% in eight of 10 countries. In short, about a quarter of the decline in agricultural employment was absorbed by displacement into non-agricultural activities.

Table I.12
LATIN AMERICA: POPULATION EMPLOYED IN NON-AGRICULTURAL ACTIVITIES
AS A PERCENTAGE OF THE EMPLOYED POPULATION IN RURAL AREAS,
1990-1999
(Percentages)

Country	Men				Women			
	1990	1994	1997	1999	1990	1994	1997	1999
Bolivia	...	...	18.2	16.5	...	...	15.6	16.8
Brazil	26	21.3	23.7	25.8	47.1	28	30.1	31.6
Chile	19.2	26.6	25.9	27.6	67.2	70.7	65.1	63.3
Colombia	30.9	35.7	32.9	31.2	71.4	77.4	78.4	77.4
Costa Rica	47.8	55.4	57.3	57.4	86.8	89.2	88.3	90.3
El Salvador	...	...	32.7	36.1	...	...	81.4	86.5
Guatemala	21.4	...	...	27.2	69.2	...	...	67.7
Honduras	18.6	24.7	21.5	23.4	88	87	83.7	87.9
Mexico	34.7	42	44.9	46.8	69.1	64.7	67.4	74.8
Nicaragua	...	25.9	...	24.5	...	80	...	73.6
Panama	25	36.6	39.3	40.3	86.1	91.5	90.3	91.9
Paraguay	...	...	...	29.9	...	...	...	57.8
Peru	...	...	18.9	18.7	...	...	32.7	27.9
Dominican Republic	...	...	54.8	...	...	...	92.4	...
Venezuela	33.9	35.4	...	...	78.2	87.2	...	...

Source: ECLAC, on the basis of special tabulations of data from household surveys conducted in the respective countries.

The growing importance of non-agricultural employment derives from a combination of factors, such as technological advances in agricultural production; investments in road infrastructure, which have enabled rural residents to commute to urban areas; constraints on the rental and purchase of agricultural land; and deficiencies in the credit and crop insurance markets. In addition, families themselves tend to seek means of diversifying their production in order to mitigate the risks inherent in agricultural activity (see ECLAC/FAO/IDB/RIMISP, 2003 and ECLAC/GTZ, 2003).

This increase in the proportion of non-agricultural rural employment is very uneven, however: in the poorest areas, for example, non-agricultural rural employment first emerges in the form of small-scale goods production on the landholding itself, using traditional, labour-intensive technologies. There follows a second phase, still in the poorest areas, in which other agriculture-based activities are added, particularly the processing, distribution and marketing of agricultural products. These activities are aided by increases in agricultural and urban incomes. The better-off rural areas then move into a third phase, which involves some elements of manufacturing and generates a rural-urban interpenetration. In this third phase, manufacturing firms move into small and medium-sized towns, rural workers are subcontracted to produce durable intermediate goods and rural services related to increases in urban income, such as services related to tourism and country homes, are expanded. In addition, this phase leads to a rise in non-agricultural employment in health and education services and in other social services for the rural population, such as construction and transport.

For many members of poor rural households, entry into non-agricultural activities is a survival strategy. What is more, a large proportion of the rural population employed in non-agricultural activities remains poor or extremely poor, depending on how far the respective country has progressed in terms of non-agricultural rural development (Reardon, Cruz and Berdegué, 1999). In most of the countries, as figure I.5 shows, poverty levels are much lower (50%) among workers employed in non-agricultural activities than among those employed in agricultural activities.

(d)   Access to land

In 2000 Latin America was still one of the regions with the highest concentration of land ownership. Three groups of countries may be distinguished in this regard. The countries in the first group (Chile, Mexico and Paraguay) have Gini indices of over 0.90; those in the second (Argentina, Brazil, Colombia, Costa Rica, El Salvador, Panama and

Venezuela) have Gini indices of between 0.79 and 0.85; and those in the third (Dominican Republic, Honduras, Jamaica, Puerto Rico and Uruguay) have indices of about 0.75.

Figure I.5
LATIN AMERICA: POVERTY AMONG THE POPULATION EMPLOYED IN
AGRICULTURAL AND NON-AGRICULTURAL ACTIVITIES
IN RURAL AREAS, 1997-1998
(Percentages)

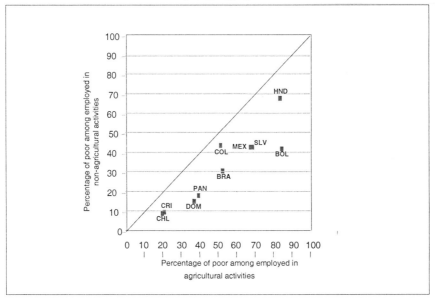

Source: ECLAC, on the basis of special tabulations of data from household surveys conducted in the respective countries.

Among the countries for which information is available, only Honduras (in the third group) had an even lower Gini index, which in the mid-1990s dropped from 0.71 to close to 0.65 (see table I.13).[10]

These levels of concentration, in combination with other factors, explain the many conflicts that arose in the 1990s over land ownership.[11]

---

[10] Gini indices take into account only the size of the landholding, not its quality. They therefore fail to consider, among other things, the landholding's distance from markets, weather conditions, access to irrigation systems and, in general, the crop yields permitted by the soil quality. In some countries the consideration of these factors could reveal trends that are at variance from those indicated with regard to the distribution of agricultural potential.

In Brazil, for example, the number of families involved in land occupations rose from 8,000 in 1990 to 63,000 in 1997. In the Dominican Republic, between 15% and 17% of the land, whether private or State-owned, is occupied on a de facto basis by poor campesinos. In Chile indigenous communities have made increasing claims on the land.

Over time, governments have taken a variety of measures to deal with the land distribution problem. In the 1960s and 1970s there were a number of attempts at agrarian reform, but these policies later gave way to other distribution arrangements. In the 1990s efforts to formalize rural land ownership through land title and registration programmes began to figure more prominently on the political agenda.

Table I.13
LATIN AMERICA AND THE CARIBBEAN (16 COUNTRIES): GINI INDICES OF LAND
CONCENTRATION, 1970-1994
(Percentages)

Group of countries [a]	Gini index		
	Circa 1970	Circa 1985	Circa 1994
Chile	0.92	...	0.92
Mexico	0.93	...	...
Paraguay	...	0.93	0.93
Brazil	0.84	0.85	0.81
Colombia	0.86	0.79	0.79
Costa Rica	0.81	0.80	...
Ecuador	0.81	...	...
El Salvador	0.80	0.83	...
Panama	0.77	...	0.85
Peru	0.88	0.83	0.86
Venezuela	0.90	0.89	...
Honduras	0.71	...	0.66
Jamaica	0.79	...	...
Puerto Rico	0.76	0.77	...
Dominican Republic	0.78	0.73	...
Uruguay	0.81	0.80	0.76

Source: ECLAC, Agricultural Development Unit, on the basis of agricultural censuses conducted in the respective countries.

[a] The countries are divided into three groups by their Gini index values.

---

[11]   In Paraguay, for example, there were over 200 land occupations between 1989 and 1996, involving more than 600,000 hectares and almost 40,000 campesino families. Between 1989 and 1991 over 3,000 arrests were made in relation to land occupations, and armed groups were set up to dissuade the campesinos involved (see Molinas, 1999).

Recent studies[12] show that transactions on the agricultural land market tend to take place within the same stratum of producers, and therefore do not modify the unequal structure of land ownership. Also, the most dynamic markets are located close to cities and in newly settled areas —not, in other words, where the poorest campesinos usually live. Changes in the structure of land ownership have therefore been limited and have not benefited the most marginalized households.

Moreover, it is acknowledged that credit markets have certain shortcomings and that the poorest campesinos lack the resources to buy land. This has led to the creation of special credit access programmes, which are up to 75% subsidized in some cases. However, in Latin America the formal land market exists alongside another market in which informal title is the prevalent form of ownership. This limits access to credit for working and investment capital.

As a fixed asset and a factor of production, land has particular features —as a geographically dispersed immovable asset whose financial value is heavily dependent on weather conditions, location, access to water and other factors— that make markets for agricultural land significantly different from markets for mass-produced goods. By their very nature, land markets are extremely imperfect and segmented, and involve high and largely fixed transaction costs (Muñoz, 1999).

In addition, most of the region's countries lack one of the most important tools for the development of a rural land market: an efficient, reliable and workable registry system that gives users the legal and financial information they need to participate in the market (Tejada and Peralta, 1999). All this has helped to perpetuate the high concentration of land markets and the shortcomings of credit markets, which impact negatively on small-scale producers and campesino families.

4. Vulnerability and poverty

(a) The concept of social vulnerability

The terms "vulnerability" and "vulnerable groups" have been used to refer to a social phenomenon of multiple dimensions which is manifested in the feelings of risk, insecurity and helplessness expressed by the population in public opinion polls. How vulnerable individuals and households are is directly related to their degree of control over

---

[12] Joint ECLAC/GTZ project on policies to develop rural land markets in Latin America, 1999.

different kinds of resources and assets, the mobilization of which enables them to make use of the existing opportunity structures at a given point in time, either to enhance their well-being or to prevent it from declining when it comes under threat (Kaztman, 1999).

The resources available to individuals and households include all the tangible and intangible assets they control, such as labour capacity, human capital, productive resources and social and family relationships. Labour, which is the most important resource of middle- and low-income groups, has been affected by external liberalization, the demands of competitiveness and the increased flexibility of the labour market.[13] In this framework, the abiding trend towards structural unemployment and informal employment has worsened, leading to more precarious employment, the weakening of trade unions and a decline in their bargaining power. With regard to human capital, there are still obstacles that hinder the process of giving new generations the capital they need for an era in which knowledge is an essential factor of production. In addition, human capital is devalued in cases where former employees of firms that have become uncompetitive and failed cannot find new jobs in firms that have stayed afloat by using new technologies and new methods of labour organization to deal with changes in their environment. Social vulnerability is also associated with a lack of access to productive resources on the part of low-productivity sectors, which have to deal with external trade liberalization and the loss of traditional markets as their outputs are displaced by newly introduced goods and services, and which moreover do not usually have the benefit of suitable protection and development policies. Vulnerability is also worsened when social relations, which form an important part of the social capital of individuals and families, are weak. These links and networks are crucial in affording access to jobs, information and positions of power. Contemporary transformations have affected traditional forms of organization, social participation and political representation, and this has even weakened social cohesiveness in many countries. Family relations, which provide individuals with support and assistance, have also been damaged by the increase in the number of failed marriages and the emergence of new, less stable types of unions.

---

[13] As stated in UNDP (2002, p. 29), it is possible to distinguish various sectors of employers and workers who have successfully withstood this trend towards greater flexibility. Also, there is a category of low-skilled workers who have always worked in flexible conditions; the discussion of increased flexibility thus refers only to other workers. This means that the problem is asymmetrical flexibility, which implies that the costs of the adjustment are unequally distributed among the population.

(b)   Measuring vulnerability

The rotation of households into or out of poverty can be a good indicator with respect to the population that can be considered vulnerable. Owing to fluctuations in household income from one year to the next, it is not unusual for the number of families below the poverty line to increase, or indeed decrease. Although longitudinal surveys that could systemically monitor this phenomenon are not conducted in Latin America, it is possible to identify households whose per capita income is between 1 and 1.25 times the poverty line or between 1.25 and 2 times the poverty line. Between 7% and 11% of the region's households —in different countries and at different times— are in the first group, and an average of about 20% are in the second. Given that national income in the different countries fluctuated widely in the 1980s and 1990s and that a significant proportion of the population experienced job loss at least once during those periods, it can reasonably be deduced that there was a more frequent rotation of households moving into or out of poverty. These figures therefore lead to the conclusion that around 30% of households may be considered vulnerable.

(c)   Policies to address vulnerability

As government policy gradually incorporates the objective of reducing vulnerability as a complement to combating poverty, new tasks begin to figure on the economic and social policy agenda. The objective of reducing vulnerability is yet another reason to develop economic policies aimed at achieving faster, steadier growth. It also calls for efforts to substantially raise the productivity of micro- and small enterprises, which, it is now clear, are no passing phenomenon. Meanwhile, it is necessary to increase the coverage, priority and efficiency of social policy. Among other things, this means targeting the low- and middle-income groups that are least able to cope with frequent economic recessions.

The variability of household income has worsened the situation of many families by forcing them to liquidate assets or to resort to extremely costly loans. This is particularly true of low- and middle-income households which, while not actually becoming poor, experience a decline in well-being and a feeling of insecurity. What is more, drops in household income can hamper families' access to social services, thereby exacerbating the downturn in their living standards and their loss of stability.

Efforts to reduce social vulnerability and continue to combat poverty are particularly hard to pursue in a context of fierce international competition that calls for macroeconomic discipline, trade liberalization and labour flexibility. It is therefore essential to develop a new social policy that is closely linked and coordinated with, rather than separate from, economic policy (ECLAC, 2000a).

In the framework of this convergence between social and economic policy, labour market-related measures must be adopted to reduce vulnerability. The fundamental measures required include the promotion and protection of employment, which, in macroeconomic terms, means maintaining relative prices that do not hurt employment; ongoing training of the labour force to prepare people to work with new technologies and thus to cope better with the restructuring of production; and the improvement of labour legislation to safeguard workers' rights and promote harmonious and equitable relations within firms. It is also necessary to provide formal education for young people to prevent them from joining the labour force prematurely; to promote women's access to the labour market in non-discriminatory conditions; and, lastly, to develop financing formulas for the implementation of unemployment insurance, in order to provide workers with effective protection during times of economic recession and productive readjustment. Labour adaptability can thus help to boost systemic competitiveness while making workers less vulnerable and enhancing their technical and professional skills.

In addition, the vast majority of low-productivity sectors consist of low-technology micro- and small enterprises whose workers lack professional or technical skills, and of equally unskilled own-account workers. In almost all the Latin American countries these sectors account for at least half of all jobs. Policies such as guaranteeing these enterprises and own-account workers ready access to credit, technology and markets, and supporting them in the areas of information, product development, marketing channels and business management, are indispensable if these productive units are to be viable concerns. At the same time, such policies should help to increase the productivity and stability of those sectors' activities in order to increase the amount of income they generate and reduce poverty and vulnerability.

Clearly, it is no easy matter to put such policies in place. First of all, microenterprises are hard to locate, both because many of them are not properly registered and because they often change addresses or cease to exist. In addition, they often fail to comply with institutional requirements, especially in the financial area. Accordingly, unless the sector can be helped to achieve at least some degree of organization of its own, measures for its benefit could be very costly.

Second, with regard to access to social services, specific measures to reduce poverty, particularly extreme poverty, should be complemented with other measures to assist low- and middle-income strata whose income is more variable and prone to decline. This means providing access to high-quality services such as education and health care. It has already been noted that vulnerable groups find their access to these services constrained in times of economic crisis because they can no longer afford health-care premiums or education costs, which are increasingly managed by the private sector. Even in boom periods, the quality of the services available to the most vulnerable sectors is far from ideal, and it worsens in times of recession. Clearly, no policy that is supposed to maintain certain minimum social standards can exclude the possibility of requiring individuals with more resources to pay for their own consumption of these services so that the benefits of public policies can be concentrated in vulnerable groups.

In particular, continuous access to quality education must be a central component of any policy for reducing vulnerability. In this respect, the gaps in the education of vast sectors of the population became apparent in the 1980s and 1990s, when education proved to be increasingly ill-adapted to productive processes based on new technologies. Education and vocational training, especially for those who are neither professionals nor technicians, are not very compatible with the demands of the new forms of production. This is particularly evident when individuals who lose their jobs try unsuccessfully to find employment in other occupations. Efforts to reintegrate such individuals into the labour market have had little success. Thus, the insufficient qualifications of a considerable proportion of the population can easily become a source of vulnerability. This should be a wake-up call for the education system and has prompted a number of reforms in this regard. Such reforms should ensure, among other things, that students have opportunities to update their knowledge on an ongoing basis.

It is also important to guarantee that retirement and other pensions, particularly those involving the lowest amounts, at least maintain their value, since their purchasing power tends to decline in times of inflation or budget cuts.

Third, the countries should design social policies that can meet the basic needs of the whole population by combining the resources, initiatives and capacities that exist in civil society and within the State. Monetary income, mainly from labour, is not the only means of enabling individuals to achieve their aspirations in terms of well-being. Factors such as housing, the surrounding environment, social infrastructure —drinking water, electricity, telephone, sewerage systems, paved roads, sports complexes, etc.— health and education, organizational networks, the instruments and tools developed by households and their initiatives are also important in this regard. These are resources which can be used by public or private initiatives to protect or further social development.

Fourth, in the 1990s the governments embarked on major efforts to increase social spending, even though economic growth was limited in most of the countries. At the same time, increasingly deregulated markets and the need to be highly competitive in economies that were becoming more and more open revealed major areas of inefficiency in the public and private sectors. For this reason, social policy must be viewed in a wider context in which more efficient use of resources is essential. In particular, it is necessary to reform social public institutions and train their staff better if social spending is to continue to expand.

In turn, efficiency improvements are closely associated with more extensive civic participation. That is to say, in addition to the proper use of fiscal resources and the implementation of operational methods that combine these resources with others from socially-oriented non-governmental organizations, it is necessary to develop a public policy that encourages the direct involvement of the citizenry. In this regard, social networks and the non-governmental organizations that support them are beginning to gain importance in some areas. The State should forge an alliance with these new organizations, in order to deal with the wide range of social problems that jeopardize public safety and social well-being.

Fifth, a number of proposals have been put forward to deal with increases in vulnerability as a result of international financial crises, through the creation of special funds or safety nets which would enable State assistance to reach the groups worst affected by the domestic recessionary impact of such crises. These funds could be financed from State savings set aside in boom periods or from international cooperation. Although such cooperation is not easy to secure, it is generally agreed that this type of measure needs some kind of permanent institutional structure that can respond quickly and effectively when crisis breaks out.

Sixth, it is necessary to create an appropriate institutional structure to implement social policy, in keeping with the conditions and requirements imposed by the new development model adopted by the Latin American countries. In this regard, it is necessary to afford social affairs the same degree of importance as economic and political affairs and to achieve a convergence between sectoral policies and programmes in the areas of health, education, housing and social security, on the one hand, and measures that target specific vulnerable groups and geographical areas, on the other. By the same token, there is a need to combine the efforts of different actors and institutions to eradicate poverty and reduce vulnerability.

In summary, the figures for the 1990s show that in many of the region's countries, a huge volume of resources could be needed to significantly reduce poverty and social vulnerability. It is therefore vital to speed up and stabilize economic growth, in view of both its direct impact on poverty and the additional leeway it affords to public revenue and spending. At the same time, economic expansion must be built, at least in part, on an improvement in low-productivity jobs, to avoid a situation in which social policy alone must compensate for slack growth and unstable income levels. Likewise, a medium-term vision for the social policy budget, together with the creation of reserve funds, would help to prevent excessive fluctuations in the resource flows of low- and middle-income strata.

Methodological annex

(a)   Method used to measure poverty

The estimated poverty rates used in this chapter were calculated using the cost of basic needs method, which is based on the calculation of poverty lines. The poverty line is the minimum income the members of a household must have in order to satisfy their basic needs. Where the necessary information was available, the poverty line for each country and geographical area was estimated on the basis of the cost of a basic food basket covering the population's nutritional needs, taking into account their consumption habits, the effective availability of food items and their relative prices. To the value of this basket was then added an estimate of the resources households need to satisfy their basic non-nutritional needs.[14]

The indigence line corresponds to the cost of the food basket, and indigents, or the extremely poor, are defined as individuals living in households whose income is so low that even if all of it were used to buy food, such households would still not be able to properly meet the nutritional needs of all their members. The value of the poverty line was obtained by multiplying the value of the indigence line by a constant factor that accounts for basic non-food costs, which was 2 for urban areas and about 1.75 for rural areas (see ECLAC, 1999c, box I.2).[15]

The differences in food prices between metropolitan areas and other urban and rural areas were taken into account in the calculation of indigence lines. In general, prices in other urban areas and in rural areas were 5% and 25% lower, respectively, than the prices registered in metropolitan areas.

With regard to sources of information, household income data were taken from household surveys conducted in the respective countries. In line with usual practice, both missing answers to certain questions on income —in the case of wage-earners, own-account workers and retirees— and probable biases arising from underreporting were

---

[14]   Information on the structure of household consumption of both food and other goods and services was obtained from surveys on household budgets conducted in the respective countries. Where no data from a recent survey of this type were available, other relevant information on household consumption was used.

[15]   The only country for which this general approach was not used was Brazil. In this case, the study used new indigence lines estimated for different geographical areas within the country, in the framework of a joint project conducted by the Brazilian Geographical and Statistical Institute (IBGE), the Brazilian Institute of Applied Economic Research (IPEA) and ECLAC.

corrected. In the latter case, the survey entries for income were compared with equivalent figures from an estimate of the household income and expenditure account from each country's system of national accounts. Income was understood to include compensation for wage labour (in cash and in kind) and own-account labour (including self-supply and the consumption value of home-made products), income from property, retirement and other pensions and other transfers received by households. For most of the countries the imputed rental value of owner-occupied dwellings was added to the income of households living in such dwellings.

To calculate the percentages of poor and indigent households and individuals, the monthly per capita value of the respective lines was compared with the total income of each household, also expressed in per capita terms. In turn, nationwide poverty and indigence indices were calculated as a weighted average of the figures corresponding to each geographical area, which means that they reflect not only the incidence of poverty in each area, but also the percentage of poverty and indigence with respect to the total population of each country.

(b)   Indicators for measuring poverty

Poverty is considered to be an eminently normative concept associated with individual well-being. Consequently, there is neither a single definition of the phenomenon nor a universal method for measuring it. There is a consensus, however, that poverty must be measured in at least two stages: the poor population must be identified, and poverty must be aggregated using a synthetic measurement.

In the first stage, a threshold known as the poverty line (z) is defined as a means of identifying the population whose per capita income (ypc) is lower than the cost of a basket of items that satisfy basic needs ($ypc < z$).

In the second stage —aggregation— an indicator is selected to reflect individuals' income shortfall in relation to the poverty line. A "good" poverty indicator should meet certain criteria, the most important of which are the following three axioms:

- Monotonicity: a reduction in the income of a poor household —ceteris paribus— should increase the poverty indicator.

- Transfer: a transfer of income from a poor household to a wealthier one —ceteris paribus— should increase the poverty indicator.

- Decomposability: it should be possible to calculate a given population's poverty indicator as the weighted sum of the indices of the different subgroups of which it is composed.

The most commonly used poverty measurements may be summarized on the basis of a parametric index family proposed by Foster, Greer and Thorbecke (1984, pp. 761-766):

$$FTG_{\alpha} = \frac{1}{n} \sum_{i=1}^{q} \left[\frac{z - y_i}{z} \right]^{\alpha} \quad (1)$$

where $\alpha > 0$ and q is the number of individuals with income lower than z.

When $\alpha = 0$, the expression (1) corresponds to what is known as the poverty incidence index (H), which represents the proportion of individuals whose income is lower than the poverty line (z).

$$H = q/n \quad (2)$$

Because it is easy to calculate and interpret, this indicator is the most commonly used of all. However, although it is decomposable, it does not satisfy the first two axioms listed above, so that its usefulness for poverty analysis is in some ways limited.

When $\alpha = 1$, however, an indicator measuring the relative shortfall in the income of poor individuals with respect to the value of z can be obtained. This indicator is known as the poverty gap (PG):

$$PG = \frac{1}{n} \sum_{i=1}^{q} \left[\frac{z - y_i}{x} \right] \quad (3)$$

The poverty gap (PG) satisfies the axiom of monotonicity, but not the axiom of transfers, which means that this indicator does not reflect unequal income distribution among the poor.

Lastly, an index reflecting both the poverty gap and income distribution is obtained when $\alpha = 2$:

$$FTG_2 = \frac{1}{n} \sum_{i=1}^{q} \left[\frac{z - y_i}{z} \right]^2$$

Although it is less intuitive than the previous indicators, this one is particularly useful for policy design and evaluation. Since it satisfies all three axioms, it serves to generate conclusive classifications of countries, geographical units or social groups in order to pinpoint the worst pockets of poverty.

(c)   Methodological considerations with respect to alternative poverty estimates

Poverty can be measured using a number of different methodologies, whose results vary widely and may even contradict one another. It is therefore important to be aware of the existence of measurements that differ from those used by ECLAC in the Social Panorama of Latin America and to take due precautions in interpreting and comparing their results. Specifically, the procedure used by the World Bank to draw up international comparisons of poverty is described below as an example of an alternative methodology for calculating poverty lines.

The World Bank uses a single poverty line to compare poverty in different countries or over time. This threshold, which reflects poverty levels in the lowest-income countries, is calculated as the median value of the world's 10 lowest national per capita poverty lines. In 2000 this value was US$ 32.74 per month in terms of purchasing power parity (PPP), or US$ 1.08 per day. Thus the threshold known as "a dollar a day" reflects a level of income low enough for the person who receives it to be considered poor anywhere in the world. The World Bank also usually includes a higher poverty line in its tables, obtained by multiplying the above value by two to reflect slightly higher standards of poverty.

When a single poverty line is used for all countries, problems of comparability inevitably arise because price levels are different in each country. This problem may be solved, at least partially, by using different exchange rates to reflect purchasing power parity (PPP). In other words, exchange rates are corrected so that a dollar has the same buying power anywhere in the world. In World Bank (2001) the poverty line is expressed in "PPP dollars" valued at 1993 prices.[16] The final step in the poverty calculation procedure is to adjust the survey data to the reference year of the poverty line by deflating those values in accordance with the consumer price index (CPI) over the period.

It is important to clarify that the purpose of the poverty line described here is to establish a common basis on which to make international comparisons. Consequently, when the objective is to evaluate or formulate policies or to analyse the characteristics of poverty in depth, the World Bank itself recommends using poverty lines that

---

[16]   The PPP exchange rates used today are estimated by the World Bank using International Comparison Programme (ICP) data from 1993, which cover a total of 110 countries. These estimates are not comparable to the PPP values used in previous years, which come from the Penn-World tables, since they can vary considerably owing to the methodology used.

reflect the specific situation in each country. The poverty lines calculated by ECLAC are of precisely this type, since they take into account each country's current energy requirements and demographic features.

Table I.14 compares ECLAC poverty estimates for the Latin American countries based on national poverty lines to World Bank poverty estimates based on international poverty lines, equivalent to US$ 32.74 (indigence) and US$ 65.48 (poverty) per month (1993 PPP). As the table shows, the World Bank's poverty and indigence estimates are almost always lower than the estimates calculated by ECLAC.

Table I.14
LATIN AMERICA: ESTIMATES BASED ON NATIONAL AND INTERNATIONAL
POVERTY LINES
(Percentages of the population)

Country	Year	National lines (ECLAC)		Year	International lines (World Bank)	
		Indigence	Poverty		Less than US$ 1 per day [a]	Less than US$ 2 per day [b]
Bolivia	1989 [c]	23.3	53.2	1990	11.3	38.6
Brazil	1996	13.9	35.8	1997	5.1	17.4
Chile	1994	8.0	28.6	1994	4.2	20.3
Colombia	1997	23.5	50.9	1996	11.0	28.7
Costa Rica	1997	7.8	22.5	1996	9.6	26.3
Ecuador	1994 [d]	25.5	57.9	1995	20.2	52.3
El Salvador	1997	23.3	55.5	1996	25.3	51.9
Guatemala	1989	41.8	69.1	1989	39.8	64.3
Honduras	1997	54.4	79.1	1996	40.5	68.8
Mexico	1996	21.3	52.1	1995	17.9	42.5
Panama	1997	13.0	33.2	1997	10.3	25.1
Paraguay	1994 [d]	18.8	49.9	1995	19.4	38.5
Dominican Republic	1997	14.4	37.2	1996	3.2	16.0
Uruguay	1990 [d]	3.4	17.8	1989	<2.0	6.6
Venezuela	1996	20.5	48.1	1996	14.7	36.4

Source: ECLAC, on the basis of special tabulations of data from household surveys conducted in the respective countries, and World Bank, *World Development Report 2000-2001: Attacking Poverty*, New York, Oxford University Press, September 2001.

[a] Equivalent to US$ 32.74 per person per month.
[b] Equivalent to US$ 65.48 per person per month.
[c] Eight departmental capitals plus the city of El Alto.
[d] Urban areas.

(d) Value of the indigence and poverty lines used to calculate the estimates

Table I.15

LATIN AMERICA (18 COUNTRIES): INDIGENCE LINES (IL) AND POVERTY LINES (PL)
(Monthly values per person)

Country	Year	Income reference period	Currency [a]	Urban IL	Urban PL	Rural IL	Rural PL	Exchange rate [b]	Urban IL	Urban PL	Rural IL	Rural PL
				Local currency					US dollars			
Argentina	1990 [e]	September	A	255 928	511 856	...	...	5 791.0	44.2	88.4	...	...
	1994	September	$	72	144	...	...	1.0	72.0	143.9	...	...
	1997 [c]	September	$	76	151	...	...	1.0	75.5	151.0	...	...
	1999	September	$	72	143	...	...	1.0	71.6	143.3	...	...
Bolivia	1989	October	Bs	68	137	...	...	2.9	23.8	47.5	...	...
	1994	June-November	Bs	120	240	...	...	4.7	25.7	51.4	...	...
	1997	May	Bs	155	309	125	219	5.3	29.4	58.8	23.9	41.8
	1999	October-November	Bs	167	333	130	228	5.9	28.0	56.1	21.9	38.3
Brazil	1990	September	Cr$	3 109	6 572	2 634	4 967	75.5	41.2	87.0	34.9	65.7
	1993	September	Cr$	3 400	7 391	2 864	5 466	111.2	30.6	66.5	25.8	49.2
	1996	September	R$	44	104	38	76	1.0	43.6	102.3	37.2	74.9
	1999	September	R$	51	126	43	91	1.9	26.7	66.2	22.7	48.1
Chile	1990	November	Ch$	9 297	18 594	7 164	12 538	327.4	28.4	56.8	21.9	38.3
	1994	November	Ch$	15 050	30 100	11 597	20 295	413.1	36.4	72.9	28.1	49.1
	1996	November	Ch$	17 136	34 272	13 204	23 108	420.0	40.8	81.6	31.4	55.0
	1998	November	Ch$	18 944	37 889	14 598	25 546	463.3	40.9	81.8	31.5	55.1
	2000	November	Ch$	20 281	40 562	15 628	27 349	525.1	38.6	77.2	29.8	52.1
Colombia	1991	August	Col$	18 093	36 186	14 915	26 102	645.6	28.0	56.1	23.1	40.4
	1994	August	Col$	31 624	63 249	26 074	45 629	814.8	38.8	77.6	32.0	56.0
	1997	August	Col$	53 721	107 471	44 333	77 583	1 141.0	47.1	94.2	38.9	68.0
	1999	August	Col$	69 838	139 716	57 629	100 851	1 873.7	37.3	74.6	30.8	53.8
Costa Rica	1990	June	¢	2 639	5 278	2 081	3 642	89.7	29.4	58.9	23.2	40.6
	1994	June	¢	5 264	10 528	4 153	7 268	155.6	33.8	67.7	26.7	46.7
	1997	June	¢	8 604	17 208	6 778	11 862	232.6	37.0	74.0	29.1	51.0
	1999	June	¢	10 708	21 415	8 463	14 811	285.3	37.5	75.1	29.7	51.9
Ecuador	1990	November	S/.	18 465	36 930	...	...	854.8	21.6	43.2	...	...
	1994	November	S/.	69 364	138 729	...	...	2 301.2	30.1	60.3	...	...
	1997	October	S/.	142 233	284 465	...	...	4 194.6	33.9	67.8	...	...
	1999	October	S/.	301 716	603 432	...	...	15 656.8	19.3	38.5	...	...
El Salvador	1995	January-December	¢	254	508	158	315	8.8	29.0	58.1	18.0	35.9
	1997	January-December	¢	290	580	187	374	8.8	33.1	66.2	21.4	42.8
	1999	January-December	¢	293	586	189	378	8.8	33.5	66.9	21.6	43.2
Guatemala	1989	April	Q	64	127	50	88	2.7	23.6	47.1	18.7	32.7
	1998	Dec.97 - Dec.98	Q	260	520	197	344	6.4	40.7	81.5	30.8	54.0
Honduras	1990	August	L	115	229	81	141	4.3	26.5	52.9	18.6	32.6
	1994	September	L	257	513	181	316	9.0	28.6	57.1	20.1	35.2
	1997	August	L	481	963	339	593	13.1	36.8	73.6	25.9	45.3
	1999	August	L	561	1 122	395	691	14.3	39.3	78.6	27.7	48.4
Mexico	1989	Third quarter	$	86 400	172 800	68 810	120 418	2 510.0	34.4	68.8	27.4	48.0
	1994	Third quarter	MN$	213	425	151	265	3.3	63.6	127.2	45.3	79.3
	1996	Third quarter	MN$	405	810	300	525	7.6	53.6	107.2	39.7	69.5
	1998	Third quarter	MN$	537	1 074	385	674	9.5	56.8	113.6	40.7	71.3
	2000	Third quarter	MN$	665	1 330	475	831	9.4	71.0	142.1	50.7	88.8
Nicaragua	1993	21 Feb.- 12 June	C$	167	334	129	225	4.6	36.6	73.3	28.2	49.4
	1997	October	C$	247	493	...	...	9.8	25.3	50.5	...	...
	1998	15 April - 31 Aug.	C$	275	550	212	370	10.4	26.3	52.7	20.3	35.5
Panama	1991	August	B	35	70	27	47	1.0	35.0	70.1	27.1	47.5
	1994	August	B	40	80	31	54	1.0	40.1	80.2	31.0	54.3
	1997	August	B	41	81	31	55	1.0	40.6	81.3	31.4	55.0
	1999	July	B	41	81	31	55	1.0	40.7	81.4	31.5	55.1
Paraguay	1990 [d]	June, July, August	G	43 242	86 484	...	...	1 207.8	35.8	71.6	...	...
	1994	August - September	G	87 894	175 789	...	...	1 916.3	45.9	91.7	...	...
	1996	July - November	G	108 572	217 143	...	...	2 081.2	52.2	104.3	...	...
	1999	July – December	G	138 915	277 831	106 608	186 565	3 311.4	42.0	83.9	32.2	56.3
Peru	1997	Fourth quarter	N$	103	192	83	128	2.7	42.1	84.3	31.6	55.3
	1999	Fourth quarter	N$	109	213	89	141	3.5	31.2	61.2	25.5	40.5
Dominican Republic	1997	April	RD$	601	1 203	451	789	14.3	42.1	84.3	31.6	55.3
Uruguay	1990	Second half	NUr$	41 972	83 944	...	...	1 358.0	30.9	61.8	...	...
	1994	Second half	$	281	563	...	...	5.4	52.1	104.1	...	...
	1997	Year	$	528	1 056	...	...	9.4	55.9	111.9	...	...
	1999	Year	$	640	1 280	...	...	11.3	56.4	112.9	...	...
Venezuela	1990	Second half	Bs	1 924	3 848	1 503	2 630	49.4	38.9	77.9	30.4	53.2
	1994	Second half	Bs	8 025	16 050	6 356	11 124	171.3	46.9	93.7	37.1	65.0
	1997 [e]	Second half	Bs	31 711	62 316	...	...	488.6	64.9	127.5	...	...
	1999 [e]	Second half	Bs	49 368	97 622	...	...	626.3	78.8	155.9	...	...

Source: ECLAC, on the basis of special tabulations of data from household surveys conducted in the respective countries.
[a] Local currencies:
Argentina: (A) Austral; ($) Peso   Bolivia: (Bs) Boliviano   Brazil: (Cr$) Cruzeiro; (R$) Real   Chile: (Ch$) Peso
Colombia: (Col$) Peso   Costa Rica: (¢) Colón   Ecuador: (S/.) Sucre   El Salvador: (¢) Colón
Guatemala: (Q) Quetzal   Honduras: (L) Lempira   Mexico: ($) Peso; (MN$) Nuevo Peso
Nicaragua: (C$) Córdoba   Panama: (B) Balboa   Paraguay: (G) Guaraní   Peru: (N$) Peso
Dominican Rep.: (RD$) Peso   Uruguay: (Nur$) Nuevo Peso; ($) Peso   Venezuela: (Bs) Bolívar
[b] International Monetary Fund "rf" series.
[c] Greater Buenos Aires.
[d] Asunción.
[e] Nationwide total.

Chapter II

Income distribution

1. Income concentration in the late 1990s

In the late 1990s, income distribution in most of the Latin American countries continued to be highly concentrated, with a substantial share of total income remaining in the hands of the richest 10% of households. In almost all countries of the region, the richest decile received more than 30% of total income, and in most of them (the exceptions being El Salvador and Venezuela), the figure was over 35% (in Brazil it was 45%). This decile's average income was 19 times higher than the average for the 40% of households with the lowest incomes, which received between 9% and 15% of total income. Uruguay is the exception in this case, in that the lowest-income group received about 22% of the total. In practically all of the countries, with the exception of Costa Rica and Uruguay, the per capita income of between 66% and 75% of the population was lower than the overall average (see table II.1).

Table II.1

LATIN AMERICA (17 COUNTRIES): HOUSEHOLD INCOME DISTRIBUTION, [a] 1990-1999

(Percentages)

Country	Year	Average income [b]	Share of total income of:				Ratio of average per capita income [c]	
			Poorest 40%	Next 30%	20% below richest 10%	Richest 10%	$D^{10}/D^{(1\ to\ 4)}$	Q^5/Q^1
Argentina [d]	1990	10.6	14.9	23.6	26.7	34.8	13.5	13.5
	1997	12.4	14.9	22.3	27.1	35.8	16.0	16.4
	1999	12.5	15.4	21.6	26.1	37.0	16.4	16.5
Bolivia	1989 [e]	7.7	12.1	22.0	27.9	38.2	17.1	21.4
	1997	5.8	9.4	22.0	27.9	40.7	25.9	34.6
	1999	5.7	9.2	24.0	29.6	37.2	26.7	48.1
Brazil	1990	9.3	9.5	18.6	28.0	43.9	31.2	35.0
	1996	12.3	9.9	17.7	26.5	46.0	32.2	38.0
	1999	11.3	10.1	17.3	25.5	47.1	32.0	35.6
Chile	1990	9.4	13.2	20.8	25.4	40.7	18.2	18.4
	1996	12.9	13.1	20.5	26.2	40.2	18.3	18.6
	2000	13.6	13.8	20.8	25.1	40.3	18.7	19.0
Colombia	1994	8.4	10.0	21.3	26.9	41.8	26.8	35.2
	1997	7.3	12.5	21.7	25.7	40.1	21.4	24.1
	1999	6.7	12.3	21.6	26.0	40.1	22.3	25.6
Costa Rica	1990	9.5	16.7	27.4	30.2	25.6	10.1	13.1
	1997	10.0	16.5	26.8	29.4	27.3	10.8	13.0
	1999	11.4	15.3	25.7	29.7	29.4	12.6	15.3
Ecuador [f]	1990	5.5	17.1	25.4	27.0	30.5	11.4	12.3
	1997	6.0	17.0	24.7	26.4	31.9	11.5	12.2
	1999	5.6	14.1	22.8	26.5	36.6	17.2	18.4
El Salvador	1995	6.2	15.4	24.8	26.9	32.9	14.1	16.9
	1997	6.1	15.3	24.5	27.3	33.0	14.8	15.9
	1999	6.6	13.8	25.0	29.1	32.1	15.2	19.6
Guatemala	1989	6.0	11.8	20.9	26.8	40.6	23.5	27.3
	1998	7.3	12.8	20.9	26.1	40.3	23.6	22.9

(Continued)

Table II.1 (concluded)

Country	Year	Average income [b]	Share of total income of:				Ratio of average per capita income [c]	
			Poorest 40%	Next 30%	20% below richest 10%	Richest 10%	$D^{10}/D^{(1\ to\ 4)}$	Q^5/Q^1
Honduras	1990	4.3	10.1	19.7	27.0	43.1	27.4	30.7
	1997	4.1	12.6	22.5	27.3	37.7	21.1	23.7
	1999	3.9	11.8	22.9	28.9	36.5	22.3	26.5
Mexico	1989	8.6	15.8	22.5	25.1	36.6	17.2	16.9
	1994	8.5	15.3	22.9	26.1	35.6	17.3	17.4
	1998	7.7	15.1	22.7	25.6	36.7	18.4	18.5
Nicaragua	1993	5.2	10.4	22.8	28.4	38.4	26.1	37.7
	1998	5.6	10.4	22.1	27.1	40.5	25.3	33.1
Panama	1991	8.9	12.5	22.9	28.8	35.9	20.0	24.3
	1997	11.0	12.4	21.5	27.5	38.6	21.5	23.8
	1999	11.1	12.9	22.4	27.7	37.1	19.5	21.6
Paraguay	1990 [g]	7.7	18.6	25.7	26.9	28.9	10.2	10.6
	1996 [f]	7.4	16.7	24.6	25.3	33.4	13.0	13.4
	1999	6.2	13.1	23.0	27.8	36.2	19.3	22.6
Dominican Rep.	1997	8.5	14.5	23.6	26.0	36.0	16.0	17.6
Uruguay [f]	1990	9.3	20.1	24.6	24.1	31.2	9.4	9.4
	1997	11.2	22.0	26.1	26.1	25.8	8.5	9.1
	1999	11.9	21.6	25.5	25.9	27.0	8.8	9.5
Venezuela	1990	8.9	16.7	25.7	28.9	28.7	12.1	13.4
	1997	7.8	14.7	24.0	28.6	32.8	14.9	16.1
	1999	7.2	14.6	25.1	29.0	31.4	15.0	18.0

Source: ECLAC, based on special tabulations from household surveys in the countries concerned.

[a] Households nationwide ranked by per capita income.
[b] Average monthly household income, in multiples of the per capita poverty line.
[c] $D^{(1\ to\ 4)}$ represents the bottom 40% of households in terms of income, while D^{10} represents the upper 10% of households in terms of income. The same notation is used in the case of quintiles (Q), which represent groupings of 20% of households.
[d] Greater Buenos Aires.
[e] Eight main cities and El Alto.
[f] Urban total.
[g] Asunción metropolitan area.

A simple comparison of the various household groups' average incomes also demonstrates how high a degree of inequity exists in Latin America. In Bolivia, Brazil and Nicaragua, the per capita income of the richest quintile (20% of households) is more than 30 times greater than the poorest quintile's. In the other countries, the average is also high (about 23 times). The ratio of the wealthiest decile's income to the income of the poorest four deciles also underscores the degree of concentration. In this case, the largest gap is seen in Brazil, where the most affluent decile's income is 32 times greater than the combined incomes of the four other deciles. The simple average difference region-wide is 19.3, which is extremely high when compared, for example, to the figures for Uruguay (8.8) or Costa Rica (12.6), the countries with the best income distribution in the region.[1]

The high degree of income concentration in Latin America can also be inferred from the Gini coefficient, which can be used to compare the overall income distribution in different countries or in different periods. A country ranking based on this indicator, calculated using the per capita income distribution for individuals,[2] confirms that, at the end of the 1990s, the highest concentration was in Brazil, which had an index of 0.64, followed by Bolivia, Nicaragua and Guatemala, in that order, with values close to 0.60; at the other end of the scale, Uruguay and Costa Rica, also in that order, again had the least inequality, with Gini indices below 0.48 (see table II.2).

Inequality nationwide does not necessarily follow the same pattern in urban and rural areas,[3] as in the majority of the countries, there tends to be less equity in urban than in rural areas. Thus, in 7 out of 13 countries, the Gini coefficient for urban areas is higher than for rural zones. The most striking cases are those of Brazil, Chile and Colombia, where the difference between the indices around 1999 was 0.049 points in Brazil and 0.042 points in the other two. Nonetheless, in some countries the situation is just the opposite, with income concentration being greater in rural areas than in urban centres. The largest gaps between urban and rural Gini

---

[1]   Although no figures are available that are comparable with those of the rest of the region, Cuba has probably maintained a less regressive income distribution than the other countries, despite the deterioration of that country's economy over the past decade.

[2]   This method of calculating the Gini coefficient is different from the one used in the *Social Panorama of Latin America*, in which the values are based on household income distribution.

[3]   As is well-known, average income levels are different in the two areas, and are invariably higher in urban zones. Although in some cases these differences are relatively small (for example, in Costa Rica), in others significant disparities are evident. In Bolivia, average income in urban areas is more than double the average income in rural areas.

coefficients are found in Bolivia and Paraguay, with 0.136 and 0.073 points respectively.[4]

Another indicator of income concentration is the percentage of persons whose per capita incomes are below the overall average. Average per capita income in Latin America falls between the seventh and eighth deciles, which means that between 67% and 77% of the population is below that threshold. In most of the countries, this proportion was smaller at the beginning of the 1980s. Thus, at present, around 75% of households have a below-average income. Moreover, because of this trend, a much larger share of increases in per capita GDP has gone to the top 25% of households in terms of income. Uruguay and Costa Rica, in that order, are the countries with the lowest percentage of persons receiving less than the average per capita income, while Brazil and Guatemala are at the opposite end of the scale (see table II.2).

Another version of this indicator is the percentage of persons whose per capita incomes are less than half of the mean; this option is particularly useful in illustrating the heterogeneity of income distribution in the region, inasmuch as it describes a more irregular portion of the distributive spectrum. For example, as can be seen from table II.2, although Uruguay and Costa Rica have practically the same percentage of persons with incomes below the mean, they are four percentage points apart when the threshold is set at half of that value.

According to this last indicator, most of the Latin American countries are in an intermediate range (between 40% and 50%), depending on what share of the population has an income of less than half of the average. Uruguay, Costa Rica, Venezuela and the Dominican Republic, in that order, have the least income concentration, since the share in question is under 40%. Brazil is the only country in the region where more than half of the population receives less than 50% of the mean income (see table II.2).

This method has been used in other countries to gauge relative poverty, which is being defined as a situation in which income is insufficient to afford a level of consumption commensurate with the prevailing standards in a given society. In this case, the indicator is used somewhat like a traditional poverty line, except that it moves in tandem with fluctuations in average income.

---

[4]   Another trait that is common to much of the region is that inequality is greater nationwide than inequality in urban and rural areas taken separately. The only exceptions are Bolivia and Paraguay, where the rural coefficient is higher than the national one. When inequality nationwide is greater than inequality in the urban and rural subgroups, this indicates that the disparities in income distribution between the two types of areas may play a very important role in shaping the pattern of income distribution.

Table II.2
LATIN AMERICA (17 COUNTRIES): INDICATORS OF INCOME CONCENTRATION,[a] 1990-1999

Country	Year	Percentage of persons with per capita incomes below:		Concentration indices			
		Average	50% of average	Gini[b]	Variance of logarithms	Theil	Atkinson
Argentina[c]	1990	70.6	39.1	0.501	0.982	0.555	0.570
	1997	72.1	43.4	0.530	1.143	0.601	0.607
	1999	72.5	44.2	0.542	1.183	0.681	0.623
Bolivia	1989[d]	71.9	44.1	0.538	1.528	0.574	0.771
	1997	73.1	47.7	0.595	2.024	0.728	0.795
	1999	70.4	45.5	0.586	2.548	0.658	0.867
Brazil	1990	75.2	53.9	0.627	1.938	0.816	0.790
	1996	76.3	54.4	0.638	1.962	0.871	0.762
	1999	77.1	54.8	0.640	1.913	0.914	0.754
Chile	1990	74.6	46.5	0.554	1.258	0.644	0.671
	1996	73.9	46.9	0.553	1.261	0.630	0.667
	2000	75.0	46.4	0.559	1.278	0.666	0.658
Colombia	1994	73.6	48.9	0.601	2.042	0.794	0.817
	1997	74.2	46.4	0.569	1.399	0.857	0.822
	1999	74.5	46.6	0.572	1.456	0.734	0.945
Costa Rica	1990	65.0	31.6	0.438	0.833	0.328	0.539
	1997	66.6	33.0	0.450	0.860	0.356	0.535
	1999	67.6	36.1	0.473	0.974	0.395	0.573
Ecuador[e]	1990	69.6	33.8	0.461	0.823	0.403	0.591
	1997	68.9	34.8	0.469	0.832	0.409	0.510
	1999	72.1	42.0	0.521	1.075	0.567	0.597
El Salvador	1995	69.7	38.4	0.507	1.192	0.502	0.695
	1997	69.9	40.2	0.510	1.083	0.512	0.583
	1999	68.5	40.6	0.518	1.548	0.496	0.798
Guatemala	1989	74.9	47.9	0.582	1.477	0.736	0.700
	1998	75.0	49.5	0.582	1.331	0.795	0.645

(Continued)

Table II.2 (concluded)

| Country | Year | Percentage of persons with per capita incomes below: | | Concentration indices | | | |
		Average	50% of average	Gini [b]	Variance of logarithms	Theil	Atkinson
Honduras	1990	75.1	52.3	0.615	1.842	0.817	0.746
	1997	72.5	45.4	0.558	1.388	0.652	0.697
	1999	71.8	46.4	0.564	1.560	0.636	0.746
Mexico	1989	74.2	43.5	0.536	1.096	0.680	0.598
	1994	73.1	44.7	0.539	1.130	0.606	0.592
	1998	72.8	43.1	0.539	1.142	0.634	0.599
Nicaragua	1993	71.5	45.9	0.582	1.598	0.671	0.802
	1998	73.1	45.9	0.584	1.800	0.731	0.822
Panama	1991	71.3	46.4	0.560	1.373	0.628	0.661
	1997	72.6	47.6	0.570	1.464	0.681	0.686
	1999	72.1	46.4	0.557	1.363	0.629	0.658
Paraguay	1990 [f]	69.2	33.4	0.447	0.737	0.365	0.468
	1996 [e]	72.9	37.9	0.493	0.916	0.515	0.544
	1999	72.3	46.3	0.565	1.555	0.668	0.716
Dominican Republic	1997	71.4	39.8	0.517	1.075	0.557	0.603
Uruguay [e]	1990	73.2	36.8	0.492	0.812	0.699	0.519
	1997	66.8	31.3	0.430	0.730	0.336	0.475
	1999	67.1	32.2	0.440	0.764	0.354	0.483
Venezuela	1990	68.0	35.5	0.471	0.930	0.416	0.545
	1997	70.8	40.7	0.507	1.223	0.508	0.985
	1999	69.4	38.6	0.498	1.134	0.464	0.664

Source: ECLAC, based on special tabulations from household surveys in the countries concerned.

[a] Calculated on the basis of individual per capita income nationwide.
[b] Includes individuals with zero income.
[c] Greater Buenos Aires .
[d] Eight main cities and El Alto.
[e] Urban total.
[f] Asunción metropolitan area.

2.   Trends over the decade

Over the past decade, the top 10% of households' share of total income continued to increase in most countries, thereby strengthening the trend towards a worsening distribution in Latin America. In fact, over that period, the share of income received nationwide by households in the top decile increased in eight countries, declined in five (although significantly so in only two, Honduras[5] and Uruguay) and held steady in one, Mexico. The countries in which the richest portion of the population's share increased include several that had been characterized by a better distribution of income. This share rose from 35% to 37% in Argentina, from 26% to 29% in Costa Rica and from 29% to 31% in Venezuela. In Chile, it remained at slightly above 40%, and in Uruguay, although it declined over the decade as a whole, it rose from 26% to 27% between 1997 and 1999. The share of the highest decile also increased in Brazil, Ecuador, Nicaragua and Panama, (from 44% to 47%, 31% to 37%, 38% to 41% and 36% to 37%, respectively) over the course of the decade. In contrast, in countries such as Colombia (between 1994 and 1999), El Salvador and Honduras, the highest-income group's share declined; the decrease was less than two percentage points in Colombia and El Salvador, but was larger in Honduras (see table II.1).

Trends differed with regard to the percentage of income received by the poorest 40% of households over the decade. This figure fell in five countries, rose in eight and held steady in one (Nicaragua). The steepest decreases were in countries that experienced major crises (Ecuador and Venezuela), but there was also a reduction in the share of the bottom 40% in Costa Rica, El Salvador and Mexico. Moreover, where there were improvements, they were relatively minor, and surpassed two percentage points in just one case (Colombia from 1994 to 1997, but with a slight deterioration from 1997 to 1999). The improvements amounted to more than one percentage point in three others (Honduras, Guatemala and Uruguay) and around 0.5% in Argentina, Brazil, Chile and Panama.

The variations exhibited by the intermediate strata —i.e., the 50% of all households positioned between the poorest 40% and the richest 10%— generally did not follow the same pattern as in the case of the top and

---

[5]   It should be noted, however, that the data for Honduras for the 1990s may not be fully comparable owing to changes in the income-measurement methodology that were introduced with the 1994 household survey. These changes, which have to do, in particular, with how broad a definition of income was used for the study, may have influenced (although in a way that is hard to pinpoint) the distribution profile of household income in 1990, compared to that of subsequent years; thus, it may have affected the analysis of the trend throughout the decade.

bottom strata. In at least seven countries, changes in income share —increases and decreases alike— amounted to two percentage points or less. The share of total income received by this group was very similar at the beginning and end of the decade in Chile, Colombia (between 1994 and 1999), Guatemala, Mexico and Venezuela. The most interesting case is that of Venezuela, where the intermediate groups maintained their share in spite of the serious crisis that hit the country in the last half of the 1990s. Only El Salvador (from 1995 to 1999), Honduras and Uruguay posted major gains in the relative income received by the intermediate strata. In the latter two cases, this was at the expense of the top decile. Brazil and Ecuador were the only countries in which relative incomes in this group fell by more than three percentage points, as a result of the strong relative gains made by the upper-income strata. In Argentina, the intermediate groups saw their share of income drop steadily throughout the decade, with the total decrease amounting to 2.6 percentage points. In Chile, this group's share declined by 0.8 percentage points from 1996 to 2000, thus undoing the cumulative gains of the first half of the 1990s. In Uruguay, however, although the share of intermediate groups also fell by 0.8 percentage points between 1997 and 1999, this decline was not large enough to reverse the strong improvement of previous years. Despite these fluctuations, the trend in the income share of intermediate groups indicates that in some countries these groups have relatively powerful means of defending their share of total income.

The above trends strengthen the impression that income distribution has worsened. Among 13 countries in which nationwide information was available for the beginning and end of the decade, eight saw an increase in the ratio between the incomes of the highest decile and those of the poorest 40%, while only four saw a decline and one showed no change. The countries in which this disparity increased the most were, in this order, Ecuador (urban area), Costa Rica, Venezuela and Argentina, while the sharpest decreases occurred in Colombia (between 1994 and 1997) and probably in Honduras as well (see figure II.1).

An analysis of the percentage of the population having a per capita income of less than 50% of the average level yields similar results. Only two countries, Honduras and Uruguay, registered a significant reduction in this indicator of inequality.[6] A number of others showed a marked increase (most notably the same countries which, as mentioned above, saw their income gap widen), while Brazil and Guatemala posted moderate upswings. In Chile, Nicaragua and Panama this indicator held fairly steady (see figure II.1).

---

[6]   This index can also be used to measure relative poverty.

The largest nationwide increases in the Gini coefficient during the decade were seen in Costa Rica and Venezuela. This indicator also deteriorated in Argentina (Greater Buenos Aires) and Ecuador (urban areas). Although to a lesser extent, inequality in income distribution was also somewhat greater at the end than at the beginning of the decade in Brazil and El Salvador (between 1995 and 1999), while in Chile, Guatemala, Mexico, Nicaragua and Panama, the situation was largely unchanged. Uruguay (urban areas) and Honduras, as well as Colombia (from 1994 to 1999), were the only countries of the region that managed to reduce income concentration, as gauged by the Gini index (see figure II.2).

Among the countries mentioned, Brazil, in particular, is faced with the serious challenge of attempting to reverse the slight rising trend in income inequality that marked the 1990s. Brazil now has the highest income concentration indices in the entire region, with a Gini coefficient of 0.64. At the other end of the scale, Uruguay has clearly consolidated the gains it made in reducing inequality, since, in addition to maintaining low poverty indicators, it has continued to make a gradual improvement in its income distribution, albeit with ups and down during the period 1997-1999; as a result, in 1999 it again posted the lowest income concentration in the region, with a Gini coefficient of 0.44 in urban areas.

Other countries that succeeded in lowering inequality indicators in urban areas over the past decade were Bolivia, Honduras, Guatemala, Mexico and Panama. In some of these cases, however, the 1999 levels are still among the highest in the region. At the same time, rural inequality, in the countries in which it could be measured, increased in six (especially in Costa Rica and Mexico and, to a lesser extent, in Brazil, Guatemala, Nicaragua and Panama) and decreased in three (Chile, Colombia and Honduras) (see figure II.2).

A comprehensive analysis turns up a number of notable features of Latin American economies and societies. First of all, in general, income distribution is not clearly related to the countries' level of development. For example, Argentina and Uruguay, which both have quite high income levels in regional terms, had very different distribution structures and trends as of the end of the decade. A similar situation is found among the economies with lower average incomes, in which the level of inequality may be high, intermediate or low (see tables II.3 and II.4). By the same token, some countries maintained the status quo in terms of distribution in the 1980s and 1990s, while in others, the situation changed substantially. Argentina and Chile, which in the 1960s stood out for their relatively good income distribution patterns, are currently close to the regional average and some of their inequality indicators are even higher.

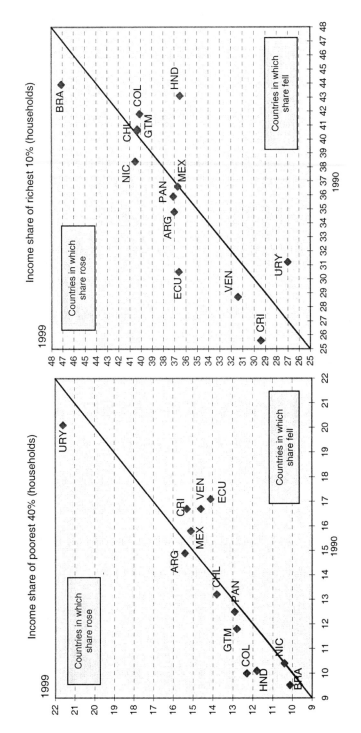

Figure II.1

LATIN AMERICA (13 COUNTRIES): CHANGES IN INCOME CONCENTRATION,[a] NATIONAL TOTAL, 1990-1999

(Percentages)

(Continued)

Figure II.1 (concluded)

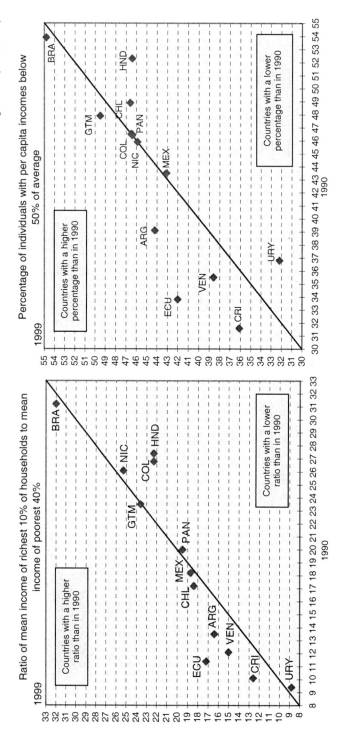

Source: ECLAC, based on special tabulations from household surveys in the countries concerned.

[a] Calculated according to the distribution of households ranked by per capita income. In the case of Argentina, the figures refer to Greater Buenos Aires, while for Ecuador and Uruguay they refer to urban areas.

(Continued)

Figure II.2

LATIN AMERICA (14 COUNTRIES): CHANGES IN THE GINI COEFFICIENT OF INCOME DISTRIBUTION,[a] 1990-1999

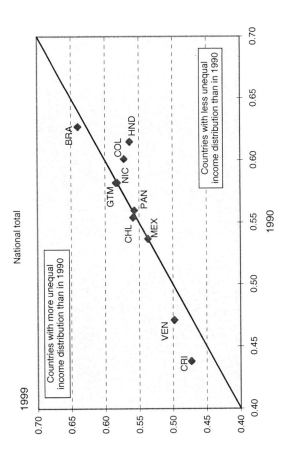

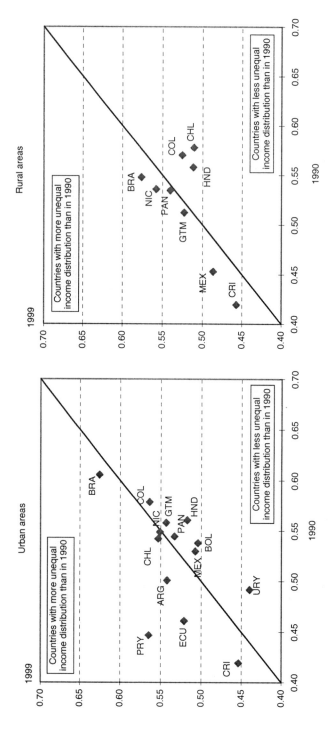

Figure II.2 (concluded)

Source: ECLAC, based on special tabulations from household surveys in the countries concerned.

[a] Calculated according to the distribution of individuals ranked by per capita income. For urban areas, in Argentina the figures refer to Greater Buenos Aires, while for Bolivia (1990) they refer to the eight main cities and for Paraguay (1990 and 1997) they refer to the Asunción metropolitan area.

In contrast, Costa Rica and Uruguay have maintained a social and political structure that is conducive to a more egalitarian income distribution, notwithstanding the changes in the domestic economy and in external economic relations that have occurred in recent years. The situation in Venezuela runs along much the same lines, since, even though it experienced a serious crisis in the second half of the 1990s and its income distribution clearly grew worse over the decade, it is still less inequitable than most of the other countries in the region.

Table II.3
LATIN AMERICA (17 COUNTRIES): PER CAPITA INCOME AND DEGREE OF INCOME
CONCENTRATION IN URBAN AREAS, 1999

Per capita income		Income concentration[a]
High		
(More than US$ 4 000)	Argentina	High
	Uruguay	Low
	Chile	High
	Mexico	Intermediate
	Brazil	High
Intermediate		
(Between US$ 2 000	Costa Rica	Low
and US$ 4 000)	Panama	Intermediate
	Venezuela	Low
	Dominican Republic	Intermediate
	Colombia	High
Low		
(Less than US$ 2 000)	El Salvador	Low
	Paraguay	Intermediate
	Guatemala	High
	Ecuador	Intermediate
	Bolivia	Intermediate
	Honduras	High
	Nicaragua	High

Source: ECLAC, based on special tabulations from household surveys in the countries concerned.

[a] Low (under 0.48), intermediate (between 0.48 and 0.54) and high (over 0.54) Gini coefficient.

Table II.4
LATIN AMERICA (18 COUNTRIES): CHANGES IN INCOME DISTRIBUTION IN URBAN
AREAS, 1990-1999

Per capita GDP growth in the 1990s [a]	$D^{10}/D^{(1\,to\,4)}$ [b]	Gini index
High (more than 4%)		
Chile	Increased	Increased
Dominican Republic	-	-
Intermediate (between 2% and 4%)		
Argentina	Increased	Increased
Panama	Decreased	Decreased
El Salvador	-	-
Peru	-	-
Uruguay	Decreased	Decreased
Costa Rica	Increased	Increased
Low (1% to 2%)		
Mexico	Decreased	Decreased
Bolivia	-	-
Guatemala	Decreased	Decreased
Brazil	Increased	Increased
Zero or negative (minus 1% to 1%)		
Colombia [d]	Decreased	Decreased
Nicaragua	Increased	No change
Honduras	Decreased	Decreased
Venezuela [e]	Increased	Increased
Ecuador	Increased	Increased
Paraguay	-	-

Source: ECLAC, based on special tabulations from household surveys in the countries concerned.

[a] Average annual variation in per capita GDP, based on 1995 prices.
[b] $D^{(1\,to\,4)}$ represents the bottom 40% of households in terms of income, while D^{10} represents the upper 10% of households in terms of income.
[c] Greater Buenos Aires.
[d] The starting year is 1994.
[e] Refers to national total.

In summary, even though many countries managed to expand their economies and substantially increase their social expenditure, Latin America as a whole has not succeeded in making any substantial improvement in income distribution. Although economic growth has made it possible to reduce absolute poverty, the increase in output has not altered the way in which the benefits of such growth are distributed. Nor are there any signs that this situation is likely to change significantly in the short or medium term.

In fact, of the 17 countries analysed, only 2 (Uruguay and probably Honduras), closed out the decade with positive results in reducing distribution inequality. Even in countries that achieved high and sustained growth rates, such as Chile, income distribution has been recalcitrant and disparities have persisted.

It is encouraging that a number of Central American countries have made progress -albeit to different degrees and on different scales- towards more even income distribution patterns in urban areas, although this subregion continues to exhibit high levels of concentration. Economic stability, more moderate financial fluctuations, the benefits brought by the economic boom in North America, the easing of demographic pressures from international migration and larger flows of remittances from nationals residing abroad are some of the factors that have contributed to this result.

3.   Factors influencing income distribution

Over the past few years, it has been found that those economies of the region that have managed to start growing again, reduce inflation substantially, raise employment levels and apply efficient public policies have nonetheless failed to improve their income distribution. This is why it is often pointed out that it is not enough to simply strengthen economic growth and boost employment; measures must also be taken that have an impact in other spheres, such as education and taxation.[7] It is also usually said that this problem can only be solved over the long term.

In this context, it would be appropriate to conduct an in-depth study of economic and social policies, with particular reference to how such policies influence poverty and income distribution, although the connection between the two phenomena is not clear. Nor is it clear whether such issues can be efficiently tackled simultaneously.

The starting point for an analysis of the relevant information is a ranking of households by per capita income. This ranking can be used not only to distinguish between indigent, non-indigent poor and non-poor households, but also to describe and assess income distribution, which can then be linked to other related variables (see figure II.3).

First of all, an examination of the average number of years of schooling of both the head of household and of all employed household members shows up a high correlation between income distribution and the distribution of education. A broad consensus exists as to the importance of achieving equality of opportunity and regarding the fundamental role of education in economic growth. Accordingly, the governments of Latin America have made an effort to improve educational coverage and to lower drop-out rates. This commitment has brought significant progress in the field of primary and secondary education.

---

[7]   This holds true at least in those countries where the tax burden is known to be low.

As may be seen from the figures, between the beginning of the 1980s and the mid-1990s the population's average number of years of schooling rose steadily, while the educational levels of heads of households and of employed household members belonging to the six or seven lowest income deciles became less uneven. The educational gap between these households and the upper deciles also widened, however. In most countries, the labour force's average number of years of schooling corresponds approximately to that of the employed household members of the seventh decile, while in the eighth decile, and especially in the ninth and tenth deciles, the number of years of schooling is significantly above the average (see figures II.3b and II.3c). Thus, the gap between the overall average, situated around the seventh decile, and that of the lowest income deciles is almost two years of schooling, whereas the gap between the former and the tenth decile is usually about four years. This illustrates the high degree of concentration existing in education, measured in terms of the number of years of schooling, as well as the fact that some social groups have managed to gain access to post-secondary formal education. At the other end of the scale, there are countries in which large sections of the population have still not managed, on average, to complete the basic cycle. However, the strategies for expanding the production sector that are now being applied in the region require educational levels comparable to those found in the most advanced countries, that is, those that are leading the field in technological innovation. It may therefore be concluded that the concentration of education contributes to a situation in which the people who have the necessary skills to work in occupations involving advanced technologies are the ones able to earn high incomes, thereby compounding the concentration of income distribution. Moreover, macroeconomic and institutional reforms are driving the expansion of this type of employment.[8]

---

[8]   In many countries the degree of concentration would certainly be even higher if the disparities existing in the quality of educational services available to the various strata of the population were added to the differences in the number of years of schooling.

Figure II.3

LATIN AMERICA (12 COUNTRIES): INDICATORS FOR INCOME, YEARS OF SCHOOLING AND INCOME FROM ASSETS BY DECILES OF INCOME, URBAN AREAS [a]

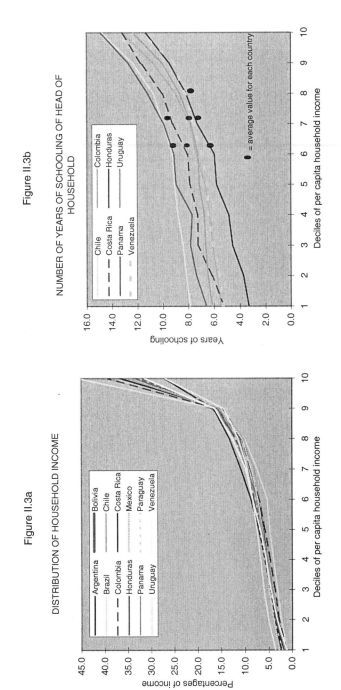

Figure II.3a

DISTRIBUTION OF HOUSEHOLD INCOME

Figure II.3b

NUMBER OF YEARS OF SCHOOLING OF HEAD OF HOUSEHOLD

(Continued)

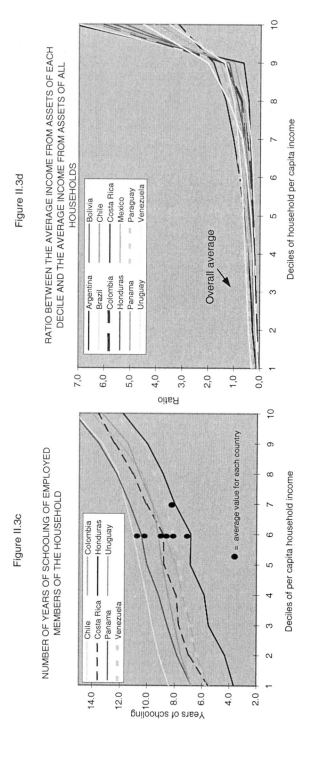

Figure II.3 (concluded)

Figure II.3d

RATIO BETWEEN THE AVERAGE INCOME FROM ASSETS OF EACH DECILE AND THE AVERAGE INCOME FROM ASSETS OF ALL HOUSEHOLDS

Figure II.3c

NUMBER OF YEARS OF SCHOOLING OF EMPLOYED MEMBERS OF THE HOUSEHOLD

Source: ECLAC, on the basis of special tabulations of data from household surveys in the countries concerned.

[a] The figures are for 1994, except in the cases of Brazil (1993) and Chile (1996).

Second, the current returns on property ownership also exhibit a distribution similar to that of total income. Household surveys capture only a portion of property income. Overall, they very probably underestimate such earnings, especially in the case of persons in the most prosperous strata. This is due to design and measurement difficulties, as a significant portion of such resources circulates within companies, in the form of capital reinvestment, although this also increases individual assets.[9] Both household surveys and national accounts can be used, however, to estimate the portion of income deriving from ownership of real estate and companies that is distributed to households.

Information from these sources (see figure II.3d) shows that the household distribution of property income is so highly concentrated that the overall average coincides with the observed value in the seventh, eighth or ninth decile, depending on the country. Although differences do exist across countries with regard to the relative share of total income that comes from this source,[10] these figures indicate that the concentration of property (and, hence, of the income deriving from such assets) plays a highly important role in the regressivity of household income distribution. In terms of future trends, this may come to be a determining factor in the reproduction of inequalities and the gaps that exist between different individuals' future opportunities for well-being.

Third, households also display a number of demographic traits that are closely correlated with the income distribution profile. With regard to household size, for example, the households with the largest number of members tend to be heavily concentrated in the lowest income deciles. This fits in with the fact that small households, i.e., households with few members, usually represent a very significant proportion of households in the high-income deciles.[11] In fact, in the highest decile of income distribution, households consisting of three persons or fewer usually account for far more than half of the total. Since the majority of larger households include a high percentage of children and consequently have high demographic dependency rates, these households' income-generating capacity relative to their size is limited. This is often compounded by the fact that large households in the poorer strata usually

---

[9]   A portion of the primary income declared by independent workers, especially those who are employers, should be recorded as returns on capital rather than as earned income.

[10]   The proportion of total household income that derives from assets varies significantly from one country to another. The percentage varies from 10% to 25%; this can be considered a minimum range given the traditional underestimation of this variable in household surveys, which more marked in this case than in that of other income flows.

[11]   This is usually reflected not only in distributions in which households are classified according to per capita income, but also, albeit to a lesser extent, in those where households are ranked by total income.

have more economic difficulty in subdividing than those situated at the other end of the scale.

Fourth, an examination of employment variables indicates that, in addition to the aspects relating to education, asset holdings and demographic features discussed above, other limitations that conspire against greater equity in the case of poor households. Just as educational factors may give rise to differences in people's income levels, the number of employed household members also affects the family's capacity to generate income. An analysis of this factor shows that the average number of employed persons per household tends to be much lower in the poorer deciles than in the upper-income deciles of the distribution. In addition, the ratio of the number of employed persons to the number of household members is at least twice as high in the richer households as in the households in the lowest income decile (see figure II.4). In other words, the gaps already noted between households belonging to different levels of the distribution are compounded by their differing capacity to generate income via employment.

Figure II.4
LATIN AMERICA (12 COUNTRIES): RATIO BETWEEN THE NUMBER OF EMPLOYED PERSONS AND THE TOTAL NUMBER OF HOUSEHOLD MEMBERS IN URBAN AREAS

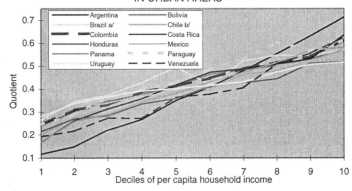

Source: ECLAC, on the basis of special tabulations of data from household surveys in the countries concerned.

[a] 1993 figures.
[b] 1996 figures.

It can thus be reasonably concluded that in a historical and structural context such as the one prevailing in Latin America, income distribution is closely associated with the household characteristics considered here. These factors are also closely interrelated. It therefore appears that, in terms of possible changes in the distributional structure over time, an improvement in one or the other of these dimensions, rather than in all of them simultaneously, would fail to trigger and/or sustain "virtuous circles" that could break the existing cycles of poverty and inequity.

Education, for example, is usually considered to have the greatest potential, in the medium and long terms, for changing the conditions that lead to the reproduction of inequalities. It is even sometimes claimed that equity in education is a sufficient condition for such change. Although it is certainly very important to make progress in this direction, it is clear that upper-income households have traditionally enjoyed socio-economic, political and cultural conditions that guarantee advantages for their children with regard to the quantity and quality of education received, as well as other sorts of resources that permit the intergenerational transfer of a significant potential for differentiation.

An analysis of the behaviour of indicators such as the educational level of heads of household and of all employed household members[12] in the various distributional strata over the past 10 years reveals, first of all, a general increase in the average number of years of schooling of both household heads and employed members. This increase amounts to between approximately six months and one year (see table II.5). This advance however has not, however, had any appreciable influence on the other variables, nor has it brought an improvement in income distribution.

Second, the distribution of years of schooling in the households in the various income deciles has varied in different ways from one country to the next. In those where the distribution of educational levels of heads and employed members of households was somewhat more equitable, the trend has been towards distributional structures similar to those found in countries where income distribution is less equitable. Thus, for example, in Costa Rica and Uruguay, the distribution of education now seems to be more concentrated than before, especially in the top income decile. Nevertheless, income distribution has remained constant in the first country and has improved significantly in the second. In the other countries, fluctuations in income distribution have, in most cases, not been very significant and have been coupled with small variations in the distribution of education. Chile constitutes a special case for at least three reasons: economic reforms are more soundly established than in many other instances; the country has experienced vigorous growth during the period considered; and its population has the highest average number of years of schooling of all the countries of the region. A comparison of the

---

[12]　The quality of education is also clearly of great importance and should also be taken into account together with the number of years of schooling. It has also been established, however, that those who accumulate more years of schooling usually have access to a higher quality of education as well, which means that the concentration of education may have been underestimated.

distribution of education in 1987 with that of 1996 shows that the average length of schooling increased by almost one year and that education is now somewhat more evenly distributed than in the mid-1980s. In addition, during the period 1987-1996 there was a significant increase in employment, as well as changes in the occupational structure. Income distribution has remained practically unchanged, however, despite the country's economic growth and the greater distributional equity of education, measured in terms of years of schooling.

Table II.5
LATIN AMERICA (7 COUNTRIES): AVERAGE NUMBER OF YEARS OF SCHOOLING
OF HEADS OF HOUSEHOLD AND OF EMPLOYED HOUSEHOLD MEMBERS,
BY INCOME DECILES, IN URBAN AREAS

Country		Total	Household deciles by per capita income									
			1	2	3	4	5	6	7	8	9	10
Chile												
Heads	1987	8.6	6.4	6.5	6.8	7.2	7.4	7.9	8.9	9.7	11.7	13.7
	1996	9.6	7.5	7.8	7.9	8.7	8.5	9.1	9.6	10.8	11.9	14.1
Employed members	1987	9.9	7.1	7.6	8.2	8.7	9.1	9.6	10.3	11.1	12.7	14.2
	1996	10.8	8.1	8.7	9.3	10.1	10.2	10.7	11.0	11.8	12.9	14.5
Colombia												
Heads	1986	7.2	5.0	5.2	5.7	6.0	6.5	6.6	7.2	8.2	9.6	12.0
	1994	7.6	5.4	5.8	6.0	6.3	6.5	6.9	7.8	8.8	10.2	12.6
Employed members	1986	8.1	5.2	5.8	6.5	6.8	7.4	7.7	8.3	9.2	10.5	12.6
	1994	8.6	5.6	6.3	6.9	7.2	7.7	8.3	9.2	10.1	11.6	13.3
Costa Rica												
Heads	1984	8.1	5.2	6.4	6.6	7.0	7.6	8.3	8.4	9.2	10.4	12.2
	1994	8.5	5.3	6.4	6.6	7.2	7.8	7.8	9.3	10.0	11.0	13.2
Employed members	1984	9.1	6.1	6.8	7.5	8.0	8.5	9.2	9.3	10.3	11.1	12.9
	1994	9.4	6.3	7.0	7.6	8.1	8.8	9.0	10.2	10.8	11.8	13.4
Honduras												
Heads	1984	6.2	3.1	4.0	3.9	4.4	4.9	5.7	6.3	7.7	9.6	12.8
	1994	6.4	3.6	3.6	4.6	4.9	5.5	6.2	7.0	8.2	9.1	11.7
Employed members	1984	7.1	3.3	4.2	4.5	4.9	5.8	6.7	7.3	8.5	10.3	12.9
	1994	7.2	3.8	4.3	5.3	5.7	6.5	7.2	7.8	8.8	9.6	11.7
Panama												
Heads	1986	8.2	4.8	5.4	6.4	6.8	7.2	8.0	8.1	9.7	11.4	13.6
	1994	9.1	6.2	6.7	7.5	7.6	8.3	9.0	9.7	10.6	11.5	14.0
Employed members	1986	9.2	4.8	6.0	7.2	7.6	8.3	9.1	9.6	11.1	12.4	14.4
	1994	10.1	6.2	7.4	8.2	8.6	9.5	10.2	10.8	11.7	12.5	14.6
Uruguay												
Heads	1986	7.0	4.8	5.5	5.6	5.9	6.4	6.7	7.3	8.0	9.0	10.4
	1994	7.3	5.6	5.8	6.1	6.1	6.4	6.7	7.0	8.3	9.4	11.5
Employed members	1986	8.2	5.6	6.5	7.0	7.5	7.9	8.2	8.7	9.1	9.8	10.8
	1994	8.8	6.4	7.2	7.6	8.0	8.3	8.8	9.0	10.0	11.0	12.4
Venezuela												
Heads	1986	7.0	5.0	5.3	5.5	5.6	6.1	6.6	7.0	7.8	9.3	11.9
	1994	7.2	5.2	5.9	6.5	6.7	7.0	6.9	6.7	7.8	8.5	10.9
Employed members	1986	7.9	5.2	5.9	6.3	6.6	7.0	7.5	8.0	8.7	10.0	12.3
	1994	8.3	6.0	6.8	7.3	7.8	8.1	7.9	8.3	9.0	9.5	11.4

Source: ECLAC, on the basis of special tabulations of data from household surveys in the countries concerned.

One reason that might be given for this is that the countries began their economic reform processes at different times. According to this line of thought, the countries in which the distribution of education has become more concentrated than before might be the same ones where the change in the economic and employment structure has brought about a redistribution of labour income whereby persons with a higher level of education have become more highly paid than before. Thus, on the one hand, the link between education and income would be strengthened in the more dynamic sectors, which employ persons with whose levels of education are far above average and, on the other hand, would reduce the dispersion of income among those with below-average levels of education. This makes the case of Chile even more interesting, since, because economic reforms have been in place for a longer time and economic growth has been so buoyant, the changes in these variables illustrate the apparent effects of the new development modality in this respect more clearly.

Although it may be too early to draw definitive conclusions, the information presented here does in some way call into question the effectiveness of attempts to modify income distribution via an educational policy designed to improve the distribution of opportunities, unless it is accompanied by other related initiatives in the areas of employment, demography and property income. In fact, all of the countries already implement policies and programmes on a regular basis in each of these areas; the challenge, however, lies in integrating them and giving greater weight to the areas previously given least attention, while at the same time strengthening those measures about which there is a greater consensus.

Thus, for example, as lower-income households benefit, simultaneously, from various sectoral policies (housing and community infrastructure, credit for productive work, land access, technical assistance, assistance for women and young people entering the labour market), the increase in years of schooling will begin to have a stronger impact and labour productivity will rise.[13] On many occasions, the effect of isolated policies is largely eroded by such factors as crowding in the home, which makes it difficult for children and young people to study properly, or a lack of capital goods and other productive resources, such as land and water, which significantly limit the level of earnings. The provision of assistance in obtaining certain assets, such as a home, can not

---

[13] See Gerstenfeld and others (1995), which demonstrates the influence on school performance of factors such as the educational capacity of the household, its economic capacity, the physical infrastructure of the home and the level of family organization. Such a package of social policies as a whole can prevent educational policies from being neutralized.

only bring about a striking improvement in households' levels of well-being, but also afford them with greater access to credit.

As noted in UNDP (2002), in the absence of policies that act simultaneously in various areas, widening wage gaps will spread to other social spheres, thereby reinforcing the trend towards segmentation in services and in the location of social groups within the urban environment. When this occurs, schools and neighbourhoods gradually lose their ability to function as significant sources of assets for families seeking a way to escape from poverty.

Methodological annex

(a)   Measuring inequality

The economic and statistical literature offers a wide range of indicators for measuring income inequality. In general, they can be classified as: (i) traditional statistical indicators (absolute and relative range, statistical indicators of order, average relative deviation, variance, variation coefficient and log variance); (ii) entropy measures (Theil index); (iii) Gini coefficient; (iv) social welfare functions (Dalton and Atkinson indices); and (v) Lorenz curve.

A good indicator of inequality is usually expected to meet the following criteria:

- "Weak" transfer principle: when income is transferred from a wealthy household to a poor one, other things being equal, the indicator should show a decrease in the degree of inequality.

- Independence of scale: the indicator should not vary in response to proportional changes or changes of scale (for example, changes in the unit used to measure income).

- Population principle: income concentration in two populations with identical Lorenz curves should be the same, regardless of the size of the populations.

- Additive decomposition: the income concentration for a population should be equal to the weighted sum of inequality among all subgroups within that population.

- "Strong" transfer principle: when income is transferred from a wealthy household to a poor one, the decrease in equality will be more pronounced as the income gap between the two households widens.

Given the importance of these criteria, and in the light of certain practical considerations, certain indices that are normally used to analyse income distribution have been chosen. Thus, the Lorenz curve is a basic statistical tool, since it shows the pattern of income distribution and the share held by the different groups in the population. In addition, given the ease with which it can be calculated and interpreted, the Gini coefficient (derived from the Lorenz curve) has become one of the most widely used indicators despite its limitations with regard to additive decomposition.

Among traditional statistical indicators, the variation coefficient and the log variance are also very useful because they take advantage of all available distribution data. In addition, the Theil and Atkinson indices are highly recommended, given their usefulness for theoretical purposes and their emphasis on lower incomes in the measurement of inequality.

As far as the comparability of findings among these indicators in concerned, it should be noted that they are all ordinal in nature, they show different ranges of variation, and they meet different criteria; hence the values obtained are not comparable. Moreover, since they all measure only partial aspects of inequality, the results they generate are normally organized differently. Consequently, a definitive ranking for a given group of distributions can only be established if the group is kept constant regardless of the index used. Inequality indices should therefore be used to complement each other and an overall analysis should be made of all the results.

Lastly, it should be noted that the values of a single index are comparable between different populations, but only as ordinal figures; in other words, they only show where greater or lesser inequality exists, but not the magnitude of the differences.

(b)   Measuring income concentration and poverty

A number of different tools can be used to measure income concentration, each of which has certain advantages and disadvantages. One simple method is to estimate the percentage of the population whose income is below the average or is a fraction of the average. The higher this percentage, the greater the difference between the higher and lower values of the distribution or, in other words, the greater the inequality of the distribution.

Some countries, particularly in Western Europe, regularly use this type of indicator to gauge relative poverty. As was noted at the beginning of this chapter, the term "relative poverty" refers to the notion that people in a given society are disadvantaged if they cannot afford certain goods that are considered basic in that society. For example, in highly developed countries, people might be classified as deprived if they cannot afford a television set, even though they have satisfied their minimum food and housing needs. This approach makes it almost impossible to establish a "poverty line" similar to the one used in the traditional, or normative, approach to poverty measurement, not only because of the difficulties involved in defining the types, amounts and prices of items to be considered, but also because the threshold has to be changed from time to time to reflect changes in living standards. Bearing this in mind, some fraction of average income might reasonably be used as a relative poverty line. This figure typically ranges between 40% and 60% of income, represented as either the mean or the median distribution.

Nevertheless, there are several practical drawbacks to this method of measuring relative poverty, two of which will be referred to here. There is the highly arbitrary choice involved in defining the income-level indicator (mean or median) and the respective cut-off fraction, and the fact that the poverty line has an elasticity of one with regard to mean income. Nevertheless, these difficulties aside, this approach underscores the strong interrelationship that exists between definitions and measurements of poverty and income distribution and the advantages of integrating the analysis of the two dimensions, as is the case in the present chapter.

In order to gain a clearer picture of the implications of these methodological considerations with regard to Latin American countries, see table II.6, which contains figures on relative poverty. Note that the countries do not vary, with regard to relative poverty, to the same extent that they do with regard to absolute poverty, and that they are broadly in agreement with the distribution criteria.

Table II.6
LATIN AMERICA (17 COUNTRIES): PERCENTAGE DISTRIBUTION OF PERSONS
HAVING INCOMES OF LESS THAN HALF THE MEDIAN INCOME LEVELS

Country	Year	50% of mean	50% of median
Argentina [a]	1990	39.1	20.5
	1999	44.2	21.4
Bolivia	1989 [b]	44.1	20.6
	1999	45.5	29.5
Brazil	1990	53.9	26.6
	1999	54.8	25.9
Chile	1990	46.5	20.3
	2000	46.4	20.3
Colombia	1994	48.9	26.0
	1999	46.6	21.8
Costa Rica	1990	31.6	19.4
	1999	36.1	20.7
Ecuador [c]	1990	33.8	17.4
	1999	42.0	18.8
El Salvador	1995	38.4	22.0
	1999	40.6	24.3
Guatemala	1989	47.9	22.7
	1998	49.5	21.7
Honduras	1990	52.3	26.1
	1999	46.4	25.7
Mexico	1989	43.5	19.7
	1998	43.1	22.9
Nicaragua	1993	45.9	27.4
	1998	45.9	26.7
Panama	1991	46.4	24.1
	1999	46.4	23.7
Paraguay [d]	1990	33.4	16.4
	1999	34.2	15.8
Dominican Republic	1997	39.8	20.8
Uruguay [c]	1990	36.8	17.4
	1999	32.2	19.0
Venezuela	1990	35.5	20.2
	1999	38.6	21.6

Source: ECLAC, based on special tabulations from household surveys in the countries concerned.

Note: The poverty levels reported here refer to the national level, except in the following cases: [a] Greater Buenos Aires. [b] Eight main cities and El Alto. [c] Urban total. [d] Asunción metropolitan area.

Chapter III

Employment

By the late 1990s it had become more difficult to generate productive employment for a rapidly expanding labour force. As a result, both low-productivity occupation and open unemployment increased. This chapter examines the causes of the still-considerable growth rate of the economically active population (EAP), the difficulties related to its productive absorption in a context of slack economic growth and technological and administrative modernization, and the consequences of these trends, particularly the increases observed in tertiary- and informal-sector employment, precarious employment and open unemployment.

1.   The labour supply

In the 1990s the EAP increased at an average annual rate of 2.6%, which, though below the levels of previous decades, was still high enough to pose a major challenge in terms of job creation. This happened because the decline in EAP growth lagged behind the decline in overall population growth, the age structure of the region's population shifted and women's participation in the labour force increased.

(a)   The demographic transition and the EAP

The population continued to expand at a high average annual rate in the 1990s (see table III.1). It should be recalled that between 1900 and

1950 the population grew at an average annual rate of 1.5%.[1] Since then the rate of population growth, though high, has trended downward: 2.7% in the 1950s and 1960s, 2.4% in the 1970s, 2.1% in the 1980s and, as mentioned earlier, 1.7% in the 1990s. As a result, the population continued to grow in absolute terms: by 50 million in the 1950s, 65 million in the 1960s, 74 million in the 1970s, 80 million in the 1980s and 70 million in the 1990s (Bajraj and Chackiel, 1995, and Bravo and Rodríguez, 1993). Consequently, in the period 1950-1999 there was an exceptionally large population increase, from 159 million to 500 million, which generated an economic and social challenge of extraordinary magnitude.

The situation varies from one country to another depending on how far the demographic transition has advanced. In the 1990s Bolivia and Haiti had high mortality and fertility rates, with average population growth of 2.1% per year. In countries at a more advanced stage of demographic transition mortality rates were lower but fertility rates remained high, generating population growth rates of 2.8%. In a number of other countries, including the most heavily populated ones, population growth had already peaked and begun to decline, since fertility had dropped to 1.9% per year. Lastly, there was a group of countries in which fertility rates had declined so far as to place average annual population growth as low as 1% (Bravo and Rodríguez, 1993).[2]

(b)   Age structure and the EAP

A drop in the population's growth rate does not immediately reduce the growth of the EAP because it has different impacts on different age groups. In effect, decreases in population growth are manifested most immediately and intensively in the under-15 age group. The growth rate of this group was 2.7% in the 1960s, but dropped to 1.7% in the 1970s, 1.1% in the 1980s and 0.3% in the 1990s. The 15-to-64 age group has evolved very differently, however: in the 1960s its growth rate was 2.7%, like that of the under-15 group, but in the 1970s the rate rose to 2.9%. Not until the 1980s did it decline to 2.6%, later falling to 2.3% in the 1990s. In turn, the 65-and-over group maintained high growth rates in all four decades: 3.5% in the 1960s, 3.3% in the 1970s, 3% in the 1980s and 3.1% in the 1990s. In other words, in the 1990s the over-15 group grew much faster than the total population, boosting the increase in the EAP (see table III.1). This phenomenon becomes even clearer when each age

---

[1]   When the Spaniards arrived the region had a population of about 50 million. During the conquest this figure dropped to around 15 million, where it remained until the early nineteenth century. It then rose to 34 million in 1850, 75 million in 1900 and 159 million in 1950.

[2]   See section 1(d).

group's share of the total population is analysed: the decline in the growth rate of the under-15 group meant that this group declined as a percentage of the total population, from 40.4% in 1950 to 31.7% in 1999, while the 15-to-64 cohort increased its share from 56.1% to 62.9% and the 65-and-over cohort, from 3.5% to 5.4%. While in the 1960s the 15-to-64 cohort accounted for just 45% of the total increase in population, in the 1990s it accounted for 80%, or 56 million of the additional 70 million people. This improved the economic dependency ratio but generated a huge challenge in terms of job creation (Chackiel, 1999).

Table III.1
LATIN AMERICA: MAIN LABOUR MARKET AGGREGATES, 1990-1999
(Millions of people and percentages)

Description	People (millions)		Average annual growth rate	
	1990	1999	1990-1994	1990-1999
Total population	429.8	499.9	1.8	1.7
Urban	305.3	374.6	2.4	2.3
Rural	124.5	125.3	0.1	0.1
Population under 15 years of age	155.2	160.2	0.4	0.3
Urban	102.8	112.2	1.1	1.0
Rural	52.4	48.0	-0.9	-1.0
Working-age population	274.6	339.7	2.5	2.4
Urban	202.5	262.4	3.1	2.9
Rural	72.2	77.3	0.8	0.8
Aged 15-64	254.6	313.2	2.4	2.3
Urban	188.0	242.2	3.0	2.9
Rural	66.6	71.0	0.7	0.7
Aged 64 or over	20.0	26.5	3.2	3.1
Urban	14.5	20.2	3.8	3.7
Rural	5.6	6.3	1.5	1.4
Economically active population[a]	167.5	211.8	2.7	2.6
Urban	120.7	161.6	3.4	3.3
Rural	46.8	50.2	0.8	0.8
Employed	159.8	193.7	2.4	2.2
Urban	114.1	144.2	2.9	2.6
Rural	45.8	49.5	1.0	0.9
Unemployed	7.6	18.1	9.1	10.1
Urban	6.6	17.5	11.2	11.4
Rural	1.0	0.7	-9.4	-4.9
Laid off	5.9	15.4	8.8	11.2
Urban	5.2	15.2	11.6	12.6
Rural	0.7	0.2	-27.4	-13.8
Seeking work for first time	1.7	2.7	10.0	5.3
Urban	1.4	2.3	9.8	5.6
Rural	0.3	0.5	10.9	3.9
Economically inactive population[a]	107.1	127.8	2.1	2.0
Urban	81.8	100.7	2.5	2.3
Rural	25.4	27.1	0.8	0.8

Source: ECLAC, on the basis of estimates prepared by the Population Division of ECLAC - Latin American and Caribbean Demographic Centre (CELADE) and special tabulations of data from household surveys conducted in the respective countries.
[a] Aged 15 or over.

According to estimates, the annual growth rate of the 15-to-64 age group in the region will continue to trend downward, reaching 0.7% around 2020, while the rate of the 65-and-over group will climb to 3.5% and that of the under-15 group will be negative. In 2020 the share represented by each age group will therefore be as follows: under 15, 23.7%; 15 to 64, 66.6%; and 65 or over, 9.7%. For subsequent decades, these projections indicate that the share of the 15-to-64 age group out of the total will change little, while that of the 65-and-over group will increase slightly and that of the under-15 group will decline somewhat. For example, in Uruguay, which is at a more advanced stage of demographic transition than the rest of the region, the proportion represented by the 15-to-64 group has varied by only a fraction of a percentage point since 1950 (Bajraj and Chackiel, 1995).

(c)   Women's participation

The participation rate, or the proportion of the working-age population incorporated into the labour force, is another factor that influences the size of the EAP. In the 1990s the total participation rate increased from 61% to 62.4%. This increase took place in urban areas and, especially, in the female workforce, which increased from 37.9% to 42% of the total (see table III.2).

Table III.2
LATIN AMERICA: RATES OF PARTICIPATION, EMPLOYMENT AND UNEMPLOYMENT, BY SEX AND PLACE OF RESIDENCE (URBAN OR RURAL),[a] 1990-1999
(Percentages)

Description	Nationwide total		Urban total		Rural total	
	1990	1999	1990	1999	1990	1999
Participation rate [b]	61.0	62.4	59.6	61.6	64.8	64.9
Men	84.9	83.6	81.4	81.0	93.7	91.5
Women	37.9	42.0	39.5	43.7	33.1	35.8
Employment rate [c]	58.2	57.0	56.4	55.0	63.4	64.0
Men	81.2	77.6	77.1	73.5	91.8	90.4
Women	36.0	37.3	37.3	37.9	32.2	35.2
Unemployment rate	4.6	8.6	5.5	10.8	2.2	1.3
Men	4.3	7.2	5.4	9.4	2.0	1.2
Women	5.1	11.2	5.7	13.3	2.9	1.6

Source: ECLAC, on the basis of estimates prepared by the Population Division of ECLAC - Latin American and Caribbean Demographic Centre (CELADE) and special tabulations of data from household surveys conducted in the respective countries.

[a] Aged 15 or over.
[b] Economically active population as a proportion of the working-age population.
[c] Employed population as a proportion of the working-age population.

The rate of women's participation in the urban EAP increased most in the 25-to-49 age group and among women with higher levels of education. In general, the participation rate increases in step with the level of formal education: the rate is only 36% among women with between 0 and 3 years of schooling and 44% among those with 4 to 6 years of schooling, but rises to 54% among those with 10 to 12 years and 71% among those with 13 or more years.

The influence of education on women's economic participation is much more marked in countries with more highly developed economies. In those countries women with little education have very low participation rates. For example, in Argentina, Chile and Uruguay about 20% of women with 0 to 3 years of schooling work, whereas the figure is much higher in less developed countries such as Bolivia, Guatemala, Honduras and Nicaragua. This difference probably reflects the fact that the higher a country's level of economic and educational development, the harder it is for women with little education to find employment because requirements in terms of work skills and formal education are more exacting. In addition, as the proportion of more highly educated women rises, less qualified women progressively lose their ability to compete. Furthermore, lack of access to childcare facilities, which is a more frequent problem among women with less schooling, represents yet another obstacle to their participation in the labour market.

Over the long term the process of demographic transition will help to reduce the labour supply and will therefore ease the pressure for job creation. The same cannot be said of the participation rate, however, since it will probably continue to increase quickly as more and more women join the workforce. In the 1990s the female EAP grew at an annual rate of 3.8%, while the male EAP expanded by 2.3%. As a result, by the end of the decade the proportion of the working-age female population that participated in the labour market approached or exceeded 50% and, in some cases, the absolute increase in women's employment was similar to or higher than the increase in men's employment. The rate of female participation will therefore help to keep the EAP growth rate high and will exert expansionary pressure on the overall labour supply.

(d)   The demographic transition and EAP growth

As shown in table III.3, the Latin American countries are at different stages of demographic transition (see ECLAC, 2000b, p. 67). One group of countries consists of those[3] that were at an early or moderate stage of demographic transition in the 1990s. These countries recorded

---

[3]   Bolivia, Guatemala, Honduras, Nicaragua and Paraguay.

rapid growth in the total population and even faster growth in the working-age population (3.2%), which increased the share of the working-age population out of the total. This increase, together with a 1.4% rise in the workforce participation rate, led to annual EAP growth of 3.5% (2.9% for men and 5% for women).

Table III.3
LATIN AMERICA: LABOUR FORCE, BY STAGE OF DEMOGRAPHIC TRANSITION
IN THE COUNTRIES, 1990-1999
(Percentages)

Stage of transition	Growth of the working-age population [a] Total	Variation in the overall participation rate [b]			Growth of the economically active population [a]		
		Total	Men	Women	Total	Men	Women
Early and moderate transition [c]	3.3	1.1	-2.7	4.6	3.5	2.9	4.9
	3.2	1.4	-2.3	4.9	3.5	2.9	5.0
Bolivia	2.7	2.0	-1.2	4.8	3.0	2.6	4.0
El Salvador	3.4	0.2	-5.5	4.8	3.4	2.8	4.9
Guatemala	3.1	2.5	-0.8	6.0	3.6	2.9	5.9
Honduras	3.5	1.6	-3.7	6.7	3.8	3.1	6.2
Nicaragua	3.8	-0.8	-3.5	1.8	3.6	3.4	4.2
Paraguay	3.1	1.0	-1.4	3.3	3.3	2.9	4.3
Full transition [c]	2.6	2.4	-0.3	5.2	3.0	2.5	4.3
	2.5	1.2	-1.8	4.2	2.8	2.3	3.8
Brazil	2.4	-0.1	-3.1	3.1	2.3	1.9	3.2
Colombia	2.3	3.2	0.8	5.4	2.9	2.4	3.8
Costa Rica	2.8	5.3	3.6	7.1	3.8	3.3	5.4
Ecuador	3.0	2.5	-1.0	6.1	3.5	2.8	5.2
Mexico	2.6	2.1	-1.3	5.5	3.0	2.4	4.5
Panama	2.4	2.7	0.4	5.3	2.9	2.4	4.2
Peru	2.5	1.7	-0.3	4.0	2.8	2.4	3.7
Dominican Republic	2.4	1.9	-0.7	4.7	2.8	2.3	3.8
Venezuela	2.8	2.3	-0.9	5.5	3.3	2.7	4.6
Advanced transition [c]	1.4	2.2	0.3	4.0	1.9	1.5	2.7
	1.7	1.7	0.0	3.3	2.1	1.7	2.8
Argentina	1.7	1.0	-0.3	2.2	1.9	1.7	2.3
Chile	1.7	3.5	0.7	6.1	2.5	1.9	3.9
Uruguay	0.8	2.2	0.4	3.8	1.2	0.9	1.8
Simple average	2.6	1.9	-1.0	4.8	3.0	2.5	4.2
Weighted average	2.5	1.3	-1.5	4.1	2.8	2.3	3.8

Source: ECLAC, on the basis of population projections prepared by the Population Division of ECLAC - Latin American and Caribbean Demographic Centre (CELADE).

[a] Annual growth rate.
[b] Difference in percentage points between the overall participation rates recorded in 1990 and 1999.
[c] The shaded figures are simple averages. The figures that follow are weighted averages.

A second group of countries[4] had reached a more advanced stage of demographic transition and had experienced a significant decline in population growth. This reduced the growth of the working-age population to 2.5%. This rate, combined with a 1.2% increase in workforce participation, translated into an annual EAP growth rate of 2.8% (2.3% for men and 3.8% for women).

Lastly, the countries[5] that are now in the final phase of demographic transition experienced a lengthy and considerable decline in their population growth rates, and the effects of this phenomenon are already fully evident. The annual growth rate of the working-age population (1.7%) offset the rapid growth in workforce participation (1.7%) and generated the region's lowest rate of EAP expansion, at 2.1% (1.7% for men and 2.8% for women).

These differences in rates of EAP expansion generated different levels of demand for job creation.

(e) Labour migration

The impact of migration on EAP growth is another point that warrants discussion. The acknowledged inability of agricultural activity to absorb the expansion of the rural labour force helps to swell migration from the countryside to the cities and, as a result, to speed the rate of non-agricultural EAP growth. The agricultural EAP grew at an annual rate of just 0.8%, while the non-agricultural EAP expanded by 3.3%.

In addition, in recent decades international migration, especially to the United States, has become much more significant, serving as an escape route from labour market difficulties. Temporary, seasonal or cyclical mobility and intraregional migration also became more common from the 1960s onward. In any event, it is clear that most of the Latin American countries, particularly those in South America, have not experienced mass emigration on a scale that could significantly alleviate the problem of productive absorption of the labour force, as it did in the European countries between 1850 and 1914.

2.   Productive employment of the labour force

The challenge of absorbing a rapidly growing labour force was compounded by an economic recession in the 1980s and low rates of

---

[4]   Brazil, Colombia, Costa Rica, Dominican Republic, Ecuador, Mexico, Panama, Peru and Venezuela.

[5]   Argentina, Chile and Uruguay.

economic expansion in the 1990s. This led to increases in both low-productivity employment and open unemployment.

(a)   The EAP, the employed EAP and labour productivity in the 1990s

The need to employ the labour force in a productive manner can be broken down into three different components: the need to supply the labour force with jobs, the need to increase its average productivity and the need to extend that increase to the entire labour force in order to even out the existing disparities within and between sectors and segments of production. This last component will be discussed later. With respect to the first two, it is undoubtedly desirable for the growth rate of the employed EAP to be as close as possible to that of the EAP as a whole. It is also desirable for GDP growth to substantially exceed the growth of the employed EAP so that the average productivity of the labour force will rise. An increase in employment without a simultaneous and generalized increase in productivity results in spurious labour absorption, where productivity gains are concentrated in just a few segments or sectors. This only serves to consolidate structural disparities and does not help to reduce poverty.

In the 1980s the annual growth of regional GDP amounted to 1%, while that of the EAP and the employed EAP was almost 3%. Although a large proportion of the workforce found employment, much of it was in low-productivity jobs, which translated into a decline in average labour productivity. Thus, in the 1990s the countries inherited the onerous task of reversing this deterioration.

These trends improved somewhat in the 1990s, since GDP expanded at an annual rate of 3.2%, while the EAP grew by 2.6% and employment, by only 2.2%. The decade began auspiciously, but between 1994 and 1997 the growth rates of GDP and employment dropped to 3.3% and 2.3%, respectively, then continued to trend downward between 1997 and 1999, reaching 1.3% and 1.6% (see figures III.1 and III.2). On the positive side, average labour productivity increased, albeit modestly, with respect to its level in the 1980s. On the negative side, even though EAP growth was slower, employment growth fell 0.4% below its level of the 1980s and, at 1.6%, again overtook GDP growth (1.3%), thereby reducing average labour productivity and increasing spurious absorption. Moreover, the gap between the EAP and the employed EAP widened (0.8%), even though EAP growth had slowed to 2.4%. As a result, the economies' performance in the 1990s did not appreciably offset the negative trends of the previous decade.

Figure III.1
LATIN AMERICA: EVOLUTION OF SOME GENERAL LABOUR MARKET VARIABLES,
1990-1999
(Percentages)

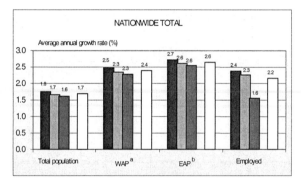

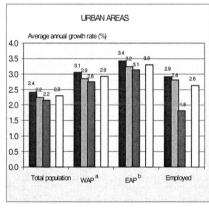

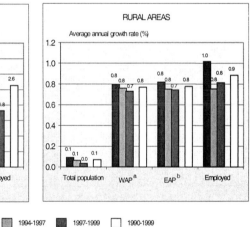

■ 1990-1994   ▨ 1994-1997   ■ 1997-1999   ☐ 1990-1999

Source: ECLAC, on the basis of estimates prepared by the Population Division of ECLAC - Latin American and Caribbean Demographic Centre (CELADE) and special tabulations of data from household surveys conducted in the respective countries.

[a] WAP: working-age population (aged 15 or over).
[b] EAP: economically active population (aged 15 or over).

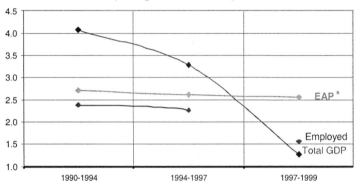

Figure III.2
LATIN AMERICA: TOTAL GROSS DOMESTIC PRODUCT (GDP)
AND EMPLOYMENT, 1990-1999
(Average annual variation)

Source: ECLAC, on the basis of special tabulations of data from household surveys conducted in the respective countries.
[a] EAP: economically active population (aged 15 or over).

(b)   Weak growth in urban areas

The slackness of economic growth in Latin America in the 1990s is particularly evident from an examination of patterns in the non-agricultural labour force. A look at the weighted average for 20 countries (see table III.4) shows that regional GDP expanded by an average annual rate of 3.3% and the employed EAP, by 2.6%. As a result, during the decade productivity increased by a modest 0.5% per year, while employment growth trailed EAP growth by 0.7%. As mentioned earlier, the agricultural EAP increased by only 0.8%. Part of the increase was absorbed by activities in this sector, but responsibility for the rest of the rural population fell, through the channel of migration, on productive activities in urban areas. The average productivity of non-agricultural activities grew even more slowly than that of total activities (0.5%, compared to 1%) and the capacity of those activities to meet the demand for employment was also lower (-0.7%, as against -0.4%).

Table III.4
LATIN AMERICA: URBAN OUTPUT, EMPLOYMENT AND PRODUCTIVITY, 1990-1999
(Annual growth rates)

Country	Gross domestic product[a]	Urban economically active population[b]		Productivity
		Total	Employed	
Argentina [c]	4.6	2.3	1.2	3.4
Bolivia [d]	4.7	4.9	5.0	-0.3
Brazil	2.3	3.1	2.1	0.2
Chile	6.1	3.0	2.7	3.4
Colombia	3.8	3.8	2.3	1.4
Costa Rica	5.0	4.7	4.5	0.4
Cuba	-1.3	2.1	2.0	-3.3
Ecuador [d]	2.5	4.8	3.6	-1.1
El Salvador	4.6	4.4	4.3	0.4
Guatemala	4.5	4.0	3.9	0.6
Haiti	-1.8	4.7	5.4	-6.8
Honduras	3.6	5.4	5.5	-1.8
Mexico	2.9	3.7	3.6	-0.7
Nicaragua	2.5	4.1	4.1	-1.5
Panama	4.6	3.7	4.4	0.2
Paraguay [e]	2.1	4.5	4.1	-1.9
Peru	4.7	3.5	3.1	1.6
Dominican Republic	5.9	3.9	4.6	1.2
Uruguay [d]	2.9	1.5	1.2	1.8
Venezuela	1.3	3.6	3.0	-1.7
Latin America	3.1	3.3	2.6	0.5

Source: ECLAC, on the basis of official figures and special tabulations of data from household surveys conducted in the respective countries.

[a] Non-agricultural output.
[b] The years taken into account are as follows: Argentina, 1990 and 1999; Bolivia, 1989 and 1999; Brazil, 1993 and 1999; Chile, 1990 and 1998; Colombia, 1991 and 1999; Costa Rica, 1990 and 1999; Ecuador, 1990 and 1999; El Salvador, 1990 and 1999; Guatemala, 1989 and 1999; Haiti, 1990 and 1999; Honduras, 1990 and 1999; Mexico, 1989 and 1998; Nicaragua, 1990 and 1998; Panama, 1989 and 1999; Paraguay, 1990 and 1999; Dominican Republic, 1990 and 1997; Uruguay, 1990 and 1999; and Venezuela, 1990 and 1999. These are years for which employment data based on household surveys were available.
[c] Estimates of the economically active population and employment are for greater Buenos Aires.
[d] Estimates of the economically active population and employment are for total urban areas.
[e] Estimates of the economically active population and employment are for Asunción and the Central Department.

These processes reveal the opposite effects of two powerful trends. On the one hand, the slower growth of the working-age population reduces EAP growth and eases the pressure to generate employment. On the other hand, agricultural activities still do not provide enough employment for the rural labour force. This leads to migration, which increases the non-agricultural EAP and intensifies the need for employment in this sector. Almost all the Latin American countries recorded significant growth in their non-agricultural EAP, in contrast to the situation in a number of English-speaking Caribbean countries, for example, where rural-to-urban migration has been much more limited.

These general trends varied from one country to another within the region. Argentina, Brazil, Colombia and Ecuador all had labour absorption shortfalls (measured as the difference between the growth of the non-agricultural EAP and that of the non-agricultural employed EAP) of 1% or more, which pointed to serious job creation problems. In the other countries the rate of urban job creation was similar to the increase in non-agricultural EAP, even where this population group expanded at an annual rate of 4% or more.[6]

With regard to trends in the productivity of non-agricultural labour, Argentina and Chile registered an appreciable rise in the corresponding annual growth rate (3.4%). Nine other countries experienced smaller increases (including Brazil, with 0.2%, and Uruguay, with 1.8%), while the remaining nine posted negative rates.

In Chile the 3.4% growth in productivity was combined with a non-agricultural job creation rate that was only 0.3% lower than the rate of increase of the EAP. Argentina's high rate of productivity growth (3.4%) was offset by a negative job creation rate (-1.1%). In other countries modest gains in productivity were accompanied by insufficient job creation: in Brazil, for example, productivity grew by only 0.2% and absorption, by -1%, while in Colombia the figures were 1.4% and -1.5%, respectively. The trend in the other countries was a relatively high rate of job creation, close to the increase in the non-agricultural EAP, accompanied by very slight or negative productivity growth.

Since rural-to-urban migration will undoubtedly persist in many countries in the coming years, the growth rate of the urban EAP will continue to be high. In nine countries the urban EAP grew at a rate of 4% or higher as a result of the combined effects of growth in the working-age population and in female participation, which were further exacerbated by the persistence of rural-to-urban migration (see table III.4). Under these conditions, sufficient productive employment in non-agricultural activities cannot be created unless GDP growth is strong.

3.   Tertiarization of the labour force

(a)   Increased employment in commerce and services

The economic doldrums of the 1990s were accompanied by sweeping changes in the employment structure. The key aspects of this transformation were sectoral changes in employment, principally a continued decline in the relative importance of the primary and secondary sectors, and an increase in the proportion of jobs created in commerce and services.

---

[6]   Costa Rica, El Salvador, Guatemala, Honduras, Nicaragua and Paraguay.

Between 1990 and 1999 agricultural employment expanded at an annual average rate of 0.7%, which raised its absolute volume from 37.2 million to 39.8 million. However, this increase was not enough to prevent it from declining as a proportion of total employment, from 23.3% to 20.5% (see table III.5). This spurred migration to the cities and increased the number of non-agricultural jobs in rural areas.

Table III.5
LATIN AMERICA: SELECTED FEATURES OF THE EMPLOYED POPULATION,[a]
1990-1999
(Thousands of people and percentages)

Description	People (thousands)		Structure (percentages)	
	1990	1999	1990	1999
Employed				
Age (in years)	159 841	193 714	100.0	100.0
15 - 24	42 741	45 275	26.7	23.4
25 - 44	79 612	96 042	49.8	49.6
45 - 59	27 724	38 216	17.3	19.7
60 and over	9 764	14 181	6.1	7.3
Years of schooling	159 841	193 714	100.0	100.0
0 - 5	73 387	72 505	45.9	37.4
6 - 9	41 366	59 066	25.9	30.5
10 - 12	22 046	37 783	13.8	19.5
13 or more	23 043	24 361	14.4	12.6
Segment of activity	159 841	193 714	100.0	100.0
Agriculture	37 227	39 789	23.3	20.5
Industry	26 911	29 065	16.8	15.0
Construction	9 499	12 284	5.9	6.3
Transport and communications	7 159	9 839	4.5	5.1
Commerce	27 747	36 968	17.4	19.1
Finance	4 581	8 932	2.9	4.6
Social services	30 325	36 695	19.0	18.9
Personal services	8 131	9 960	5.1	5.1
Domestic services	7 886	9 754	4.9	5.0
Not classified	374	429	0.2	0.2
Size of establishment [b]	100 116	113 051	100.0	100.0
(owners and employees)				
1 - 5	26 538	34 621	30.7	32.3
6 - 10	9 242	11 687	10.7	10.9
11 - 49	28 267	31 572	32.7	29.4
50 or more	22 514	29 352	26.0	27.4
Not classified	13 554	5 818	-	-
Secondary income earners [c]	71 404	82 393	44.7	42.5

Source: ECLAC, on the basis of estimates prepared by the Population Division of ECLAC - Latin American and Caribbean Demographic Centre (CELADE) and special tabulations of data from household surveys conducted in the respective countries.

[a] Aged 15 or over.
[b] By number of people employed. Percentage structure excludes segments not classified.
[c] Refers to employed people whose income is lower than that of the household's primary breadwinner.

Notwithstanding the increase in the urban labour supply, the growth of industrial employment fell below the average rate of employment growth. As a result, its share of total employment dropped from 16.8% to 15%, while employment in construction rose from 5.9% to 6.3% of the total. The combined share of the two sectors thus fell from 22.7% to 21.3%. Accordingly, although another 4.7 million people found employment in the production of primary and secondary goods, their relative share of total employment declined from 46% to 41.8%.

By contrast, employment in commerce increased from 17.4% of total employment in 1990 to 19.1% in 1999, thanks to the creation of 9.2 million jobs, which was double the number of jobs created in the primary and secondary sectors combined. The share of services out of the total increased from 31.9% to 33.6% over the same period, absorbing 14.4 million people. Within services, the largest absolute increase took place in social services, which absorbed 6.3 million, while employment in financial services also increased at a very high annual rate, almost doubling the number of people employed in this segment even though it is still quite small in relative terms. Personal and domestic services remained stable as a proportion of the labour force, although both increased in absolute terms, by a total of 3.2 million people. Lastly, employment in transport and communications increased from 4.5% to 5% of the total, absorbing 2.7 million workers.

In conclusion, of the 33.8 million new jobs created during the decade, agriculture accounted for 7%; industry, 6.5%; construction, 8.3%; transport and communications, 8%; commerce, 27.2%; and services, 42.9%. The services portion can be broken down as follows: financial services, 13%; social services, 18.9%; personal services, 5.3%; and domestic services, 5.7%. Thus, more than 78% of the new jobs created in the 1990s were in the tertiary sector, with the result that this sector came to represent an even bigger proportion of the employment structure.

As a result of these developments, in 1999 the sectoral distribution of the Latin American workforce was as follows: agriculture, 20.5%; industry and construction, 21.3%; transport and communications, 5.1%; commerce, 19.1%; and services, 33.6%. In turn, the services workforce was divided as follows: financial services, 4.6%; social services, 18.9%; personal services, 5.1%; and domestic services, 5%.

The countries exhibit no major differences with regard to the decline in the relative importance of employment in goods-producing sectors. The agricultural sector shrank in all the countries and the industrial sector contracted in most of them. The biggest downturns in industry were seen in countries with a large industrial base, such as Argentina, Brazil, Chile, Colombia, Uruguay and Venezuela. In Mexico the opposite occurred, since the industrial sector expanded. Another way to view this process is to examine trends in manufacturing employment, which declined more in countries with higher per capita GDP and higher rates of GDP growth (ECLAC, 2001b, chapter VI).

(b)   Productive absorption and sectors producing tradable and non-tradable goods

It is particularly interesting to review employment trends in sectors that produce tradable and non-tradable goods and services. In most Latin American countries employment expanded faster in sectors that produce non-tradable goods and services than in tradable goods-producing sectors, except in Brazil and Peru, where the two sectors grew at similar rates, and in Costa Rica, Ecuador, Mexico, Nicaragua and Venezuela, where employment in tradables sectors grew faster (see table III.6).[7] In addition, the two sectors' respective capacities to increase productivity and generate employment tend to evolve separately. In general, the tradables sector absorbs little labour but achieves productivity gains. By contrast, the non-tradables sector usually has a greater capacity to generate employment, but at the cost of nil or negative rates of productivity growth.

The low rate of job creation in the tradables sector was evident even in those countries where the sector's output increased relatively quickly. In Argentina, for example, the GDP of the tradables sector expanded at an annual rate of 3.6%, while the variation in total employment was -1.3%. In Brazil these figures were 2.4% and 0.2%, respectively; in Chile, 5.6% and -0.4%; in Colombia, 1.7% and -0.1%; in Costa Rica, 5.5% and 1.3%; in Mexico, 3.4% and 1.7%; in Panama, 3% and -0.6%; in Uruguay, 1.1% and -1.1%; and in Venezuela, 2.7% and 0.7% (see table III.7). In some smaller and less developed countries, however, the tradables sector diverged from this trend. In El Salvador employment in this sector grew by 3.6%, while total employment expanded by 3.5%. In Honduras employment in tradables expanded by 3.2% and total employment, by 2.9%; in Nicaragua these figures were 4.3% and 3.9%, respectively. This atypical behaviour can be attributed to the development of the maquila industry, stimulated by the proximity of the United States market.

---

[7]   In a number of countries some non-tradable services, such as segments of the tourism sector, may be significant. However, since most of the countries' national accounts estimates do not identify the amounts corresponding to these segments, growth rates in the tradables sector may be to some extent underestimated, in cases where they are representative and have expanded rapidly.

Table III.6
LATIN AMERICA: GROSS DOMESTIC PRODUCT (GDP) IN THE 1990s

	Annual variation			
	GDP	GDP goods and services [a]	Tradable and non-tradable sectors	
			Tradable sectors [b]	Non-tradable sectors [c]
	1991-1999	1991-1999	1991-1999	1991-1999
Argentina	4.5	4.5	3.6	4.8
			(3.4)	(2.5)
Bolivia	4.1	4.4	3.4	5.1
			(3.9)	(3.1)
Brazil	2.9	2.3	2.4	2.3
			(2.2)	(1.9)
Chile	6.3	6.0	5.6	6.3
			(4.7)	(3.7)
Colombia	3.1	3.4	1.7	4.3
			(1.1)	(6.2)
Costa Rica	5.0	4.9	5.5	4.5
			(6.3)	(3.0)
Cuba	-1.5	-1.5	0.4	-3.0
			(1.0)	-(0.3)
Ecuador	2.3	2.5	3.3	1.8
			(4.1)	-(0.2)
El Salvador	4.7	4.1	3.6	4.4
			(5.1)	(2.4)
Guatemala	4.2	4.2	3.0	4.7
			(2.8)	(4.1)
Haiti	-1.4	-1.6	-4.0	0.2
			-(6.9)	(1.9)
Honduras	3.2	3.4	3.2	3.4
			(4.0)	(1.3)
Mexico	2.8	2.8	3.4	2.6
			(3.9)	(1.6)
Nicaragua	3.4	3.4	4.3	2.5
			(1.6)	-(1.4)
Panama	4.2	4.4	3.0	4.7
			(3.4)	(2.3)
Paraguay	2.3	2.3	2.0	2.5
			(0.8)	(0.1)
Peru	4.9	4.8	4.9	4.8
			(4.0)	(2.6)
Dominican Republic	5.6	5.6	3.9	6.4
			(4.4)	(3.1)
Uruguay	3.7	3.0	1.1	3.7
			(0.1)	(1.5)
Venezuela	2.1	1.2	2.7	0.4
			(0.9)	(0.7)
Total	3.3	3.0	2.9	3.0
			(2.8)	(2.1)

Source: ECLAC, regressions on the basis of official figures provided by the countries.

[a] The total is the sum of the output generated by the tradable goods- and services-producing sector and that generated by the non-tradable goods- and services-producing sector. It is therefore not the same as gross domestic product, since it does not include adjustments for banking services, value-added taxes or import duties.
[b] The figures shown in brackets are for the manufacturing industry.
[c] The figures shown in brackets are for social, community and personal services.

Table III.7

LATIN AMERICA (16 COUNTRIES): TOTAL AND WAGE EMPLOYMENT, 1990-1999
(Annual rates of variation)

	Total	Total employment		Waged employment [a]		
		Tradable sector [b]	Non-tradable sector [c]	Total	Tradable sector [b]	Non-tradable sector [c]
	1990-1999	1990-1999	1990-1999	1990-1999	1990-1999	1990-1999
Costa Rica	3.7	1.3	5.2	4.5	3.2	5.2
		(2.1)	(3.7)		(2.9)	(3.5)
El Salvador [d]	4.3	3.5	4.6	4.8	4.0	5.1
		(4.1)	(2.2)		(5.2)	(3.7)
Guatemala	3.6	2.2	5.6	2.7	2.9	2.6
		(6.0)	(2.3)		(4.4)	-(0.3)
Honduras	3.9	2.9	5.2	3.0	2.3	3.4
		(6.6)	(4.4)		(7.3)	(3.8)
Mexico	3.0	1.7	3.9	2.6	1.7	2.1
		(4.0)	(4.6)		(3.4)	(3.9)
Nicaragua	3.5	3.9	3.3	3.6	5.8	2.5
		(1.2)	(1.6)		(4.0)	(3.2)
Panama	3.5	-0.6	5.6	4.1	1.7	4.8
		(3.5)	(2.7)		(3.5)	(2.4)
Subtotal (weighted average)	3.2	1.8	4.1	2.8	2.0	2.7
		(4.1)	(4.3)		(3.6)	(3.6)
Argentina [d]	1.2	-1.3	1.7	1.6	-1.4	2.5
		-(1.5)	(2.2)		-(1.6)	(2.4)
Bolivia [d]	5.0	7.6	4.4	3.8	3.6	3.9
		(8.1)	-(0.9)		(4.9)	(1.5)
Brazil	1.6	0.2	2.4	1.7	0.2	2.5
		(0.3)	(2.4)		(0.2)	(2.8)
Chile	2.3	-0.4	3.6	2.8	-0.1	4.3
		-(0.2)	(4.6)		(0.0)	(6.0)
Colombia	1.7	-0.1	2.8	1.2	0.2	1.9
		-(0.4)	(3.1)		-(0.4)	(2.1)
Ecuador [d]	3.6	2.2	4.1	3.5	1.6	4.1
		(1.4)	(4.2)		(0.6)	(3.1)
Paraguay [e]	4.1	3.9	4.1	4.7	4.7	4.7
		(4.5)	(3.3)		(5.6)	(3.5)
Uruguay [d]	1.2	-1.1	1.8	1.5	-0.3	2.0
		-(1.8)	(1.0)		-(2.0)	(1.1)
Venezuela	2.7	0.7	3.4	1.5	0.1	2.0
		(1.6)	(2.5)		-(0.3)	(1.3)
Subtotal (weighted average)	1.8	0.2	2.6	1.8	0.1	2.5
		(0.2)	(2.5)		-(0.1)	(2.6)
Total (weighted average)	2.2	0.8	3.0	2.1	0.7	2.6
		(1.5)	(2.9)		(0.9)	(2.9)

Source: ECLAC, estimates based on special tabulations of data from household surveys conducted in the respective countries.

[a] Figures are for wage earners between the ages of 25 and 59, working 20 hours or more per week.
[b] The figures in brackets refer to the manufacturing industry.
[c] The figures in brackets refer to government, social, community and personal services.
[d] Total for urban areas.
[e] Asunción and the Central Department.

In Mexico technology-intensive production was combined with the development of the maquila industry. Manufacturing output expanded at an annual rate of 3.9% but productivity dropped (-0.1%), since total employment increased by 4%. The productivity of wage employment alone increased at a positive, albeit modest, rate (0.5%), since this type of employment grew more slowly (3.4%). The combination of considerable labour absorption and slight or negative productivity growth was attributable to the growing importance of the maquila sector. In 1989 this sector had accounted for just over 10% of wage employment in manufacturing, but it expanded so quickly (at an average annual rate of 10.4%) that by 1998 it represented almost 19% of manufacturing employment. Maquila accounted for 46% of all new jobs in the manufacturing sector over this period. At the same time, employment in non-maquila manufacturing expanded much more slowly (2%), with the result that this subsector's share of total wage employment in manufacturing slid from almost 90% in 1989 to 81% in 1998.

It can therefore be concluded that although the upturn in the production of tradable goods has helped to drive economic growth and increase productivity, its effects on employment have been weak except in countries with a growing maquila sector (Mexico and some of the Central American and Caribbean countries). At the same time, although the maquila industry generates employment, it has shown little or no capacity to increase productivity, and must therefore be ruled out as the basis of a regional strategy for economic growth and the creation of productive employment.

In general, the responsibility for generating employment has fallen on the non-tradables sector, although in Argentina, Colombia and Uruguay this sector also generated too few jobs, with the inevitable result that open unemployment went up. Also, in a number of countries tradable services, such as transport and certain tourism segments, expanded briskly and had significant effects on output and employment.

This asymmetry between the tradables and non-tradables sectors, with the exceptions mentioned above, not only accentuated the heterogeneity of the Latin American economies but also had an impact on the labour market. Furthermore, it has been exacerbated by the fact that the gap between the incomes of wage earners with higher and lower levels of schooling has tended to widen.

4.   Modernization and informalization of the labour force

Another key feature of the transformation of the employment structure in the 1990s was the growing contrast between the few branches and sectors in which productivity grew strongly and the other branches and sectors —the majority— in which productivity increased only slightly or not at all. In other words, the modernization of certain occupations took place alongside an increasingly marked informalization of the workforce.

In conditions of slack or modest economic growth, a large part of the workforce faces the dilemma of remaining unemployed or accepting employment in low-productivity occupations. Since there is little unemployment protection in Latin America, most workers prefer to avoid unemployment by resorting to low-productivity jobs. This was the pattern in the 1980s and also in the 1990s, although in the latter decade open unemployment also rose.

Much debate has surrounded the question of whether or not the tertiarization of the employment structure is conducive to modernization. The answer to this depends on whether the tertiarization derives from economic growth or, on the contrary, from a lack of momentum in the economy, which drives workers to seek employment in commerce and services. The two processes exist side by side in Latin America, but informalization prevails over modernization.

In effect, the 1990s were a time of intensive tertiarization, when 66% of all new jobs in urban areas were generated in the informal sector (see table III.8; the breakdown by country is given in tables A.6 and A.7 of the statistical appendix). The proportion of unskilled own-account workers in commerce and services displayed the largest increase (24.2%), followed by increases in the shares of workers (employers and employees) in microenterprises (18.2%), domestic workers (9.4%) and unskilled own-account workers in industry and construction (8.1%) and in primary occupations (6%).[8] Most of these new jobs were of low quality, evincing the urban economy's poor capacity to raise average labour productivity. This conclusion holds true for most of the 17 countries considered, particularly the most heavily populated ones, such as Brazil, Colombia and Mexico. In Argentina and Chile, by contrast, most new jobs were in

---

[8]   In the formal sector, which generated 34.1% of all new jobs, the biggest increases in employment were for wage- or salary-earning professionals and technicians (20.1%), entrepreneurs and independent professionals and technicians (6.5%), wage or salary earners other than professionals and technicians (5.4%) and public-sector employees (2.1%).

the formal sector, although Argentina also recorded a substantial increase in open unemployment.

As a result of these patterns, informal employment expanded from 41% of the total in 1990 to 46.3% in 1999 (see table III.8). The contraction of the formal sector reflected a decline in the proportion of private-sector employees other than professionals and technicians, from 35.9% to 29.1%, and in the proportion of public-sector employees, from 16% of the labour force in 1990 to 12.9% in 1999. These relative decreases were not fully offset by the increases observed in the share of professionals and technicians working in the private sector (from 4.7% to 7.8%) and in that of employers and independent professionals and technicians (from 3.8% to 4.3%).

Table III.8
LATIN AMERICA: DISTRIBUTION OF THE EMPLOYED POPULATION IN URBAN AREAS, BY LABOUR MARKET SEGMENT AND LABOUR STATUS, 1990-1999
(Percentages of the total employed population in urban areas and thousands of employed persons)

Type of labour status	Composition of urban employment		Share of each category between 1990 and 1999	
	1990	1999	Percentages	Thousands of employed persons
Total employed persons	100.0	100.0	100.0	26 216
Total formal sector	58.9	53.6	34.1	8 933
Public sector	16.0	12.9	2.1	551
Private sector	44.4	41.3	32.0	8 382
Employers, independent professionals and technicians	3.8	4.3	6.5	1 703
Employees	40.6	36.9	25.5	6 679
Professionals and technicians	4.7	7.8	20.1	5 260
Non-professional, non-technical workers	35.9	29.1	5.4	1 419
Total informal sector	41.0	46.3	65.9	17 284
Employment in microenterprises [a]	14.7	15.5	18.2	4 784
Domestic employment	5.4	6.3	9.4	2 466
Unskilled own-account workers	22.3	25.8	38.3	10 034
In agriculture, forestry, hunting and fishing	2.2	3.0	5.9	1 559
In industry and construction	4.3	5.2	8.1	2 131
In commerce and services	15.8	17.7	24.2	6 344

Source: ECLAC, on the basis of special tabulations of data from household surveys conducted in the respective countries.

[a] Includes employers and employees in firms with up to five workers.

The wage gap between different segments of the workforce also widened. In general, occupational earnings were slow to increase, and grew at a lower rate than per capita income. Moreover, in most of the countries these increases were too small to bring earnings back up to the levels recorded before the crisis of the 1980s. In almost every case, upturns in income reflected the combination of a large jump in the earnings of workers employed in the fastest-growing activities of the modern sector and the slower (or even negative) growth of the earnings of all other urban workers. As a result, the income gaps between the formal and informal sectors and between more and less skilled workers yawned even wider (ECLAC, 2000b).

Wage disparities between the formal and informal sectors increased in all the countries for which data are available (see table III.9). The same was true of the average income of workers in these two sectors in all the countries except Costa Rica, Honduras and Panama. Within each sector, income disparities between workers in higher- and lower-skilled jobs also increased everywhere except Argentina, although that country's situation is not fully comparable to those of the other countries owing to the upsurge in its open unemployment rate. By contrast, and with few exceptions, income disparities between men and women tended to narrow. The main exception was Panama, where these disparities are smaller than in any other country of the region.

Table III.9

LATIN AMERICA: INCOME DISPARITIES [a] IN URBAN AREAS, 1990-1999

(Percentages of the total employed population in urban areas)

Country	Year	Wage disparity between private professional and technical workers and non-professional, non-technical workers in the formal sector	Wage disparity between private professional and technical workers and non-professional, non-technical workers in the informal sector	Wage disparity between private-sector wage earners in the formal and informal sectors	Disparity in average wages between the formal and informal sectors	Wage disparity between men and women	Wage disparity between men and women with more than 12 years of schooling
Argentina [b]	1990	211	211	139	93	155	161
	1999	180	174	147	115	154	152
Bolivia	1989	237	173	161	138	176	205
	1999	205	208	191	203	171	154
Brazil	1990	223	165	135	138	184	194
	1999	234	171	168	163	163	175
Chile	1990	217	200	167	136	159	183
	1998	279	237	188	138	150	159
Colombia	1991	221	...	...	...	150	148
	1999	243	...	...	...	136	135
Costa Rica	1990	218	209	146	164	145	152
	1999	215	194	148	157	145	141
Ecuador	1990	221	148	147	189	165	180
	1999	175	153	184	204	162	141
El Salvador	1995	250	155	161	180	164	139
	1999	232	183	195	195	137	137
Guatemala	1989	207	229	172	152	154	...
	1998	265	216	175	209	190	161

(Continued)

Table III.9 (concluded)

Country	Year	Wage disparity between private professional and non-technical workers and non-professional, non-technical workers in the formal sector	Wage disparity between private professional and technical workers and non-professional, non-technical workers in the informal sector	Wage disparity between private-sector wage earners in the formal and informal sectors	Disparity in average wages between the formal and informal sectors	Wage disparity between men and women	Wage disparity between men and women with more than 12 years of schooling
Honduras	1990	257	244	191	264	170	158
	1999	152	155	201	170	160	135
Mexico	1989	223	...	...	...	182	158
	1998	235	247	164	125	181	179
Nicaragua	1993	210	209	135	133	131	153
	1998	248	274	170	186	161	149
Panama	1991	234	285	168	255	115	132
	1999	236	289	200	206	122	141
Paraguay [c]	1990	189	211	153	125	183	174
	1999	208	178	162	183	137	149
Dominican Republic	1997	222	213	157	121	133	134
Uruguay	1990	210	192	166	120	204	177
	1999	241	169	181	178	154	172
Venezuela	1990	186	140	162	111	155	140
	1999[d]	230	200	166	128	131	135

Source: ECLAC, on the basis of special tabulations of data from household surveys conducted in the respective countries.

[a] The disparity is obtained by dividing the average income of the higher-income category by the average income of the lower-income category and multiplying by 100.
[b] Greater Buenos Aires.
[c] Asunción and the Central Department.
[d] Nationwide total.

5.   Increased precariousness of labour conditions

In the 1990s labour conditions underwent a number of changes, including a decline in formal employment contracts; the proliferation of temporary and part-time jobs; the lack of social security coverage; the expansion of permissible grounds for dismissal; the reduction of severance pay; and restrictions on the right to strike, collective bargaining and union membership.

One of the ways in which more precarious employment conditions have been manifested is the increase in the proportion of wage or salary earners employed in temporary jobs. For example, in urban areas of Chile, Colombia and Costa Rica there was a substantial increase in non-permanent jobs, especially in microenterprises, where the proportion of temporary jobs is twice the proportion found in larger firms. Workers in the tertiary sector —the fastest-growing— are the ones most strongly affected by the increase in temporary hiring. Workers in low-skilled occupations are also particularly likely to be hired on a temporary basis, thus broadening the gap between more and less skilled workers.

According to data from seven countries in the region, towards the mid-1990s more than 40% of employees in Brazil, Paraguay and Peru, and more than a third in Argentina and Colombia, lacked open-ended contracts. More recent data show that 20% of employees in Chile and 33% in Mexico did not have such contracts. This trend intensified throughout the decade, as demonstrated by developments in Argentina, Brazil and Peru. The worst affected were microenterprise employees; data show that the differences between these workers and those employed in larger firms were 60 points in Mexico, about 40 points in Chile and Paraguay and a little over 30 points in Brazil.

Precarious labour conditions translate into a sharp downturn in wages (see table III.9). In all the countries considered the employment income of non-permanent employees was much lower than that of permanent employees. A similar gap exists between employees with and without a contract of employment. The biggest differences were observed in Mexico, where the earnings of workers without contracts amounted to 41% of the earnings of workers with contracts.

Another form of precariousness occurs when workers lack social security coverage or health insurance. Microenterprise employees are again the worst off in this respect, although the situation varies substantially from one country to another (see table III.10). In Bolivia and Paraguay over 60% of employees have no social security coverage, while in Argentina, Brazil, El Salvador, Mexico and Venezuela the figure is just

over a third. The countries with the broadest coverage are Chile, Costa
Rica —here social security covers between three quarters and four fifths
of the labour force— and Uruguay, where only a tiny percentage of the
population is not covered.

Table III.10
LATIN AMERICA (10 COUNTRIES): EMPLOYEES WITHOUT
SOCIAL SECURITY COVERAGE
(Percentages)

| Country | Year | Total | Size of establishment | |
			Up to 5 workers	More than 5 workers
Argentina	1990	29.9	64.8	18.2
	1997	37.3	74.1	22.7
Bolivia	1989	57.3	88.5	40.3
	1997	61.8	90.7	46.9
Brazil	1990	26.9	-	-
	1996	34.9	68.4	22.4
Chile	1990	20.1	42.5	13.2
	1996	19.6	43.6	13.1
Costa Rica	1990	22.5	66.2	11.8
	1997	26.2	71.2	14.0
El Salvador	1997	45.6	85.2	28.4
Mexico	1989	36.3	-	-
	1996	35.6	79.1	20.3
Paraguay	1995	64.4	94.3	47.2
Uruguay	1981	2.8	5.9	1.9
	1997	3.9	7.0	2.8
Venezuela	1997	38.8	79.1	24.5

Source: ECLAC, on the basis of special tabulations of data from household surveys conducted in the
respective countries.

6.   Open unemployment

(a)   Economic growth and unemployment

It is very probable that the main cause of the disparity between
labour supply and labour demand is the decrease in the proportion of jobs
created in the primary and secondary sectors, as well as the fact that some
subsectors   —such   as   financial   establishments,   telecommunications,
insurance and business services— have modernized through the intensive
use of new technologies, which has reduced their capacity to generate
employment.

The jump in unemployment in the 1990s was not, however, a
universal phenomenon in the region, although most of the South
American countries felt its effects. Unemployment climbed steadily in

Argentina, Brazil and Colombia, although in Brazil it reached levels equivalent to only half the rates recorded in the other two countries. Unemployment also worsened in Bolivia, Chile, Ecuador, Paraguay, Uruguay and Venezuela. In Chile it did not begin to rise until 1998, after having gone down systematically since the beginning of the decade. By contrast, unemployment tended to subside in Mexico and most of the Central American and Caribbean countries. Once it had recovered from the effects of the 1995 crisis, Mexico saw a clear downturn in urban unemployment, which returned to a rate of about 2.5%. The figure also dropped in some Central American countries, such as El Salvador, Honduras and Nicaragua, while in Costa Rica it stayed relatively moderate (see figure III.3 and tables III.11 and III.12).

(b) Unemployment by income level, sex and age group

Unemployment continues to affect the lower income bands the most. As shown in table III.13, in 17 Latin American countries and in the group of eight countries that experienced a more rapid increase in unemployment between the mid- and late 1990s,[9] the percentage of unemployed people in the poorest 40% of the population (quintiles I and II), which continued to be considerably higher than the overall rate of unemployment, increased significantly between 1994 and 1999. This phenomenon is thus one of the main determinants of poverty and inequality. Unemployment also rose in another 40% of households (quintiles III and IV), particularly in the eight countries worst affected by the crisis. The increase in urban unemployment even impinged on the highest-earning quintile. At the end of the decade the three quintiles with the highest incomes recorded rates of unemployment twice as high —and in some countries three times as high— as the rates posted in the middle of the decade.

---

[9]   Argentina, Brazil, Chile, Colombia, Ecuador, Paraguay, Uruguay and Venezuela.

Figure III.3
LATIN AMERICA: TRENDS IN ECONOMIC GROWTH AND URBAN OPEN
UNEMPLOYMENT,[a] 1980-2000

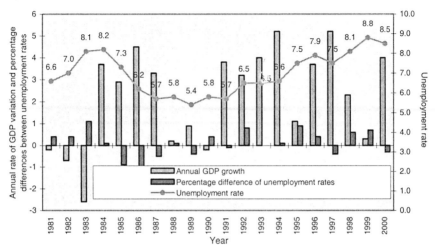

Source: ECLAC, on the basis of official government figures.

[a] The figures relating to economic growth correspond to the weighted average of 19 countries of the region.

Table III.11
LATIN AMERICA: LEVEL AND COMPOSITION OF UNEMPLOYMENT, 1990-1999
(Thousands of people and percentages)

	People (thousands)		Annual rate of variation (%)
	1990	1999	1990-1999
Unemployed	7 643	18 118	10.1
Urban areas	6 600	17 457	11.4
Rural areas	1 043	661	-4.9
Laid off	5 932	15 391	11.2
Urban areas	5 225	15 204	12.6
Rural areas	708	186	-13.8
Seeking work for the first time	1 711	2 728	5.3
Urban areas	1 376	2 253	5.6
Rural areas	335	475	3.9

Source: ECLAC, on the basis of estimates prepared by the Population Division of ECLAC - Latin American and Caribbean Demographic Centre (CELADE) and special tabulations of data from household surveys conducted in the respective countries.

Table III.12
LATIN AMERICA AND THE CARIBBEAN: URBAN UNEMPLOYMENT, 1990-2000
(Average annual rates)

Country	1990	1991	1992	1993	1994	1995	1996	1997	1998	1999	2000[a]
Latin America and the Caribbean											
Weighted average	5.8	5.7	6.5	6.5	6.6	7.5	7.9	7.5	8.1	8.8	8.5
Simple average	9.5	9.6	9.8	10.0	9.5	10.1	10.5	9.9	9.7	10.6	10.8
Argentina [b]	7.4	6.5	7.0	9.6	11.5	17.5	17.2	14.9	12.9	14.3	15.1
Barbados [c]	14.7	17.3	23.0	24.3	21.9	19.7	15.6	14.5	12.3	10.4	9.2
Bolivia [b]	7.3	5.8	5.4	5.8	3.1	3.6	3.8	4.4	6.1	8.0	7.6
Brazil [b]	4.3	4.8	5.8	5.4	5.1	4.6	5.4	5.7	7.6	7.6	7.1
Chile [d]	9.2	8.2	6.7	6.5	7.8	7.4	6.4	6.1	6.4	9.8	9.2
Colombia [b e]	10.5	10.2	10.2	8.6	8.9	8.8	11.2	12.4	15.3	19.4	20.2
Costa Rica	5.4	6.0	4.3	4.0	4.3	5.7	6.6	5.9	5.4	6.2	5.3
Cuba [c]	...	7.7	6.1	6.2	6.7	7.9	7.6	7.0	6.6	6.0	5.5
Ecuador [e]	6.1	7.7	8.9	8.9	7.8	7.7	10.4	9.3	11.5	15.1	14.1
El Salvador	10.0	7.9	8.2	8.1	7.0	7.0	7.5	7.5	7.6	6.9	6.5
Guatemala	6.0	4.2	1.6	2.6	3.5	3.9	5.2	5.1	3.8	...	...
Honduras [c]	7.8	7.4	6.0	7.0	4.0	5.6	6.5	5.8	5.2	5.3	...
Jamaica [c]	15.3	15.4	15.7	16.3	15.4	16.2	16.0	16.5	15.5	15.7	15.5
Mexico	2.7	2.7	2.8	3.4	3.7	6.2	5.5	3.7	3.2	2.5	2.2
Nicaragua	7.6	11.5	14.4	17.8	17.1	16.9	16.0	14.3	13.2	10.7	9.8
Panama [d e]	20.0	19.3	17.5	15.6	16.0	16.6	16.9	15.5	15.2	14.0	15.2
Paraguay	6.6	5.1	5.3	5.1	4.4	5.3	8.2	7.1	6.6	9.4	10.7
Peru [f]	8.3	5.9	9.4	9.9	8.8	8.2	8.0	9.2	8.5	9.2	8.5
Dominican Republic	...	19.6	20.3	19.9	16.0	15.8	16.5	15.9	14.3	13.8	13.9
Trinidad and Tobago [c e]	20.1	18.5	19.6	19.8	18.4	17.2	16.2	15.0	14.2	13.1	12.5
Uruguay [f]	9.2	8.9	9.0	8.3	9.2	10.3	11.9	11.5	10.1	11.3	13.6
Venezuela	11.0	9.5	7.8	6.6	8.7	10.3	11.8	11.4	11.3	14.9	14.0

Source: ECLAC, prepared on the basis of ECLAC, *Statistical Yearbook for Latin America and the Caribbean, 2000* (LC/G.2118-P), Santiago, Chile, February 2001. United Nations publication, Sales No. E.00.II.G.1; and *Current conditions and outlook: Economic survey of Latin America and the Caribbean 2000-2001* (LC/G.2142-P), Santiago, Chile. United Nations publication, Sales No. E.01.II.G.121.

[a] Preliminary figures.
[b] Main urban areas.
[c] Nationwide.
[d] Metropolitan region.
[e] Includes hidden unemployment.
[f] Capital city.

Table III.13
LATIN AMERICA: RATE OF URBAN UNEMPLOYMENT IN 17 COUNTRIES AND
IN 8 COUNTRIES WITH A STEEP RISE IN UNEMPLOYMENT, 1994-1999

	Latin America (17 countries)		Eight countries with a steep rise in unemployment[a]	
	1994	1999	1994	1999
Rate of unemployment:				
Both sexes	7.1	10.6	6.6	13.1
Men	6.7	9.4	5.8	11.3
Women	7.7	12.3	7.8	15.5
Young people aged 15-24	14.0	20.0	14.0	24.8
Quintile I (lowest 20% income quintile)	14.8	22.3	15.8	27.8
Quintile II	8.1	12.7	8.3	15.6
Quintile III	5.6	9.4	5.5	11.2
Quintile IV	3.9	6.5	3.7	8.0
Quintile V (highest 20% income quintile)	2.3	4.3	2.0	4.6

Source: ECLAC, on the basis of special tabulations of data from household surveys conducted in the respective countries.

[a] Countries with rising rates of unemployment in the period, of close to or higher than 10%: Argentina, Brazil, Chile, Colombia, Ecuador, Paraguay, Uruguay and Venezuela.

In addition, unemployment continues to be particularly rife among young people between the ages of 15 and 24, who represent between a quarter and a fifth of Latin America's workforce. Even before the Asian crisis the unemployment rate in this group was almost double the regional average, and in most countries these young people represented almost half the total number of unemployed workers. Between 1994 and 1999 this age group's unemployment rate rose from 14% to 20%, and to 24.8% in the eight countries hardest hit by the crisis. This group's relative share of total unemployment dropped slightly, owing to an increase in unemployment among the primary labour force.

Lastly, gender differences with regard to employment worsened. In the urban areas of 17 countries in the region, female unemployment rose, on average, from 7.7% to 12.3%, while male unemployment climbed from 6.7% to 9.4%. These gaps widened even more, to women's disadvantage, in the eight countries hardest hit by the crisis.

(c)   Unemployment and well-being

The impact of unemployment on the well-being of the different population groups depends not only on the level of unemployment, but also on the average duration of periods of unemployment and the wage losses suffered by workers who subsequently manage to find employment (see figure III.4).

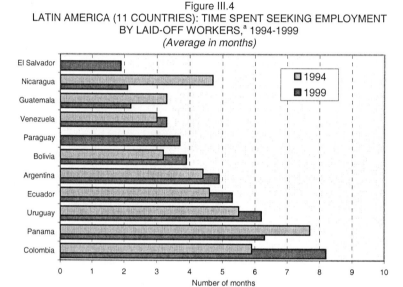

Figure III.4
LATIN AMERICA (11 COUNTRIES): TIME SPENT SEEKING EMPLOYMENT
BY LAID-OFF WORKERS,[a] 1994-1999
(Average in months)

Source: ECLAC, on the basis of special tabulations of data from household surveys conducted in the respective countries.

[a] Does not include unemployed persons who have been seeking work for more than two years.

In economies with high rates of unemployment, the prolongation of a period of unemployment impacts negatively in three different ways: it hurts unemployed workers themselves, owing to the loss of human capital or reintegration into the labour force at lower wages; the families of unemployed workers suffer a loss of well-being if they are forced to liquidate assets, engage in child labour or drop out of school; and the economy at large suffers because of the decline in the average level of wages, the contraction in demand for goods and the resulting recessionary effects. An examination of the situation in six of the region's countries where unemployment practically doubled shows that the out-of-work period increased from an average of 4.4 to 5.3 months for men and a little more, from 4.7 to 5.7 months, for women. The duration of the period of unemployment increased by the same amount of time —about a month— among both heads of household and workers who were not heads of household.

Although differences in the size of the reserve wage could largely account for the marked differences in the average duration of unemployment observed between unemployed workers with different levels of schooling, the fact that less skilled workers spend more time seeking work also seems to reflect problems with the supply and loss of jobs in the region's economies. Although more highly skilled workers spent much longer periods out of work than less skilled ones in the 11 countries for which data are available and in the six countries that registered the largest increases in unemployment, between 1994 and 1999 the average length of unemployment increased faster among less skilled workers; that is, those with fewer than 10 years of schooling.

One final point that warrants discussion is the loss of income workers are forced to accept in order to find a new job. According to a study on Uruguay conducted by Bucheli and Furtado (2001), the wage loss faced by workers aged 23 to 59 who managed to find a new job represented between 23% and 34% of the amount they had earned in their previous employment. This serves to illustrate what happens in urban markets where the labour force is largely wage-dependent and unemployment persists at relatively high rates.

Chapter IV

Occupational stratification

The occupational stratification that prevailed in Latin America in the late 1990s reflects the inequality existing in the region with respect to productive assets, professional qualifications and occupational income. Grouped on the basis of these criteria, the occupational strata may be divided into three relatively homogeneous levels: upper, middle and lower. The upper level accounts for 10.3% of the employed workforce, with incomes considerably higher than those corresponding to the other levels, which clearly set them apart from the latter. The middle level includes only 14.5% of the employed workforce, but the lower group encompasses 75% of the employed, many of whom earn an income that is insufficient in itself to maintain a typical four-member Latin American family above the poverty line.

1.   The basic structure of occupational stratification

The expansion of non-manual and urban occupations in the postwar period and the concomitant reduction in manual and agricultural work caused a marked change in the structure of the workforce. This process has continued over the last two decades, but unlike the pattern in the past, it has not brought major changes in occupational income, so that a more in-depth study needs to be carried out on the integration and characteristics of the different occupational strata, especially those that group together non-manual and urban occupations.[1]

The information available on the earnings of the different occupations makes possible a more realistic evaluation of the situation of each level, particularly in the case of non-manual occupations, which were regarded as the clearest expression of upward social mobility between 1950 and 1980. This information shows how difficult it is for many occupations, both manual and non-manual, to increase earnings and thus bring the persons in question fully into the middle classes. Owing to these factors, the prevailing occupational stratification in Latin America is still characterized by a large lower stratum, although currently this stratum is not composed predominantly, as was the case in the past, of manual and agricultural occupations. This process of relative reduction in the income obtained by non-manual middle-level occupations is consistent with the fact that in most countries average household income has shifted in the last two decades from about the 66th percentile to about the 75th percentile, which indicates that 75% of households receive incomes below the mean.

As already noted, the occupations employing most of the workforce of Latin America in the late 1990s may be ordered in three levels, upper, middle and lower, when examined on the basis of certain basic variables, such as ownership of productive assets, level of qualifications, authority exercised in the workplace, and occupational income. The upper level accounts for 10.3% of the workforce employed in the eleven countries under consideration and comprises non-manual occupational categories that must possess either productive assets (employers), a high level of professional skills (professionals), or authority in the workplace (managers). The average occupational income corresponding to this level is equivalent to 12.5 times the poverty line and its members have an average educational level of 11.6 years of schooling. The middle level is also made up of non-manual occupations: its members have an intermediate degree of professional skills or authority (supervisors, middle level professionals, technicians) or are administrative employees. This level accounts for 14.5% of the workforce and the average occupational income is equivalent to 4.9 times the poverty line, with an average of 11.2 years of education. The lower level encompasses a vast and heterogeneous group of manual and non-manual occupations, whose members do not have productive assets or positions of authority and have a relatively low degree of professional skills. This level covers 74.5% of the workforce, with an average occupational income

---

[1]   Some conceptual aspects of occupational stratification are dealt with in the methodological annex.

equivalent to 2.4 times the poverty line and an average educational level of 5.5 years of schooling. This level can be broken down into two groups of roughly the same size which, although both lack sufficient levels of income and education to have access to a reasonable degree of well-being, may be clearly differentiated from each other by the levels of these characteristics. The first group is made up of commercial employees and blue-collar workers, artisans and drivers, who have an average income equivalent to 3 times the poverty line and 6.5 years of schooling, while the second group, consisting of workers providing personal services and agricultural workers, has an average income equivalent to 1.8 times the poverty line and 4.3 years of schooling (see table IV.1).

Table IV.1
LATIN AMERICA (11 COUNTRIES): SOME CHARACTERISTICS OF THE DIFFERENT
OCCUPATIONAL STRATA, 1999

Occupational stratum	Employed labour force		Average income	Average years of schooling
	Persons	%		
Total	148 737 944	100.0	3.8	6.9
1. Employers	6 589 655	4.4	14.1	8.9
2. Executives and managers	3 069 273	2.1	11.9	11.7
3. Professionals	5 676 632	3.8	11.1	14.6
1 + 2 + 3	15 335 560	10.3	12.5	11.6
4. Technicians	12 004 237	8.1	5.7	11.5
5. Administrative employees	9 502 927	6.4	3.8	10.9
4 + 5	21 507 164	14.5	4.9	11.2
6. Workers in commerce	18 888 087	12.7	2.8	7.1
7. Blue-collar workers, artisans, drivers	40 126 684	27.0	3.1	6.2
6 + 7	59 014 771	39.7	3.0	6.5
8. Personal services workers	22 792 347	15.3	2.1	5.9
9. Agricultural workers	29 168 673	19.6	1.6	3.1
8 + 9	51 961 020	34.9	1.8	4.3
6 + 7 + 8 + 9	110 975 791	74.6	2.4	5.5
10. Armed Forces	897 701	0.6	7.2	10.6
11. Unclassified	21 728	0.0	5.2	10.6

Source: ECLAC, on the basis of special tabulations of household surveys of the respective countries.

As this basic structure of occupational stratification in Latin America shows, only one out of every ten members of the employed workforce is equipped to obtain an income that will enable him or her to enjoy a high standard of living. Below this occupational elite, a little less than 15% have attained an intermediate position on the occupational pyramid, thanks mainly to their educational attainments, which are similar to those of the upper level, although their occupational income is much lower. Lastly, the base of the pyramid is made up of three-quarters of the workforce, whose members, despite their considerable labour heterogeneity, obtain occupational incomes very similar to each other and far removed from those received by the other two levels.

These three levels constitute the basic structure of the occupational stratification of the region and give a general idea of its features. Clearly, in order to carry out a more detailed analysis of this structure, an examination must be made of the internal composition of each of these levels and of the variations that occurred in this structure in each of the countries during the 1990s. However, an analysis of this kind will not show any major variation from the overall picture. Similarly, the validity of the criteria used to classify the occupations may be open to question, but given the differences in the occupational income of the three levels, and especially between the upper category and the two others, it is difficult to imagine that a change in the classification criteria would lead to any substantial change in the general view of this basic structure.

(a) The upper level

The upper level consists of three occupational strata: i) employers; ii) senior officials and private and public managers, and iii) professionals. Employers account for 4.4% of the workforce and receive average occupational incomes that are much higher than any of the other strata (14.1 times the poverty line), although they have an average educational level (8.9 years of schooling) which is lower than that of the middle strata. Two-thirds of all employers are micro-entrepreneurs, since they employ fewer than 5 persons; most of them are engaged in non-agricultural activities, with an average income of 12.1 times the poverty line, while the remaining employers are engaged in agricultural activities with a slightly lower average income (8.8 times the poverty line). The remaining third of employers employ six or more persons and, as may be supposed, their occupational income rises as the number of employees increases. Those that employ between 6 and 9 persons have an average income equivalent to 15.6 times the poverty line, when they work in non-agricultural activities, and 12.1 times the poverty line when they work in agricultural activities; those who employ 10 or more persons earn an income

27.3 times the poverty line (non-agricultural) and 29.3 times the poverty line (agricultural). Employers who employ ten or more persons make up the occupational stratum with the highest income of the entire workforce, far outpacing all the rest. However, employers with smaller businesses also receive a high income compared with the rest of the workforce, which shows the decisive importance of ownership of productive assets in determining the place that one occupies in the occupational stratification pyramid.

Senior officials and private and public executives represent 2.1% of the total workforce, and the vast majority work in businesses that employ 10 persons or more. Their average occupational income is equivalent to 11.9 times the poverty line, but varies considerably if we take into account the size of the business in which they work: those employed in businesses with 10 or more employees have an income equivalent to 14 times the poverty line, which is almost twice that of the minority working in smaller businesses. Not all surveys differentiate between employees on the basis of whether they belong to the public or private sector, which prevents us from presenting figures for all the countries together. According to available information, private executives in some countries, such as Chile, El Salvador, Guatemala and Paraguay, earn more than their public counterparts; in others, such as Colombia and Costa Rica, the reverse is true, while in Panama and Venezuela, there is not much difference in income between the two. The average years of schooling of the members of this stratum (11.7 years) is not particularly high, so that their level of income depends significantly on the degree of authority they wield within the private or public organization where they work (see table IV.1).

Professionals account for 3.8% of the workforce and earn an average occupational income equivalent to 11.1 times the poverty line, for an average of 14.6 years of schooling. As in the case of executives and managers, 75% of them work in businesses that employ 10 or more persons, although in this stratum, the remaining 25% work independently. The few professionals who are engaged in enterprises of up to nine persons earn considerably less than those who work in larger establishments or who are independent. In this respect, there is no clear trend among independent professionals, since in some countries they have a higher income than those working in medium-sized or large firms, while in other countries, the reverse is true.

(b)   The middle level

This level is made up of occupational strata that do not own productive assets. One of the strata is made up of persons with a middle level of professional skills (technicians) or of authority (supervisors); the other is made up of administrative employees.

Technicians and supervisors account for 8.1% of the workforce, and on average their occupational income is 5.7 times the poverty line and they have an educational level of 11.5 years' schooling. As already noted, their educational level is similar to that of the higher level, but their income is much lower. Close to 75% of technicians and supervisors work in companies that employ 10 or more persons; the remaining 25% are divided up among those who work in smaller enterprises or as independent workers. The occupational income of technicians and supervisors who work in enterprises of up to nine persons is markedly lower than that of their counterparts who work in larger businesses or who are independent.

Administrative employees make up 6.4% of the workforce and have an average income equivalent to 3.8 times the poverty line and 10.9 years of schooling. Almost all the members of this stratum work as wage earners, and most belong to establishments that employ ten or more persons. In the latter case, the earnings of administrative employees are equivalent to 4.3 times the poverty line, but those that are employed in micro-enterprises or small enterprises have much lower earnings, between 2.6 and 3 times the poverty line, similar to those obtained by manual workers of the lower level. As in the case of technicians and supervisors, administrative employees derive little benefit in terms of occupational income from their years of schooling.

(c)   The lower level

As already noted, the lower level is made up of a heterogeneous set of occupations, predominantly manual, which includes workers in commerce; blue-collar workers, artisans, operatives and drivers; workers in personal services, and agricultural workers.

Workers in commerce are divided into three basic subcategories of occupations, which are not always clearly discernible in the household surveys: i) independent merchants who do not employ any staff but have their own premises; ii) wage-earning salesmen or women, and iii) street vendors. The available information indicates that, as a whole, this stratum accounts for 12.7% of the workforce; its members have, on average, 7.1 years of schooling and occupational income equivalent to 2.8 times the poverty line. This stratum, together with that of agricultural workers, has the particular feature of being made up of a higher proportion of own-account workers than of wage earners, with a not insignificant proportion of unpaid workers. Of the total of this stratum, 37% are wage earners, 53% are own-account workers and 10% are unpaid workers. Almost half of the wage-earning salespersons in the commercial sector work in establishments that employ up to five persons; this is quite important, because the average income for these occupations increases in proportion to the size of the establishment: in establishments of up to 5 employees, the average occupational income is 1.9 times the poverty line; in those of 6 to 9 employees, it is 2.6, and in those of 10 or more, it is 3.3. Own-account salespersons in the commercial sector have a higher income than that of wage earners (3.4 times the poverty line), which is due to the fact that this category encompasses, as already noted, both established independent merchants and street vendors. In those countries whose surveys distinguish between the two groups of occupations in terms of occupational income, it is possible to pinpoint the differences between them: in Brazil, for example, the average income of established merchants is 4.5 times the poverty line, while that of street vendors is 2.3 times the poverty line; in Colombia, the incomes are 2.5 and 1.8 times the poverty line, respectively. It is hard to estimate the quantitative weight of independent merchants who do not employ hired labour, but it is probable that in Latin America as a whole it may vary between 1.5% and 2% of the total of the workforce, with an average income closer to the middle than the lower level.

Blue-collar workers, artisans, operatives and drivers account for 27% of the workforce and have an average income 3.1 times the poverty line and an educational level of 6.2 years of schooling. More than 40% of these workers are employed in establishment of 10 employees or more and earn an average occupational income equivalent to 3.5 times the poverty line. Almost 30% are own-account workers, with an income 3.3 times the poverty line, while the rest work in enterprises with up to nine employees, where income ranges between 2.3 and 2.6 times the poverty line. Admittedly, the members of this stratum have different levels of qualifications and different degrees of authority in the firm, and this naturally has consequences from the point of view of occupational income, but unfortunately it is hard to analyse this aspect with the information available. In the few countries where it is possible to explore the subject, the differences in terms of skills and authority are seen to have a similar impact on income to that linked to the size of the establishment (small, medium-sized or large). At all events, given the gap between the average income of this group and the income of the middle level, it is very unlikely that this group includes more highly skilled occupations which might make it possible for such employees to move up to the middle level.

Workers in personal and security services account for 15.3% of the workforce, with an occupational income equivalent to 2.1 times the poverty line and an average of 5.9 years of schooling. The vast majority are wage earners, divided up fairly evenly between micro- and small enterprises, on the one hand, and medium-sized and large enterprises, on the other. As in most of the remaining strata, those working in medium-sized and large enterprises earn higher incomes, followed by independent workers and finally, with the lowest average incomes, those employed in micro- and small enterprises.

Agricultural workers make up 19.6% of the total workforce and have, on average, an occupational income equivalent to 1.8 times the poverty line and an educational level of 3.1 years of schooling. Approximately half of them are own-account workers, 30% are wage earners and the rest are unpaid family members. There are no major differences between the occupational income of the first two subgroups, although those working as wage earners in medium-sized and large enterprises earn more.

The basic occupational stratification structure described above reveals the high degree of inequality between the incomes of the different strata: a result which coincides with the data on income distribution in the region. The strata that make up the upper level, in particular medium- and large-scale employers, earn an income that sets them apart from the rest, forming an elite characterized by its high standard of living. The strata of the middle level earn incomes which, although only 40% of those obtained by the upper level strata, still afford employees in this category in the countries with the highest average income levels a reasonably comfortable standard of living. This strata's share of total employment is not as significant as might have been assumed, because of the weakening of the State's employment capacity, which has reduced the number of technicians and professionals that it employs, and because of the loss of status by some occupations corresponding to employees in commerce and some administrative employees, which means that they can no longer be included in the middle level strata. Thus, the incomes received by the workers in commerce and administrative employees in question are not sufficient to enable them to improve their living conditions substantially. The lower level, for its part, comprises all those occupations which provide such a low occupational income that it leaves many workers highly vulnerable to poverty. Among the persons employed in these occupations, independent merchants and more highly skilled blue-collar workers and operatives are in a slightly better situation, but at the base of the stratification system, in many of the countries considered, there are many salespersons in commerce and personal services workers and agricultural workers whose occupational income scarcely keeps them above the poverty line.

The basic structure of occupational stratification did not change significantly in the 1990s. In 1999, the share of the upper level was 0.3% smaller than in 1990, following a slight decline in the percentage of professionals and employers. The share of the middle level also declined by 0.2%, because the decline in the percentage of administrative employees (1.5%) was not offset by the increase in technicians and supervisors. The share of the lower level, however, increased by 2.3%. In this level, the percentage corresponding to agricultural workers (0.6%) diminished, while that of blue-collar workers, artisans, operatives and drivers remained more or less stable and there was an increase in workers in commerce (1.4%) and in personal services and security (1.8%). Admittedly, the changes were not substantial, perhaps partly because the 1.3% of unclassified workers listed in the 1990 figures was eliminated in the 1999 figures. At all events, the changes indicated here are compatible with the trends pointed out in other studies, such as the absence of occupational mobility, the persistent relative reduction in agricultural workers and the likewise relative increase in low-productivity urban occupations in the tertiary sector.

The occupational income of the workforce as a whole fell, on average, by only 0.1%, although as may readily be supposed, it increased in some strata and diminished in others. It diminished slightly, by the equivalent of 0.3% of the poverty line, among employers, but increased among executives and senior officials (0.5), professionals (1.2) and technicians (0.4). Apart from personal services and security workers, for whom a small increase was recorded (0.2), occupational income declined in all the other strata: administrative employees (0.2 times the poverty line); blue-collar workers, artisans, operatives and drivers (0.1); workers in commerce (0.6), and agricultural workers (0.4). These changes, although moderate, indicate the existence of a process of concentration of occupational income in the upper level occupations within a context of reduction of average occupational income (see table IV.1).

Finally, attention should also be drawn to the higher educational level of the workforce, which increased from 6.2 years of schooling in 1990 to 6.9 years in 1999. This process, which will be examined in more detail below, shows that there is a persistent inconsistency between, on the one hand, the increase in the educational level and, on the other, the relative lack of labour opportunities in the middle and upper levels and the reduction in the occupational income of most of the manual and non-manual occupations of the lower level.

2.   Basic structure and national situations

The occupational stratification structure prevailing in Latin America corresponds to a relatively low degree of development and a high degree of structural heterogeneity, which is evident when one compares the different occupational strata and analyses the composition of each of them. In the countries where the average occupational income increased significantly during the 1990s, the proportion of the workforce employed in the upper and middle levels of stratification increased while the workforce in the lower level decreased. The opposite occurred in those countries where average occupational income diminished. Generally speaking, however, two trends predominated: one towards a decrease in the proportion of the workforce employed in the upper and middle levels and the other towards an increase in that of the lower level, both as a result of the decline in average occupational income, which shows the scant upward structural mobility registered in the 1990s in most of Latin America.

The basic structure described does not merely represent the statistical average of national situations, which could possibly be very different from one another: on the contrary, it is a true reflection of reality, since there is a great similarity in this respect between the majority of countries, even the most heavily populated. Thus, according to the general structure, the workforce of Latin America was distributed in such a way that 10.3% were in the highest level, 14.5% in the middle level and 74.6% in the lower level, and if we look at some representative individual cases we see that the distributions were very similar. For example, the proportions existing in Brazil at the end of the 1990s were 9.3%, 14.2% and 75.4%, respectively; in Colombia, they were 9.5%, 14.4% and 76.1%, and in Mexico, they were 10%, 16,7% and 73.1% (see table IV.2). This similarity stems from the fact that there is a fairly close relationship between the degree of economic development of a country and the distribution among the three levels of stratification. In most countries in the region, the average occupational income of the workforce is between 3 and 4 times the poverty line, and this is faithfully reflected in the general average of 3.8 times the poverty line. This average is consistent with the above-mentioned percentage distribution of the workforce by occupational level. If the average occupational income were higher, the proportion represented by the lower level in the workforce would be smaller, and concomitantly, that corresponding to the middle and upper levels would be higher. This stands out clearly when we look at the stratification structure of the countries under consideration. Chile, for example, is the country where the average level of occupational income is highest (7.3 times the poverty line) and the lower stratum is smallest, since it represents 65.5% of the workforce; next comes Costa Rica with 6.2 times the poverty line and 68.7%; Panama, with 5.4 and 67.9%; Brazil, with 3.9 and 75.4%; Mexico with 3.7 and 73.1%; Venezuela, with 3.6 and 72%; El Salvador, with 3.4 and 78.2%; Colombia with 3.2 and 76.1%; Paraguay, with 2.9 and 78.5%; Nicaragua, with 2.8 and 82.5%, and Guatemala, with 2.8 times the poverty line and 84.9%. The greater part of the workforce of Latin America is employed in economies that reflect the basic stratification structure, but when we look at countries which depart from this more generalized degree of development, the differences between them stand out quite markedly, so that the country with the highest occupational income has a lower level which is almost 20% smaller than that of the country where occupational income is lowest. Clearly, the pattern of occupational stratification is affected by a number of factors, but it does correspond to a great extent to the country's average occupational income, for the development process and occupational income are linked to the distribution of workers among the different economic sectors, to their manual or non-manual and wage-earning or own-account status, and to the relative importance of the different sizes of establishments, i.e., large, medium-sized or small (see table IV.2).

If we compare more closely the situation of Chile and Guatemala, which are the countries with the highest and the lowest average occupational income, respectively, the differences between them in this respect stand out clearly. As already noted, in Guatemala the lower level accounts for almost 20% more of the workforce than in Chile, which is due largely to the fact that agricultural workers account for a much larger share of the total than in Chile (36.2% compared with 13%). In addition, the composition of these workers varies significantly between one country and the other. In Guatemala, 35% are own-account workers and more than 20% are unpaid; the rest are wage earners, but only half of them work in enterprises with 10 or more workers. In Chile, own-account, workers represent only 25% of the total, there are practically no unpaid workers, and the remaining 75% are wage-earners, most of whom work in medium-sized and large enterprises.

The proportion of persons working in the personal services and security category is higher in Chile (16.6%) than in Guatemala (10%), which, as will be shown later in greater detail, indicates that the increase in average occupational income in Chile has tended to be concentrated in the upper level, which results in a greater demand for employees in security work and personal services to serve those belonging to that level. The percentage of blue-collar workers, artisans and drivers is not very different in the two countries: 22.9% in Guatemala and 26.4% in Chile, but

Table IV.2
LATIN AMERICA (11 COUNTRIES): EMPLOYED WORKFORCE BY OCCUPATIONAL STRATUM, 1999
(Percentages)

Occupational stratum	Brazil	Chile	Colombia	Costa Rica	El Salvador	Guatemala	Mexico	Nicaragua	Panama	Paraguay	Venezuela	Total
Total	100.00	100.00	100.00	100.00	100.00	100.00	100.00	100.00	100.00	100.00	100.00	100.00
Employers	4.22	4.13	4.11	8.20	4.51	3.43	4.77	3.86	2.92	5.42	5.20	4.43
Executives and senior officials	2.23	4.57	1.48	3.44	1.48	1.17	1.63	1.87	5.65	1.15	2.30	2.06
Professionals	2.87	8.77	11.28	5.95	2.70	4.58	3.60	2.58	7.27	2.39	12.01	4.75
Technicians and supervisors	8.32	7.54	-	5.85	7.51	3.01	9.94	6.53	5.82	5.86	-	7.14
Administrative employees	5.84	8.84	7.05	7.56	5.33	2.93	6.79	2.45	10.46	6.55	8.14	6.39
Workers in commerce	11.27	9.46	15.20	10.06	16.71	15.97	13.02	14.88	10.73	15.67	17.39	12.70
Blue-collar workers, artisans, drivers	25.39	26.40	23.85	26.54	27.77	22.87	31.78	22.56	23.64	21.43	28.34	26.98
Personal services and security workers	16.92	16.62	16.74	16.16	14.09	9.99	12.05	14.63	17.10	12.89	16.87	15.30
Agricultural workers	21.81	12.99	20.30	15.95	19.64	36.02	16.29	30.44	16.38	28.46	9.45	19.61
Armed Forces	1.14	0.54	-	-	-	0.03	0.11	0.14	-	0.16	0.28	0.60
Others	0.01	0.15	-	0.29	0.27	-	-	0.05	0.02	0.04	0.02	0.02

Source: ECLAC, on the basis of special tabulations of household surveys of the respective countries.

once again, there is a contrast in their composition, although not as much as in the case of agricultural workers. The percentage of independent workers is quite similar in the two countries —between 25% and 30% of the total— and in both cases there are few unpaid workers. Therefore, the percentage of wage earners is also quite similar, but the major difference stems from the fact that in Chile most wage earners work in medium and large-scale enterprises, while in Guatemala they work predominantly in micro- and small enterprises. There is also a marked contrast between the two countries with respect to vendors in the commercial sector, since in Guatemala they account for a higher percentage (16%), than in Chile (9.5%) and more than 80% of them are own-account workers or are unpaid. In Chile, 60% of the sales personnel in the commercial sector are wage earners and half of them work in medium-sized or large enterprises.

In the middle level, the differences between the two countries are observed not so much in the internal composition of the strata as in the proportion that they represent. In Guatemala, technicians, supervisors and administrative employees together make up only 5.9% of the workforce, whereas in Chile they account for 16.3%. In both countries, however, they are mostly wage earners who work in medium-sized and large enterprises. The nature of the work of technicians is such that a certain percentage operate as own-account workers, but the same does not apply to supervisors and administrative employees. Any increase in these occupations depends on the emergence and expansion of productive establishments and State agencies which bring about economic and social development. This leaves little room for own-account workers.

At the upper level, the occupation of senior official or private or public-sector manager is also related to the development of productive organizations and government agencies, so that their expansion depends on the degree of development attained by each country; in Chile, senior officials and private or public managers account for 4.6% of the workforce, compared with 1.2% in Guatemala. The comparison between the two countries is particularly interesting in the case of employers. The first point to note is that the proportions are not too different: 4.1% in Chile and 3.4% in Guatemala, and in both countries the majority of employers devote themselves to non-agricultural activities: 88% in Chile and 73% in Guatemala. The two countries are also similar on another score, since more than 80% of agricultural employers are micro- or small entrepreneurs, while in non-agricultural activities, the corresponding percentages are 70% in Chile and 90% in Guatemala. In other words, the proportion of entrepreneurs is slightly higher in Chile and most of them are engaged in non-agricultural activities. Moreover, in Chile there is a higher percentage of employers with establishments that employ ten or more persons, but the differences between the two countries are not very significant in this respect. These figures reveal that the increase in average occupational income does not raise substantially the proportion of employers. As the degree of development rises, the amount of productive assets increases, but their ownership becomes more concentrated, leading to the appearance of large-scale employers who account for much of the ownership of such assets. Finally, economic and educational development increases the number of professionals. In Chile they represent 8.8% of the workforce and in Guatemala, only 4.6%, In both countries, the vast majority of professionals are wage-earners in medium-sized and large private and State-owned enterprises, so that those who work independently account for only about 10% of the total number of professionals.

A comparison of the countries that occupy the extremes in terms of average occupational income is instructive because it gives a clear idea of the impact of the degree of economic development on the distribution of the workforce in the different levels and strata and allows us to pinpoint some of the features of the internal composition of those strata. However, none of these features fully reflects the predominant stratification structure in the region. In the predominant structure, which is similar to that of Brazil and Mexico, the average occupational income is somewhat less than four times the poverty line, which is closer to the level of Guatemala than that of Chile, and with a productive system characterized by a higher degree of heterogeneity in terms of productivity, income and distribution of the workforce among the strata. Countries such as Brazil and Mexico display a higher degree of heterogeneity, since characteristics typical of the two extremes in development, such as those that occur in Guatemala and Chile, coexist side by side.

In Brazil and Mexico, the proportion of the workforce situated in the upper level is 9.3% and 10%, respectively; these figures are similar to those for Guatemala and are almost half those of Chile. Although Brazil and Mexico have highly developed economic sectors with a predominance of large establishments and a large State apparatus compared with the regional average, the professionals, executives and senior officials employed in these establishments and in State agencies are proportionally few in relation to the size of their workforce. Moreover, as already mentioned, whatever the degree of development of the countries, the percentage share of the upper level should not be expected to grow through an increase in employers, who account for a little more than 4% in Brazil and Mexico. Conversely, the proportion represented by the middle level strata in Brazil and Mexico is similar to that of Chile and more than double that of Guatemala, which highlights the importance of educational development in those countries and the significant number of occupational opportunities that the urban economy has managed to provide in them.

In Brazil and Mexico, structural heterogeneity is a feature of the lower level too. In Brazil, agricultural workers still represent close to 22% of the workforce (a percentage intermediate between that of Chile and that of Guatemala); of this percentage, only 25% work in medium-sized or large enterprises, 50% are own-account workers, and the remaining 25% are unpaid workers. In other words, 16% of the employed workforce in Brazil is made up of peasants who work on their own account or are unpaid. The corresponding figure in Mexico is almost 10%, that is, lower than in Brazil, but three times as high as in Chile. Moreover, Brazil and Mexico have a higher percentage of own-account or unpaid salespersons in commerce than Chile, but there are no major differences between those two countries and Chile as regards the percentage of persons who work in personal and security services. As regards blue-collar workers, artisans, operatives and drivers, there are no appreciable differences compared with Chile and, in fact, among the 11 countries considered in this chapter, Mexico has the highest percentage of employed persons in this stratum (31.8%) and also the highest percentage of those who work in medium-sized and large enterprises (14.8%). In short, with respect to the distribution of the workforce in the levels and strata, the different situations observed in Latin America are due in particular to the different degrees of economic development achieved by the countries.

The figures showing the evolution between 1990 and 1999 illustrate clearly the effects of economic growth on the distribution of the workforce in the various strata and occupational levels. In those countries, like Chile and Costa Rica, where the average occupational income increased most between those years, the percentage represented by the lower level diminished considerably, while that of the other two levels increased concomitantly. In Chile, where the highest increase in average occupational income during the period was recorded, the share of all the strata of the upper and middle levels rose from 15.3% to 25% of the total workforce, setting Chile apart from the remaining countries. In Costa Rica, where this increase was more moderate, the share of the strata of the upper and middle levels together rose from 26.5% to 31.1% over the period. In countries such as Mexico where the average occupational income grew very little in the 1990s, the proportion of the workforce belonging to the upper and middle levels only grew from 25.2% to 26.7%. Finally, in the countries where the occupational income diminished, such as Venezuela, the proportion of those strata declined from 33.7% to 27.6%.

With respect to the lower level strata, the proportion of agricultural workers fell in all the countries, and in most of them the proportion of workers in commerce and in personal services and security increased. No clear trend was discernible with regard to the percentage of blue-collar workers, artisans, operatives and drivers, since it rose in some countries and declined in others. The predominant overall trend for the eight countries for which information is available for the years 1990 and 1999 was the decline in the workforce belonging to the upper and middle levels and the increase in the percentage employed in the lower level, which is a reflection of the decline in the average occupational income and the scant occupational mobility existing in the 1990s.

3. Inequality in occupational stratification

Most of the eleven countries examined in this chapter have very uneven occupational income distribution structures. In particular, unlike the situation in the more developed countries, the upper level strata obtain an average income that is considerably higher than the rest, especially compared with the lower level, which encompasses, as we know, the majority of employed persons. In most countries, the low level of average occupational income is combined with marked inequality, in sharp contrast to the situation in Costa Rica, where occupational income distribution is much more egalitarian.

Unlike the distribution of the workforce, the distribution of occupational income in the different countries is not determined by the level of average occupational income, since there are countries with similar incomes which have different degrees of inequality and, conversely, countries with very different income levels which have similar degrees of inequality. For example, if the countries are ranked on the basis of the average occupational income recorded in 1999 and examined according to the number of times that the income of medium-sized and large non-agricultural employers exceeded the national average, we obtain values that vary between 2.2 and 16.1 times the poverty line (see table IV.3).

Table IV.3
LATIN AMERICA (8 COUNTRIES): SOME FEATURES OF THE PREVAILING
OCCUPATIONAL STRATA, 1990 AND 1999

Occupational strata		Employed working force		Average income	Average years of schooling
		Persons	%		
		1999			
	Total	142 866 679	100.0	3.9	6.9
1.	Employers	6 315 967	4.4	14.3	9.0
2.	Executives and managers	2 983 465	2.1	11.9	11.7
3.	Professionals	5 526 415	3.9	11.1	14.5
	1 + 2 + 3	14 825 847	10.4	12.6	11.6
4.	Technicians	11 613 214	8.1	5.8	11.5
5.	Administrative employees	9 209 179	6.4	3.8	10.9
	4 + 5	20 822 393	14.6	4.9	11.2
6.	Workers in commerce	17 957 391	12.6	2.8	7.2
7.	Blue-collar workers, artisans, drivers	38 710 353	27.1	3.1	6.2
	6 + 7	56 667 744	39.7	3.0	6.5
8.	Personal services workers	21 981 791	15.4	2.1	5.9
9.	Agricultural workers	27 662 488	19.4	1.6	3.1
	8 + 9	49 644 279	34.7	1.8	4.3
	6 + 7 + 8 + 9	106 312 023	74.4	2.5	5.5
10.	Armed Forces	886 257	0.6	7.2	10.6
11.	Not known	20 159	0.0	5.5	10.7
		1990			
	Total	109 709 636	100.0	4.0	6.2
1.	Employers	4 941 431	4.5	14.6	7.8
2.	Executives and managers	2 262 655	2.1	11.4	11.1
3.	Professionals	4 313 580	3.9	10.2	14.0
	1 + 2 + 3	11 517 666	10.5	12.3	10.8
4.	Technicians	7 851 736	7.2	5.4	11.0
5.	Administrative employees	862 557	7.9	4.0	10.2
	4 + 5	16 473 293	15.0	4.7	10.6
6.	Workers in commerce	12 258 753	11.2	3.4	6.4
7.	Blue-collar workers, artisans, drivers	29 810 385	27.2	3.2	5.3
	6 + 7	42 069 138	38.3	3.3	5.6
8.	Personal services workers	14 898 839	13.6	1.9	4.5
9.	Agricultural workers	22 141 485	20.2	2.0	2.6
	8 + 9	37 040 324	33.8	2.0	3.4
	6 + 7 + 8 + 9	79 109 462	72.1	2.7	4.6
10.	Armed Forces	1 226 196	1.1	5.5	9.5
11.	Not known	1 383 019	1.3	3.2	6.3

Source: ECLAC, on the basis of special tabulations of household surveys of the respective countries.

Among these countries, the distributive structure of Costa Rica is particularly worthy of note, first, because none of the strata in that country have occupational incomes less than 3.6 times the poverty line, and second, because the income is distributed in a fairly egalitarian manner, since the vast majority hover around the general average. Underlying this distribution are a number of different factors, one of the most important of which is the occupational structure in Costa Rica. The percentage of employers —agricultural and non-agricultural— is almost double the regional average. Furthermore, agricultural workers account for a lower percentage than the regional average, quite apart from the fact that the Costa Rican agricultural sector stands out within Latin America for its better land distribution, substantial diversification of production and significant assimilation of technical progress. For these reasons, agricultural wage earners in Costa Rica have an income equivalent to 4.6 times the poverty line, which is three times the regional average and is the highest of all the countries studied. These factors, among others, explain why occupational incomes in Costa Rica have a much more limited spread than in other countries of the region and are therefore much closer to the national average. Moreover, the income of medium-sized and large-scale entrepreneurs is only 2.2 times above the national average; that of managers of medium and large-scale enterprises is 2.1 times above the average; that of administrative employees is similar to the average; that of blue-collar workers and artisans is equivalent to 85% of the average, and that of agricultural workers, to 75% (see table IV.4).

In Chile, for example, there are no occupational strata with incomes less than 3.3 times the poverty line, but this positive fact is combined with considerable inequality in the distribution of occupational income. As already noted, in Chile the occupational income of medium and large-scale non-agricultural employers is almost seven times the national average and that of medium and large-scale agricultural employers is 16 times the average, while that of medium and large-scale managers is five times as high. In contrast, the occupational income of administrative employees is equivalent to only 70% of the national average, that of blue-collar workers and operatives, 64%, and that of personal services, security and agricultural workers, around 45% of the average.

When we compare the incomes for the same occupations in Chile and Costa Rica, the degree of inequality can be seen to increase as one goes up the occupational stratification scale. Thus, the average occupational income of all the lower strata, measured as multiples of the poverty line, is higher in absolute terms in Costa Rica than in Chile, and the same applies even to administrative employees. Technicians and supervisors receive the same occupational income in the two countries,

Table IV.4
LATIN AMERICA (11 COUNTRIES): EMPLOYED WORKFORCE, BY OCCUPATIONAL STRATUM, 1999
(Average income, in multiples of the per capita poverty line)

Occupational stratum	Brazil	Chile	Colombia	Costa Rica	El Salvador	Guatemala	México	Nicaragua	Panama	Paraguay	Venezuela	Total
Total	3.9	7.3	3.2	6.2	3.4	2.8	3.7	2.8	5.4	2.9	3.6	3.9
Employers	14.5	34.8	8.2	10.9	7.2	14.8	15.2	10.1	12.5	11.3	9.2	14.2
Executives and senior officials	11.4	14.9	8.3	12.2	11.8	8.5	14.8	8.0	11.7	8.9	7.7	11.8
Professionals	14.8	16.2	6.3	11.8	9.9	5.1	7.4	7.9	12.8	8.0	5.3	9.6
Technicians and supervisors	6.1	8.9	-	8.9	6.1	4.0	5.4	4.1	8.3	4.5	-	5.9
Administrative employees	4.3	5.3	3.2	6.0	4.6	3.3	3.0	3.2	5.6	3.4	3.0	2.8
Workers in commerce	2.9	3.8	2.0	4.6	2.8	1.9	2.8	2.3	3.4	2.3	3.0	2.8
Blue-collar workers, artisans, drivers	3.1	4.7	2.5	5.3	3.0	2.1	2.9	2.6	4.6	2.6	3.3	3.0
Personal services and security workers	2.0	3.3	2.2	3.6	2.9	1.9	2.1	2.3	3.1	1.9	2.3	2.1
Agricultural workers	1.2	3.5	2.6	4.6	1.3	2.0	1.4	1.5	2.4	1.2	2.0	1.5
Armed Forces	7.5	7.1	-	-	-	15.0	4.0	5.9	-	5.0	4.6	7.2
Others	5.1	5.6	-	6.4	4.5	-	-	1.2	2.3	1.2	3.3	5.1

Source: ECLAC, on the basis of special tabulations of household surveys of the respective countries.

but differences, and quite marked ones, emerge in the three strata which make up the upper level. Managers and senior officials in Chile earn 25% more than those in Costa Rica; professionals 37% more and employers more than three times the income of those in Costa Rica. It would be beyond the scope of this study to consider the causes of the different degrees of inequality existing in the two structures; they are probably due to a combination of technical/economic and political/institutional causes. The latter play a decisive role in the distribution of economic and political power in the two societies, and hence in the capacity of each of the strata to defend and increase their income.

The comparison between the two countries also serves to define more accurately the influence of economic growth on occupational stratification. It has already been noted that growth has an important impact on the proportion that each of the strata represents in the workforce as well as on the internal composition of each of them. This also influences to an appreciable extent the absolute occupational income that such strata earn; however, its influence is considerably smaller as regards the distribution of the increases in occupational income among the different strata. Chile enjoyed rapid growth over most of the last 15 years, boosted by a significant transformation in its economic structure. Because of this, as already noted, the occupational structure was modified in the sense of an increase in upper and middle-level occupations and a reduction in the lower level. These structural modifications have not, however, brought with them a more equitable distribution of occupational income. The occupations of the upper level have broken away from the rest as a result of the sharp increase in their occupational income, making them an extremely affluent group. In contrast, while the number of occupations that make up the middle level has increased significantly, their income is getting closer to that of the lower level. In the lower level, for its part, the majority of the workforce obtains occupational incomes close to half of the national average. At all events, there is no doubt that the increase registered in average occupational income in the 1990s reached all occupational strata, thus helping to raise consumption and reduce poverty.

Unfortunately, the more egalitarian distribution of occupational incomes prevailing in Costa Rica is rare in Latin America, since most countries show a considerable degree of inequality. It may also be noted that while the buoyant economic growth in Chile has not translated into a more equitable distribution among the occupations, the situation in other countries has been even more negative, with lower average occupational income being combined with marked inequality.

In Brazil, where average income is equivalent to 3.9 times the poverty line, in 1999 those employed in personal services and security earned an average income equivalent to only twice the poverty line, while agricultural workers received only 1.2 times the poverty line, showing that large segments of the employed did not earn enough to keep an average-sized family above the poverty line. This situation coexists with a high degree of inequality. The income of medium and large-scale non-agricultural employers was almost six times the average for the workforce as a whole, and that of executives and managers in the same types of establishment was more than three times the national average and the average income of professionals. For its part, the income of the middle-level strata exceeds the national average by close to 50% and that of technicians and administrative employees exceeds it by close to 10%, but 75% of the workers belonging to the lower level obtain an income that is below the average (agricultural workers, for example, only earn the equivalent of 30% of the national average) (see table IV.4).

In Mexico, where the average occupational income in 1999 was 3.7 times the poverty line, personal services and security workers and agricultural workers also received incomes close to or less than twice the poverty line, which shows the difficulties that these employees face in trying to bring their families out of poverty. This situation is also accompanied by marked inequality. The average occupational income of medium and large-scale non-agricultural employers in Mexico is more than ten times that of the workforce as a whole, and in the case of managers and senior officials of medium and large establishments, it is nearly five times as high. From the level of administrative employees downwards, occupational income falls sharply: this category obtains only 80% of the national average, but agricultural workers are in an even worse position, earning barely 38% of the average. If we consider the two extremes, it may be noted that a medium-sized or large-scale non-agricultural employer in Mexico obtains, on average, an occupational income more than 20 times as high as that of an agricultural worker, while in Chile, it is 14 times as high but in Costa Rica, only 3 times as high.

In short, the foregoing analysis reveals that a high degree of inequality in the distribution of occupational income may be observed in situations which are very different in terms of the actual amount of the average occupational income. This confirms the idea stated in many ECLAC studies that an increase in income is not necessarily accompanied by greater equality in its distribution. As already noted, analysis of the recent Chilean experience reveals two contrasting points: first the substantial rise in average occupational income has enabled almost all of the occupations of the lower level to obtain relatively high average incomes compared with the Latin American average, and this has made a decisive contribution to poverty alleviation. However, in contrast with the above, this higher income has not been distributed equitably among the occupational strata, because the higher the position attained in the occupational stratification, the greater the resources available for obtaining occupational income and the greater the capacity for defending them.

At all events, if inequality persists or increases in a structure, but at the same time the average occupational income increases, many lower-level strata can earn sufficient income to have access to goods and services considered typical of the middle level. Thus, an apparently paradoxical effect is produced: on the one hand, a very uneven stratification structure develops, which seems to favour the polarization of occupational income between the upper level and the group formed by the middle and lower levels, but on the other, both manual and non-manual occupations of the middle level and some of the lower level provide sufficient income for a good number of persons to accede to goods and services that can make them feel part of the middle strata. If we look at this process from the perspective of the relative distribution of occupational income among the strata, it is clear that we are dealing with a stratification structure made up of a minority with very high incomes, a broad base with much lower income, and a middle level which, although growing in size, obtains incomes not much different from those of the lower level. Conversely, if it is viewed from the perspective of the increase in absolute income, as already noted it will be seen that poverty is reduced and a part of the lower strata feel that their level of consumption has improved sufficiently to enable them to consider themselves part of the middle strata.

As most of the countries in the region did not enjoy rapid economic growth in the 1990s, they do not reflect the contrast between a rising occupational income and inequitable income distribution. Therefore, the main problem in most of the countries is not whether it is more important to have growth in absolute occupational income or an improvement in its equitable distribution among the strata, but rather how to wrestle with a situation in which there is a low level of occupational income, very slow or zero economic growth and considerable distributive inequality.

4.   Occupational income of the lower strata

In the eleven countries considered, approximately 30% of occupations provide, on average, an income lower than the minimum estimated to be necessary to maintain a typical four-member household above the poverty line. However, the relationship between occupational income and poverty is not linear, because the percentage of open unemployment varies from one country to another and, in addition, because relatively low occupational incomes can permit some of the households to overcome poverty, especially in those countries where the average number of employed persons per household is high and the amount of non-labour income earned by households is significant.

A substantial proportion of the occupations belonging to the lower level provide occupational income that is not sufficient in itself to keep a family with four members above the poverty line. The lower the average income corresponding to a given occupation is, compared with a certain minimum level, the greater the probability that the worker's household will be poor. However, the relationship between the level of occupational income and the incidence of poverty in a given country is not so simple or linear as it might appear at first sight, because other factors exist that help households to reduce the negative influence of the lower individual wages on the family's living conditions. National poverty percentages are influenced above all by the level of open unemployment and the average occupational income. Two countries may have a fairly similar average occupational income, but if in one of them the rate of open unemployment is higher, the proportion of poor households will also be higher. Households differ also in the number of members and the number of persons employed and in terms of the proportion of non-labour income in the family income. These factors affect the relative importance that occupational incomes have as determinants of the household's poverty status, so that it is advisable to consider only as a tentative approximation the establishment of a level of occupational income which would, supposedly, be sufficient in all countries to maintain a household above the poverty line.

Nevertheless, this does not detract from the importance of seeking to raise the occupational income of jobs at the lower level, because although this is not the only determining factor of poverty, it is one of the most important.

In the light of the above-mentioned facts, we may consider, as a tentative estimate, that 2.5 times the poverty line is the minimum occupational income necessary to place a household with 4 members above the poverty line. According to this criterion, in Chile and Costa Rica, where occupational income reached an average of 7.3 and 6.2 times the poverty line, respectively, in 1999, all occupations receive occupational incomes above the minimum. In Panama, with an average income 5.4 times the poverty line, only the agricultural occupations (16.4% of the employed) provide incomes below the minimum. El Salvador, although it has a level of average income considerably below that of Panama (3.4 times the poverty line), is in this respect in almost the same situation as the latter country, since only the agricultural occupations (19.6% of the total) do not attain a minimum income of 2.5 times the poverty line. In Brazil, Mexico and Venezuela, which have average occupational incomes of 3.9, 3.7 and 3.6 times the poverty line, respectively, persons employed in personal services, security and agricultural activities do not earn the necessary minimum; they account for 39% of employed persons in Brazil, more than 28% in Mexico and 26% in Venezuela (see tables IV.3 and IV.4).

In Colombia, where the average income is 3.2 times the poverty line, workers in commerce and those engaged in personal and security services (32% of the workforce) earn incomes below the minimum, but the other occupations of the lower level earn incomes that barely exceed the limit. Finally, in those countries where the average occupational income of the workforce is less than three times the poverty line, almost all the occupations of the lower level receive incomes below the minimum: these occupations account for 57% of the workforce in Paraguay, 60% in Nicaragua, and 85% in Guatemala.

In short, as might be expected, the occupations belonging to the middle and upper levels all obtain incomes above the minimum. In addition, when the average occupational income is more than six times the poverty line (Chile and Costa Rica), all the occupations receive average incomes which are sufficient in themselves to keep a typical household above the poverty line. In the remaining countries, where the average occupational income is lower than that of the above-mentioned countries, the incomes of the occupations of the lower level generally fall as average income declines. When countries have an average income that varies between three and four times the poverty line, it is very probable that agricultural workers and employees in personal and security services will receive occupational incomes below the minimum and it is very probable also that the incomes corresponding to the remaining occupations of the lower level will be very close to this limit. In those countries where the average occupational income is below three times the poverty line, the most likely situation is that all lower level occupations will have average incomes that do not by themselves allow a family to stay above the poverty line.

Between 1990 and 1999, there were some variations in the countries owing to the different evolution of the respective average occupational income. Costa Rica and Venezuela were the only countries of the eight for which information was available where all the occupations obtained income above the minimum in 1990. In Costa Rica, this condition was maintained in 1999, owing to the favourable trend in the average occupational income and the equitable pattern of income distribution among occupations. In Venezuela, on the other hand, the fall in average occupational income from 4.5 times the poverty line in 1990 to 3.6 times in 1999 meant that in 1999, workers in personal and security services and agricultural workers had incomes less than 2.5 times the poverty line. In Chile, thanks to the sharp improvement in average occupational income, it was possible to raise the income of workers in personal services and security, which was below the minimum in 1990, and at the same time to move agricultural workers a little further from the poverty threshold. The sound economic performance recorded in Panama in the 1990s meant that the occupational income of personal services and security workers rose above the minimum and also brought the income of agricultural workers almost to the point of passing that level. In 1999, the situation in Brazil and Mexico did not differ from that prevailing in 1990, since personal services and security workers and agricultural workers continued to earn less than the minimum. In Colombia, on the other hand, all the strata of the lower level continued to obtain earnings less than or just over the minimum in 1999, while in Guatemala there was a regressive trend, since workers in commerce, who earned more than the minimum in 1990, lost this position, and in 1999 all the occupations of the lower level earned incomes below 2.5 times the poverty line.

5. Occupational income and educational level

The educational level of the workforce continued its upward trend during the 1990s, but the majority had still not achieved enough years of schooling to move out of the lower occupational income levels, while there was still a high degree of educational inequality among the different strata, although less so than with respect to income.

On the basis of the weighted averages of 10 countries, the workforce as a whole had 6.9 years of schooling in 1999. The stratum with the highest level of education was that of the professionals, who had 14.6 years of schooling, followed by executives and managers (11.7 years), technicians (11.5), administrative employees (10.9), employers (8.9), workers in commerce (7.1), blue-collar workers, artisans, operatives and drivers (6.2), workers in personal services and security (5.9), and agricultural workers (3.1). The general average rose from 6.2 years of schooling in 1990 to the above-mentioned level of 6.9 years at the end of the decade (weighted averages of eight countries) and an increase was recorded in all the strata: in the stratum of employers, the average increased by 1.2 years of schooling; in that of executives and managers, 0.6, as also in the case of professionals; for technicians, 0.5; for administrative employees, 0.7; for workers in commerce, 0.7; for blue-collar workers, artisans, operatives and drivers, 0.9; for personal services and security workers, 1.4, and for agricultural workers, 0.5 years (see table IV.5).

During the 1990s, along with the rise in the educational level of the workforce, there was a continued increase in the disparity (already very significant in the 1980s) between that rise and the decline in occupational income (from 4 to 3.8 times the poverty line between 1990 and 1999). In some countries where the workforce had a relatively low educational level, a great effort was made to raise it, but this has not yet translated into an increase in average occupational income. In El Salvador and Paraguay, for example, the average number of years of schooling of the workforce at the end of the decade was 6.6 and 7.2, respectively: figures close to those of countries like Costa Rica, whose educational development is of longer standing, and where the average is 8 years of schooling. Nevertheless, the average occupational incomes of all three continue to be very different, since in El Salvador and Paraguay they were 3.4 and 2.9 times the poverty line, respectively, while in Costa Rica, the average was 6.2 times the poverty line. In other words, El Salvador and Paraguay have an educational gap of less than two years of schooling compared with Costa Rica, but their occupational income is only half that of the latter country. This type of trend should point to the need for caution vis-à-vis strategies which place too much emphasis on educational development as the preferred method of increasing occupational income.

In various studies by ECLAC, attention has been drawn to the fact that the relationship between the rise in the educational level of the workforce and the increase in occupational income is not linear. It has also been emphasized that in most countries, 12 years of schooling seem to constitute the minimum threshold for education to play a significant role in the improvement of occupational income and in poverty reduction. Anyone who has an educational level of less than 12 years of schooling and does not own productive assets will find it very difficult to move up from the lower occupational strata, with their correspondingly low incomes. However, as the above data show, the mere fact of attaining an educational level similar to that of the middle strata is no guarantee either of attaining a correspondingly higher occupational level. In order to have some chance of acceding to a middle or upper occupational level, it is necessary to have close to or more than 12 years of schooling, and to enhance this chance, it is necessary to reach the highest educational level, with 14 or more years of schooling. It is therefore clear that families and the State must make an enormous effort to raise the educational qualifications of the workforce.

Table IV.5
LATIN AMERICA (11 COUNTRIES): EMPLOYED WORKFORCE, BY OCCUPATIONAL STRATUM, 1999
(Average years of schooling)

Occupational stratum	Brazil	Chile	Colombia	Costa Rica	El Salvador	Guatemala	Mexico	Nicaragua	Panama	Paraguay	Venezuela	Total
Total	6.4	10.6	7.4	8.0	6.6	4.3	-	5.5	9.7	7.2	8.5	6.9
Employers	9.1	12.7	8.2	8.4	6.6	6.7	-	6.4	11.0	9.0	8.9	9.0
Executives and senior officials	11.1	10.7	13.1	13.2	15.1	12.3	-	10.6	13.7	12.9	14.4	11.7
Professionals	14.7	16.5	13.4	14.7	16.7	12.2	-	14.5	16.5	16.4	14.1	14.3
Technicians and supervisors	10.8	13.7	-	12.5	13.0	9.5	-	11.5	13.8	12.3	-	11.1
Administrative employees	10.6	12.6	11.0	11.0	11.6	10.4	-	10.2	12.7	11.8	11.2	10.9
Workers in commerce	6.9	10.5	7.4	7.7	5.9	4.1	-	5.7	9.4	7.1	8.0	7.1
Blue-collar workers, artisans, drivers	5.7	9.6	6.9	6.9	6.2	4.1	-	5.9	8.8	6.8	7.5	6.2
Personal services and security workers	5.5	9.2	6.4	6.4	5.7	4.4	-	4.7	7.9	6.6	6.8	5.9
Agricultural workers	2.8	6.7	3.6	4.8	2.9	2.2	-	2.5	5.0	4.4	4.1	3.1
Armed Forces	10.5	12.7	-	-	-	14.7	-	7.2	-	13.9	11.4	10.6
Others	10.8	10.7	-	10.5	7.8	-	-	4.3	18.0	9.1	10.5	9.9

Source: ECLAC, on the basis of special tabulations of household surveys of the respective countries.

With regard to the educational levels of the different occupational strata, professionals have attained a level of education which puts them clearly above the strata forming the upper level, standing out as a true elite in terms of education, just as medium and large-scale employers are with respect to income. The latter have an occupational income which is considerably higher than that corresponding in theory to their relatively low educational level, which shows the importance of owning productive assets in order to obtain high income, even with few years of schooling. A point which should also be taken into consideration is the fact that there are major differences in the educational levels of the different types of employers: employers owning medium-sized and large establishments usually have a much higher educational level than that of the owners of small businesses and above all those of micro- and small enterprises. Furthermore, as is well known, in this latter stratum occupational income is mingled with the returns on wealth, thus distorting the value of the first type of income.

Another interesting point is that in educational stratification, occupations are ranked differently from the stratification based on income; in the latter, the main cut-off point occurs between the upper level —whose average income is 12.5 times the poverty line— and the remaining levels, in which the best-paid occupation is that of technician, with an average remuneration of 5.7 times the poverty line. In educational stratification, however, the main cut-off point is located between the occupations of the upper and middle levels, on the one hand, and those of the lower level on the other. This difference in terms of the place where the main cut-off point is located in the two stratification structures —that based on income and that based on education— reveals that the occupations of technician, supervisor and administrative employee are the most affected, in this respect, since on average they have a level of education very similar to that of executives and managers and substantially higher than that of employers, yet they obtain a much lower income than these two groups.

Although educational expansion, as already noted, has led to a situation where many countries have substantially increased the number of years of schooling of the workforce, there are still important differences between them, which show up for example in the disparity existing in 1999 between the average of 10.6 years of schooling recorded in Chile and the average for Guatemala of 4.3 years. However, it is clear that there is a tendency for the occupations of the middle and upper levels of all countries to converge with respect to the educational level. A professional, manager, technician or administrative employee will tend to have an educational level that is fairly similar in all countries. For example, while the average years of study in Chile are more than double those in Guatemala, Chilean professionals only have on average 35% more years of schooling than Guatemalans, and in the case of administrative employees only 20% more. However, all the occupations of the lower level in Chile have more than twice as many years of schooling as those in Guatemala. Nevertheless, although as already noted the educational level has risen in all the strata of all countries, major differences still exist between the various levels within the same country. In Guatemala, for example, a professional has eight years more schooling than a blue-collar worker, and in Chile, seven years more, although this difference is less today than it was a few decades ago.

6.   Stratification of occupations and of households

If households are classified on the basis of the occupation of the main breadwinner, average per capita household income reproduces in a fairly proportional way the order of average incomes of the occupational strata. This highlights the importance of the occupation of the main breadwinner for household stratification. However, the fact that almost half of Latin American households have more than one breadwinner affects the per capita income of the household, depending on the occupations and the country involved. In the case of lower-income occupations of the lower level, the fact of having more than one employed person per household reduces poverty or the percentages of poverty, depending on the average income of the country and the size of the households. In the upper level, having another employed person does not have much impact in view of the high income of the main breadwinner. The greatest influence shows up in the middle level and in the higher part of the lower level, where households with more than one employed person usually have higher average incomes than those of households with only one employed person.

The occupation of the main breadwinner has a sufficiently strong influence on family income to cause the per capita income of households classified on the basis of this occupation to maintain, in a fairly proportional way, the order of the average incomes of the occupational strata. Thus, as we can see from table IV.6, the weighted averages for the overall employed population in the eight countries for which data were available for 1990 and 1999 indicate that when the main breadwinners are employers, senior officials, executives or professionals, the per capita income of the households varies between 5.4 and 5.9 times the poverty line, while the figures for the remaining occupations are as follows: technicians or supervisors, 3.1 times the poverty line; administrative

Table IV.6
LATIN AMÉRICA (11 COUNTRIES): PER CAPITA LABOUR INCOME OF HOUSEHOLDS, BY OCCUPATIONAL STRATUM OF THE MAIN BREADWINNER, 1999
(Number of poverty lines)

Occupational stratum	Brazil	Chile	Colombia	Costa Rica	El Salvador	Mexico	Panama	Venezuela	Total (8 countries)	Guatemala	Nicaragua	Paraguay	Total (11 countries)
Employers	6.4	13.9	3.6	4.4	2.6	5.8	5.4	3.5	5.9	4.6	4.0	4.1	5.8
Directors and managers	5.5	6.5	4.8	5.3	4.3	6.3	5.4	3.5	5.6	3.8	2.5	3.7	5.5
Professional	8.0	8.1	3.0	5.8	4.7	3.6	6.4	2.6	5.4	2.4	2.8	3.6	5.3
Technicians	3.3	4.4	-	4.0	2.6	2.6	3.9	-	3.1	2.2	1.6	2.0	3.1
Administrative employees	2.5	2.5	1.5	2.9	2.2	1.6	2.8	1.3	2.1	1.4	1.1	1.7	2.1
Workers in commerce	1.7	1.9	1.1	2.4	1.4	1.7	1.8	1.5	1.6	1.2	1.1	1.2	1.6
Blue-collar workers, artisans, drivers	1.4	1.9	1.0	2.2	1.3	1.2	2.0	1.3	1.4	0.9	1.0	1.2	1.3
Personal services workers	1.2	1.6	1.0	1.8	1.2	1.2	1.6	1.1	1.2	1.2	0.9	1.0	1.2
Agricultural workers	0.8	1.5	1.1	1.9	0.6	0.7	1.1	0.9	0.9	0.8	0.6	0.6	0.8
Armed Forces	3.2	2.6	-	-	1.8	1.3	-	1.5	3.1	3.8	1.4	1.4	3.0
Unclassified	8.1	3.0	-	2.7	-	-	11.6	1.2	3.6	-	2.1	1.0	3.5
Total													
Households with employed persons	2.2	3.5	1.6	2.9	1.6	1.9	2.7	1.7	2.1	1.3	1.2	1.4	2.1
All households	2.0	3.0	1.4	2.6	1.4	1.8	2.4	1.6	1.9	1.2	1.1	1.3	1.4

Source: ECLAC, on the basis of special tabulations of household surveys of the respective countries

employees, 2.1; workers in commerce, 1.6; blue-collar workers, artisans and drivers, 1.4; personal services and security workers, 1.2, and agricultural workers, 0.9 times the poverty line. In other words, although households can improve their income by having more of their members in the workforce, their basic position will continue to be determined fundamentally by the occupation of the main income earner.

In many households in Latin America, the per capita income of the household has improved thanks to the incorporation of more than one member in the workforce. The increasing incorporation of women into the labour force, the classic involvement of unpaid family members in rural areas or the forced incorporation of children and young people in times of crisis, are some of the mechanisms through which households manage to improve per capita income. At the end of the 1990s, the number of employed persons per household, in the group of households with employed persons, stood at an average of 1.8, a figure which falls to 1.6 if we take into consideration households without employed persons. The number is smaller in countries with higher average occupational income: if we take into account all households, the figure is 1.4 in Chile and 1.5 in Costa Rica and Panama, and 1.6 in the rest of the eight countries under consideration, except Venezuela, where it is 1.7.

These figures conceal widely differing situations. In the set of eight countries examined, 47.6% of households have more than one breadwinner, while 41.6% have one breadwinner and 10.8% have none. In those with none, 9.2% are headed by inactive heads and 1.6% by unemployed heads (see table IV.7). As might be expected, there tends to be a higher percentage of households without employed persons in the countries where there is a higher average occupational income: for example, taking the two extremes in this respect, 14% of households in Chile are in this situation and only 6.2% of those in Guatemala. This is due to the fact that in countries where there is higher occupational income, there is a higher proportion of heads of household who are aged 65 years or more and/or who can afford not to work. Admittedly, the proportion of households with an unemployed head also has an impact, but this proportion does not vary according to the greater or lesser average occupational income prevailing in each country.

The analysis by countries does not reveal exactly which households resort most frequently to the strategy of increasing the number of employed persons. As already noted, countries with a higher average occupational income tend to have a lower number of employed persons per household, owing to their higher proportion of households without employed persons; but if we consider only the households with employed

Table IV.7
LATIN AMERICA (11 COUNTRIES): DISTRIBUTION OF HOUSEHOLDS BY NUMBER OF EMPLOYED PERSONS, TYPE OF HEAD AND POVERTY STATUS, 1999
(Percentages)

| Country | Distribution of households | | | | | | Proportion of poor households in each category | | | | |
| | Total | No employed persons | | | One employed person | More than one employed person | Total | No employed persons | | One employed person | More than one employed person |
		Inactive head	Unemployed head	Total				Inactive head	Unemployed head		
Brazil	100.0	10.7	1.8	12.4	38.6	49.0	29.9	18.9	72.4	35.2	26.5
Chile	100.0	12.1	2.5	14.6	45.5	39.9	16.6	14.7	67.2	21.7	8.2
Colombia	100.0	7.7	3.1	10.7	43.9	45.4	48.7	48.1	81.6	57.5	38.0
Costa Rica	100.0	9.3	0.8	10.2	46.4	43.4	18.2	54.1	86.7	20.2	7.2
El Salvador	100.0	8.4	1.3	9.8	43.2	47.1	43.5	53.9	80.4	51.1	33.6
Guatemala	100.0	5.8	0.3	6.2	37.4	56.5	53.5	54.1	50.0	55.2	52.3
Mexico	100.0	7.6	0.3	7.9	45.4	46.7	33.3	29.8	44.9	37.4	29.7
Nicaragua	100.0	6.2	2.7	8.9	40.0	51.1	65.1	84.1	83.0	72.8	55.8
Panama	100.0	10.5	1.7	12.2	46.5	41.3	25.0	35.4	76.4	30.0	14.6
Paraguay	100.0	7.2	1.4	8.7	39.4	51.9	51.7	55.6	75.2	57.6	46.0
Venezuela	100.0	5.5	2.5	8.0	39.6	52.4	44.0	79.5	93.0	55.7	29.1
Total (8 countries)	100.0	9.2	1.6	10.8	41.6	47.6	33.1	26.7	74.5	38.9	27.9
Total (11 countries)	100.0	9.1	1.6	10.7	41.4	47.9	34.1	27.8	74.5	39.8	29.0

Source: ECLAC, on the basis of special tabulations of household surveys of the respective countries.

persons, the figures vary very little from one country to another. Nor are there substantial differences in the number of persons employed in the households, when these are grouped according to the occupational stratum of the main breadwinner, although this number tends to be slightly higher in the strata of the middle and upper levels, where it amounts to a simple average of 1.8 in the eight countries under consideration, than in the lower-level strata, where the average goes down to 1.7 (see table IV.8).

If we simultaneously consider the number of employed persons and the size of the household, we can determine to what extent the increase in the number of employed household members is a necessary survival strategy for a large household or whether, unlike this situation of necessity, it is a means adopted by households to increase their well-being still further, even when the main breadwinner is able on his/her own to place the household in the middle or upper level.

Occupational density, which is the ratio of the number of employed members to the total number of members in the household, is a suitable indicator for understanding the relative intensity of employment in the different strata. As shown in table IV.8, the overall group of households of the eight countries under consideration has an occupational density of 0.44, but this rises to 0.49 if we take into account only those households in which there is at least one employed member. In this respect, there are appreciable differences between the countries, varying from a maximum of 0.53 for all households in Brazil and a minimum of 0.44 in the case of El Salvador and Venezuela, but such differences are due to complex factors associated more with the willingness to accept different types of work, especially low-productivity work, than with the average occupational income existing in each country.

The differences in occupational density are better understood if we consider them from the standpoint of the occupational hierarchy of the household, this being understood as the greater or lesser capacity to generate income as a result of education, wealth or social factors. Thus, we can see that occupational density is lower in low-level households than in those of the middle or high level, since the latter are in a position to find employment for a larger number of members, having received a better education and benefited from a network of social relationships that make it much easier for various members to find employment. In the households in which the main breadwinner has a upper level occupation, the occupational density is 0.51, declining to 0.49 for a middle level occupation and to 0.45 for a lower level occupation.

Table IV.8
LATIN AMERICA (11 COUNTRIES): NUMBER OF EMPLOYED PERSONS AND OCCUPATIONAL DENSITY OF HOUSEHOLDS, BY OCCUPATIONAL STRATUM OR GROUP OF THE MAIN BREADWINNER, 1999

	Brazil		Chile		Colombia		Costa Rica		El Salvador		Mexico		Panama		Venezuela		Total (8 countries)		Guatemala		Nicaragua		Paraguay		Total (11 countries)	
	EPHᵃ	ODᵇ	EPH	OD	EPH	OD	EPH	OD	EPH	OD	EPH	OD	EPH	OD	EPH	OD	EPH	OD	EPH	OD	EPH	OD	EPH	OD	EPH	OD
Employers	2.0	0.58	1.8	0.53	2.0	0.52	1.9	0.48	1.8	0.45	1.9	0.51	1.8	0.53	2.1	0.47	2.0	0.54	2.0	0.47	1.9	0.42	2.1	0.48	2.0	0.54
Directors and managers	1.8	0.54	1.8	0.52	1.8	0.54	1.7	0.47	1.7	0.43	1.7	0.47	1.8	0.52	2.0	0.50	1.8	0.52	2.0	0.48	1.8	0.41	2.0	0.49	1.8	0.52
Professionals	1.7	0.58	1.7	0.53	1.7	0.51	1.7	0.52	1.8	0.50	1.8	0.52	1.8	0.53	1.9	0.48	1.8	0.53	1.9	0.49	1.7	0.39	2.1	0.51	1.8	0.53
Technicians	1.8	0.55	1.7	0.49	-	-	1.8	0.48	1.9	0.47	1.8	0.15	1.8	0.49	-	-	1.8	0.52	2.1	0.51	1.7	0.39	2.0	0.48	1.8	0.52
Administrative employees	1.8	0.54	1.6	0.47	1.8	0.47	1.7	0.49	1.9	0.50	1.9	0.52	1.9	0.51	1.8	0.45	1.8	0.51	2.2	0.47	1.9	0.38	1.8	0.52	1.8	0.51
Workers in commerce	1.8	0.53	1.7	0.46	1.6	0.46	1.7	0.45	1.8	0.49	1.8	0.52	1.6	0.48	1.9	0.46	1.8	0.51	2.1	0.49	2.1	0.44	1.9	0.47	1.8	0.51
Personal service workers	1.8	0.48	1.6	0.41	1.7	0.42	1.7	0.43	1.8	0.44	1.8	0.44	1.6	0.43	1.9	0.41	1.8	0.45	2.0	0.39	1.9	0.38	1.8	0.45	1.8	0.45
Blue-collar workers, artisans and drivers	1.7	0.50	1.6	0.45	1.6	0.44	1.6	0.42	1.8	0.44	1.7	0.49	1.6	0.45	1.8	0.42	1.7	0.48	2.0	0.45	2.0	0.39	1.7	0.46	1.7	0.48
Agricultural workers	2.1	0.57	1.5	0.42	1.8	0.44	1.5	0.41	1.5	0.37	1.8	0.43	1.5	0.48	1.7	0.44	1.9	0.50	2.0	0.39	1.8	0.36	1.9	0.49	1.9	0.49
Armed Forces	1.7	0.49	1.5	0.39	-	-	2.1	-	2.1	0.41	1.1	0.32	-	-	1.4	0.35	1.7	0.50	1.9	0.37	2.1	0.49	1.4	0.35	1.7	0.50
Unclassified	1.0	0.68	1.5	0.47	-	-	1.9	0.42	-	-	-	-	2.0	0.50	2.3	0.43	1.6	0.49	-	-	2.0	0.50	1.0	0.61	1.6	0.50
Total employed	1.8	0.53	1.6	0.45	1.7	0.46	1.7	0.45	1.8	0.44	1.8	0.47	1.7	0.48	1.9	0.44	1.8	0.49	2.0	0.42	1.9	0.39	1.9	0.46	1.8	0.49
Total (includes households without employed members)	1.6	0.46	1.4	0.39	1.6	0.41	1.5	0.40	1.6	0.40	1.6	0.43	1.5	0.42	1.7	0.41	1.6	0.44	1.9	0.40	1.7	0.35	1.7	0.42	1.6	0.44

Source: ECLAC, on the basis of special tabulations of household surveys of the respective countries.

ᵃ EPH: Number of employed persons per household.
ᵇ OD: Occupational density.

Thus, households whose heads belong to occupational strata of the upper and middle levels have a slight difference in their favour in terms of the chance of finding employment for other members of the family and a much more substantial advantage with respect to occupational density. This difference in the occupational density of households according to the stratum of the main breadwinner is seen in all the countries under consideration, although it tends to be greater in those where the average occupational income is higher (see table IV.8).

As may be inferred to some degree from the above, the impact of the number of employed persons on household income varies considerably depending on the occupational stratum of the main breadwinner. In those strata which are at the lower end of the scale, especially agricultural workers, this impact is quite weak, since the households tend to be very large and to have a relatively small number of employed members, so that the occupational density is also low. Clearly, as the number of employed persons increases so does the average income of any household, thus ensuring an improvement in its living conditions. Nevertheless, if the household is very large, the increase in per capita income coming from the higher number of employed members will not be significant and often will not exceed that of smaller households with only one employed person. In general, an increase in the number of employed persons in larger households relieves the extreme poverty that having only one employed person would imply, but does not make it possible to raise substantially their per capita income, especially in those countries where there is a large mass of poor peasants. In Brazil, for example, households in which the main breadwinner is an agricultural worker have the highest average of employed persons (2.1) of all the strata in all countries, but there is no difference in the average income of these households regardless of whether they have only one or more than one member employed, which shows that large households or those where the main breadwinner receives an extremely low income have no choice but to have other members join the labour force.

At the other extreme of the stratification scale, households whose main breadwinner has a upper level occupation can in theory benefit even more from the incorporation of other members into the workforce, because generally such households are smaller than those of the lower strata. However, this is not usually the case. When these households have more than one employed member, the average income does not increase very significantly, owing largely to the fact that additional workers usually earn much lower occupational incomes than that of the main breadwinner.

In reality, the greater impact of the increase in the number of employed persons on average income does not occur in households in which the main breadwinner belongs to the extremes of the job stratification scale, but in those that are in the middle level and in the upper part of the lower level, such as those corresponding to administrative employees, workers in commerce and urban manual workers. In these households, if other members join the workforce, it adds substantially to the household's average income. On the basis of the available information, it may be stated that in many households whose heads belong to these strata, a significantly higher income has been achieved than in the case of just one employed member, which has contributed to their upward social mobility. Although this is a common occurrence, it cannot be said to apply to the region as a whole, since it does not occur in Mexico and only occurs to a limited degree in Brazil. Furthermore, owing to the difference in occupational income existing between the occupations of the middle and upper level, the increase generated by the higher occupational density is not sufficient to enable middle-level households to receive incomes as high as those of the upper level. This situation occurs only in Costa Rica, where the differences between the occupational incomes of the different strata are slight. Nor is it easy for a household whose main breadwinner has a lower-level job to obtain the income characteristic of a middle-level occupation by increasing the number of employed persons, although there have been examples of this. Consequently, the increase in household income owing to a higher number of employed persons does not generally enable a household to cross the income barrier between the different occupational levels.

Naturally, poverty is more prevalent in households without employed persons, since it affects 68.9% of them, followed by those with inactive heads (41.6%) and by households that have only one employed person (41.2%), declining to 31.9% in those where there is more than one employed person.

The greater occupational density helps to reduce poverty, especially in households where the main breadwinner has a lower-level occupation, because obviously, when the occupational income is higher, this is often sufficient in itself to keep the household above the poverty line. However, when the income of the main breadwinner is very low, the incorporation of new members into the workforce may alleviate poverty but not succeed in overcoming it. This is particularly evident when the main income earners of the household are agricultural workers, since in this case the low occupational income is compounded by the fact that an important proportion of the other members are unpaid family workers (see table IV.8).

In households where the main breadwinners work in non-agricultural manual jobs, the proportion of unpaid family members is usually much less and the household smaller than in the case of agricultural occupations, so that the addition of another member into the workforce usually means a more significant improvement in total household income. The chance of this permitting the household to overcome poverty depends on the occupational income obtained by the employed members of the household, however, which is quite low in some countries in the case of some urban occupations, such as personal services jobs.

In any event, as already noted, the fact that greater occupational density is not sufficient to reduce the proportion of poor households in those situations where occupational income is very low does not mean that this higher density does not help to improve living conditions by at least relieving the gravity of their poverty.

Methodological annex

Criteria applied in defining occupational strata

Studies on occupational stratification usually use a variety of variables to define the main occupational groups or strata. The most important of these variables are those relating to i) the relationship between persons and the means of production, which makes it possible to distinguish between the basic categories of owners or employers —subdivided in turn according to the size of the firm— and of wage-earners and own-account workers; ii) the nature of the work (manual and non-manual); iii) the degree of skills, divided generally into three levels: high, middle and low; iv) the degree of authority exercised in the enterprise, also divided generally into three levels; v) the type of contract —service, middle and labour, according to Goldthorpe's classification— and lastly, vi) the branches and sectors of activity to which people belong. In the vast majority of empirical studies on the subject, the classification of strata or major occupational groups has been made on the basis of some of these variables, although the emphasis may be placed on certain variables in particular, according to each author's implicit or explicit theoretical orientation. For example, the occupational classifications used by some official agencies, such as the Registrar General of the United Kingdom, the first of which dates back to 1911, pay special attention to the level of skills and authority and the nature of the work carried out; those of neo-marxists, such as Wright, place emphasis on the ownership of the means of production, while not ignoring the level of skills and authority; while neo-Weberians, such as Goldthorpe, combine the relationship with the means of production with the level of skills and authority, the separation into agricultural and non-agricultural branches and, especially, the nature of the contract: a criterion which they use to establish their well-known division between the service class, the middle class and the working class. Of course, another point of great importance in defining the strata that are used is the universe to which the study will apply (for example, for obvious reasons, the studies carried out in the developed countries pay much less attention to the agricultural occupations than those carried out in Latin America). It is also important to determine whether the study will use first hand data or data drawn from censuses or household surveys. When second-hand information is used, as is the case in this study, it must respect the classification contained in the original study, which may be modified or adapted, but always within narrow limits.

Based on the above-mentioned criteria, the classification of strata used in this study is as follows:

i) Employers, divided on the basis of size of enterprise into micro-employers (up to four or five employees, depending on the country), small-scale employers (from four or five to nine or ten employees) and medium and large-scale employers (from ten or eleven employees and up).

ii) Senior officials, managers and directors.

iii) Highly skilled professionals.

iv) Middle-level professionals, technicians and supervisors.

v) Administrative or clerical employees.

vi) Workers in commerce.

vii) Blue-collar workers, artisans, operatives and drivers.

viii) Personal services and security workers.

ix) Agricultural workers.

In general, these are the occupational strata that are usually used in household survey classifications, but in this study it was necessary in some cases to adjust the data to match this classification, in order to ensure that the data corresponding to eight countries in the 1989-1990 period and to eleven countries in the 1999-2000 period were comparable.

The nine strata mentioned constitute the basic categories used here for the analysis of occupational stratification, although, in so far as the information allowed it, additional variables were also used to obtain a more detailed overview of each of the strata. This is particularly relevant, since the strata are large conglomerates of occupations, and although they display a basic degree of homogeneity, it is always possible to discern various sub-strata among them, depending on the level of skills, the size of the enterprise in which the persons are employed, whether they are wage-earners or own-account workers, public or private employees, and other similar parameters. Finally, the strata, and whenever possible the sub-strata, were studied and compared on the basis of three main variables: the proportion that they represented in the labour force, the average occupational income of each of them (measured in multiples of the poverty line), and the average years of schooling.

Chapter V

Intergenerational transmission of opportunities for attaining well-being

This chapter, which covers 18 countries of the region, shows how, despite the efforts made to extend the coverage of the formal education system, the socioeconomic and family origin of individuals continues to be a determining factor in their present and future opportunities for education and for social and economic integration. The fact that educational opportunities —and consequently, opportunities for access to more stable and better-paid employment— are to a high degree inherited is a key element in the reproduction of socioeconomic inequalities, and limits the potential for taking advantage of competitiveness strategies based on technological progress and the accumulation of knowledge.

1.   Transmission of opportunities for well-being

The opportunities for well-being of more than half of all Latin Americans are restricted at an early stage by the nature of the intergenerational transmission of educational capital and work opportunities, which is one of several determining factors in the high and persistent level of socioeconomic inequality in the region.

Around 75% of young people in urban areas are from households in which the parents have inadequate educational capital (less than 10 years of schooling) and, on average, more than 45% do not reach the educational threshold required for attaining well-being, which, while varying from country to country, is currently around 12 years of schooling (see figure V.1 and table V.1).

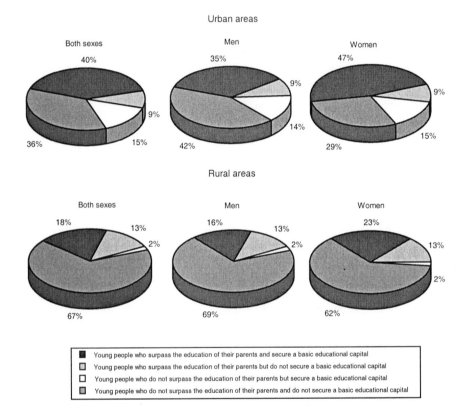

Figure V.1
LATIN AMERICA: EDUCATIONAL ATTAINMENT OF YOUNG PEOPLE AGED 20 TO 24
YEARS COMPARED WITH THAT OF THEIR PARENTS, 2000
(Percentages)

Source: ECLAC, on the basis of special tabulations of data from household surveys of the respective countries.

Table V.1
LATIN AMERICA (GROUPS OF COUNTRIES): INTERGENERATIONAL EDUCATIONAL
BETTERMENT OF CHILDREN AGED FROM 20 TO 24 YEARS, BY SEX,
URBAN AND RURAL AREAS, 2000
(Percentages)[a]

			Geographical area							
			Urban areas					Rural areas		
		Total	Educational betterment				Total	Educational betterment		
			Young people who surpass the education of their parents		Young people who do not surpass the education of their parents			Young people who surpass the education of their parents		Young people who do not surpass the education of their parents	
Group of countries[b]	Sex		And secure basic educational capital	And do not secure basic educational capital	And secure basic educational capital	And do not secure basic educational capital		And secure basic educational capital	And do not secure basic educational capital	And secure basic educational capital	And do not secure basic educational capital
Low group	Both sexes	100	41	9	12	37	100	13	10	0	77
	Men	100	37	9	12	42	100	13	11	0	76
	Women	100	47	10	12	31	100	13	9	0	77
Intermediate group	Both sexes	100	40	9	14	36	100	19	13	3	65
	Men	100	34	9	13	43	100	16	11	3	70
	Women	100	47	9	15	29	100	24	15	3	57
High group	Both sexes	100	43	9	18	31	100	25	18	3	54
	Men	100	36	9	18	38	100	20	19	3	59
	Women	100	51	8	18	23	100	33	18	3	46
Total, all countries	Both sexes	100	40	9	15	36	100	18	13	2	67
	Men	100	35	9	14	42	100	16	13	2	70
	Women	100	47	9	15	29	100	23	13	2	62

Source: ECLAC, on the basis of special tabulations of data from household surveys of the respective countries.

[a] Simple averages of the country data.
[b] The countries are grouped according to the gross enrolment ratio for the secondary cycle in the mid-1990s, according to figures from the UNESCO Institute for Statistics (UIS). The low group consists of Bolivia, El Salvador, Guatemala, Honduras, Paraguay and Venezuela; the intermediate group includes Brazil, Colombia, Costa Rica, Ecuador, Mexico, Nicaragua and the Dominican Republic, and the high group consists of Argentina, Chile, Panama, Peru and Uruguay.

The opportunities for young people who live in rural areas are even more limited, as around 80% do not manage to accumulate the minimum educational capital, even when a lower threshold is considered (see table V.2).[1] This high proportion of young people inherit an inadequate education which, in the course of their lives, results in badly paid jobs and reduces their own opportunities for well-being and those of their families.

---

[1] For rural areas, the threshold for children was set at 9 years, while for the parents, less than 6 years of schooling was considered inadequate.

Table V.2
LATIN AMERICA (GROUPS OF COUNTRIES): CHILDREN AGED FROM 20 TO 24 YEARS
WHO DID NOT SURPASS THE EDUCATION OF THEIR PARENTS AND WHO
COMPLETED LESS THAN 12 YEARS OF SCHOOLING, BY SEX AND
EDUCATIONAL LEVEL OF THEIR PARENTS,
URBAN AND RURAL AREAS, 2000
(Percentages)[a]

Group of countries[b]	Sex	Geographical area											
		Urban areas						Rural areas					
		Total	Educational level of parents					Total	Educational level of parents				
			0-2 years	3-5 years	6-9 years	10-12 years	13-15 years		0-2 years	3-5 years	6-9 years	10-12 years	13-15 years
Low group	Both sexes	37	55	48	31	21	10	77	82	72	58	13	16
	Men	42	59	55	34	25	13	76	80	70	63	11	13
	Women	31	48	40	27	16	7	77	84	72	52	10	18
Intermediate group	Both sexes	36	52	48	35	24	11	65	75	62	48	20	9
	Men	43	59	52	42	30	12	70	79	67	56	20	15
	Women	29	44	42	28	18	10	57	69	53	37	20	7
High group	Both sexes	31	41	44	38	21	15	54	63	56	46	32	34
	Men	38	51	53	47	24	18	59	67	64	47	39	41
	Women	23	30	33	29	17	13	46	56	43	43	21	28
Total, all countries	Both sexes	36	51	48	36	23	11	67	75	64	51	20	17
	Men	42	57	55	42	28	14	70	77	68	57	23	19
	Women	29	43	40	29	18	9	62	72	58	43	15	17

Source: ECLAC, on the basis of special tabulations of data from household surveys of the respective countries.

[a] Simple averages of the country data.
[b] The countries are grouped according to the gross enrolment ratio for the secondary cycle in the mid-1990s, according to figures from the UNESCO Institute for Statistics (UIS). The low group consists of Bolivia, El Salvador, Guatemala, Honduras, Paraguay and Venezuela; the intermediate group includes Brazil, Colombia, Costa Rica, Ecuador, Mexico, Nicaragua and the Dominican Republic, and the high group consists of Argentina, Chile, Panama, Peru and Uruguay.

The intergenerational factor is even more apparent from the low proportion of young people who significantly exceed the educational level of their parents, despite the notable extension in educational coverage between the two generations.[2]

The average years of schooling of young people have risen from 7.1 to 10.4 years in urban areas, and from 3 to 6.8 in rural areas, yet only a little over 33% of urban young people and 20% of rural young people have achieved a significant and sufficient increase in education compared with their parents (see figure V.2).

---

[2]   Although there are other important factors, such as the demographic, asset ownership and employment aspects of households, for most people educational capital is the main determining factor of their opportunities for future well-being.

Figure V.2
LATIN AMERICA: AVERAGE YEARS OF SCHOOLING OF YOUNG PEOPLE AGED
20 TO 24 AND OF THEIR PARENTS, 1999

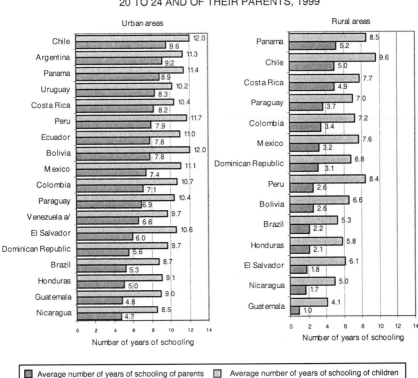

Urban areas

Country	Parents	Children
Chile	9.6	12.0
Argentina	9.2	11.3
Panama	8.9	11.4
Uruguay	8.3	10.2
Costa Rica	8.2	10.4
Peru	7.9	11.7
Ecuador	7.8	11.0
Bolivia	7.8	12.0
Mexico	7.4	11.1
Colombia	7.1	10.7
Paraguay	6.9	10.4
Venezuela a/	6.6	9.7
El Salvador	6.0	10.6
Dominican Republic	5.6	9.7
Brazil	5.3	8.7
Honduras	5.0	9.1
Guatemala	4.8	9.0
Nicaragua	4.7	8.5

Number of years of schooling

Rural areas

Country	Parents	Children
Panama	5.2	8.5
Chile	5.0	9.6
Costa Rica	4.9	7.7
Paraguay	3.7	7.0
Colombia	3.4	7.2
Mexico	3.2	7.6
Dominican Republic	3.1	6.8
Peru	2.6	8.4
Bolivia	2.6	6.6
Brazil	2.2	5.3
Honduras	2.1	5.8
El Salvador	1.8	6.1
Nicaragua	1.7	5.0
Guatemala	1.0	4.1

Number of years of schooling

◼ Average number of years of schooling of parents   ▢ Average number of years of schooling of children

Source: ECLAC, on the basis of special tabulations of data from household surveys of the respective countries.

[a] National total.

In the following sections of this chapter, data will be presented on the chain that determines the different opportunities for well-being according to the social stratum of the household of origin, together with data on the way in which this is reflected in income distribution. When the information is presented by groups of countries, details of the figures for each country may be found in the statistical appendix.

2.   The transmission of educational capital

Despite the significant extension of educational coverage in the region over the past 15 years, young people from the lower social strata have had few opportunities to achieve a level of education that would allow them subsequently to attain a minimum level of well-being. At present, just over 30% of young people whose parents did not complete their primary education manage to finish the secondary cycle. In contrast, the secondary cycle is completed by 75% of children whose parents had at least ten years of schooling.

The continuing link between access to education and the social stratum of origin indicates that the well-being opportunities of young people today have already been shaped to a large extent by the pattern of inequalities that prevailed in the previous generation. This results in a rigid social structure and little social mobility. This inequality even limits opportunities to improve income distribution in the medium term, because educational capital —the number of years of schooling and the quality of education— is the main route, and for the majority the only route, to obtaining well-paid employment.

Analysis of the intergenerational transmission of educational inequalities is particularly important with regard to the possibilities of completing the secondary cycle, which today is the threshold for avoiding poverty. There are very sharp differences in the proportion of young people who complete 12 or more years of schooling according to the level of education of their parents. Thus, among the countries for which information is available, in those with relatively lower levels of coverage for secondary education —Bolivia, El Salvador, Guatemala, Honduras, Paraguay and Venezuela— only one in every three young people whose parents completed less than six years of education manage to complete their secondary education. In contrast, three out of every four young people whose parents completed more than 12 years of schooling reach at least this level (see table V.3).

In countries with higher secondary enrolment ratios —Argentina, Chile, Panama, Peru and Uruguay— there are also differences of educational level among young people according to the educational capital of their household of origin. In these countries, the proportion of urban young people who complete 12 or more years of schooling reaches, on average, 60%: a figure which is higher than the average for the first group of countries in the table (53%). This gap is also apparent in rural areas (37% compared to 11%). In these countries with higher ratios, while only 36% of children of parents with less than six years of schooling complete secondary education, over 90% of the children of parents who completed secondary school reach that level (see figure V.3).

Table V.3
LATIN AMERICA (GROUPS OF COUNTRIES): YOUNG PEOPLE AGED 20 TO 24 YEARS
WITH A MINIMUM OF 9, 12 AND 14 YEARS OF SCHOOLING, BY EDUCATIONAL
LEVEL OF THEIR PARENTS, URBAN AREAS
(Simple average of the countries, percentages)

Group	Years of schooling	Year	Total	Educational level of the parents[a]			
				0-5	6-9	10-12	13 or more
Low group[b]	At least 9 years	1990	65	49	81	90	96
		2000	69	51	81	94	96
	At least 12 years	1990	43	28	53	74	84
		2000	53	33	63	77	91
	At least 14 years	1990	19	10	21	39	57
		2000	20	8	18	31	57
Intermediate group[c]	At least 9 years	1990	62	49	76	93	96
		2000	70	51	79	89	96
	At least 12 years	1990	43	29	53	75	88
		2000	54	32	59	75	92
	At least 14 years	1990	16	7	20	39	60
		2000	23	7	22	36	62
High group[d]	At least 9 years	1990	77	58	80	91	96
		2000	79	58	75	94	97
	At least 12 years	1990	52	30	51	72	88
		2000	60	36	51	75	90
	At least 14 years	1990	16	6	12	26	48
		2000	22	6	12	29	54

Source: ECLAC, on the basis of special tabulations of data from household surveys of the respective countries.

[a] Average years of schooling of the head of household and his/her spouse.
[b] Bolivia, El Salvador, Guatemala, Honduras, Paraguay and Venezuela.
[c] Brazil, Colombia, Costa Rica, Ecuador, Nicaragua and Mexico. The Dominican Republic was excluded, as comparable data were not available for both years.
[d] Chile, Panama and Uruguay. Argentina and Peru were excluded, as comparable data were not available for both years.

The data for rural areas also show differences deriving from the prevailing educational climate in the home. As in urban areas, throughout the 1990s a gap remained between the percentages of young people from households of different educational levels who completed at least nine years of schooling. Between the beginning and end of the decade, there was a certain rigidity in the distribution of educational opportunities, due largely to the educational climate of the home (see table V.4).

Figure V.3
LATIN AMERICA: YOUNG PEOPLE AGED 20 TO 24 YEARS WITH A MINIMUM OF 9,
12 AND 14 YEARS OF SCHOOLING, ACCORDING TO THE EDUCATIONAL
LEVEL OF THEIR PARENTS, URBAN AREAS, 1990-2000
(Percentages)

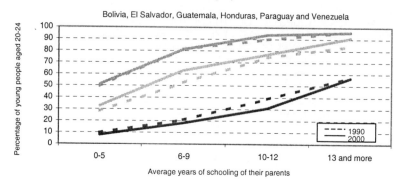

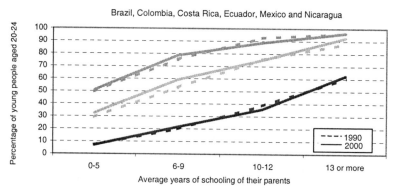

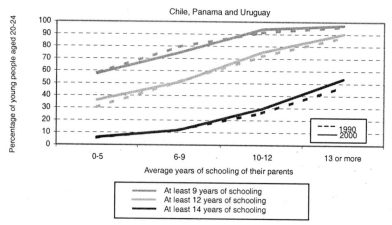

Source: ECLAC, on the basis of special tabulations of data from household surveys of the respective
countries.

It is disturbing to note that the efforts made to extend educational coverage over the past ten years have not succeeded in reducing the gap between young people from different social strata. If all of the data relating to the urban areas of 15 countries at the beginning and end of the 1990s are considered, it will be seen that the differences in the proportions of young people aged 20 to 24 with 12 years of schooling from households with different educational capital remained virtually unchanged (see table V.4).

Table V.4
LATIN AMERICA (GROUPS OF COUNTRIES): YOUNG PEOPLE AGED 20 TO 24 YEARS WITH A MINIMUM OF 9 AND 12 YEARS OF SCHOOLING, BY EDUCATIONAL LEVEL OF THEIR PARENTS, RURAL AREAS
(Simple average of the countries, percentages)

Group	Years of schooling	Year	Total	Educational level of the parents[a]		
				0-5	6-9	10 or more
Low group [b]	At least 9 years	1990	14	12	64	69
		2000	21	18	59	90
	At least 12 years	1990	7	6	34	58
		2000	11	9	41	65
Intermediate group [c]	At least 9 years	1990	24	20	55	90
		2000	34	28	63	94
	At least 12 years	1990	13	10	32	64
		2000	22	15	44	87
High group [d]	At least 9 years	1990	44	31	72	89
		2000	55	41	70	92
	At least 12 years	1990	28	17	52	76
		2000	37	24	49	78

Source: ECLAC, on the basis of special tabulations of data from household surveys of the respective countries.

[a] Average years of schooling of the head of household and his/her spouse.
[b] El Salvador, Guatemala and Honduras. Bolivia, Paraguay and Venezuela were excluded, as comparable data were not available for both years.
[c] Brazil, Colombia, Costa Rica, Nicaragua and Mexico. Ecuador and the Dominican Republic were excluded, as comparable data were not available for both years.
[d] Chile and Panama. Argentina, Peru and Uruguay were excluded, as comparable data were not available for both years.

The above shows that, for the majority of young people in the region, educational capital continues to depend on the education of their parents and the economic capacity of their household of origin. Two aspects are worthy of note in this respect. First, the inequality of educational opportunities already manifests itself at the primary school level. In urban areas of Bolivia, El Salvador, Guatemala, Honduras, Paraguay and Venezuela, the percentage of young people who did not complete more than 8 years of schooling fluctuated between 11% and 47%, and most of them were from homes where the parents had not surpassed that educational level either. In Brazil, Colombia, Costa Rica, Ecuador, Nicaragua, Mexico and the Dominican Republic, these percentages fluctuated between 20% and 49%, and in Argentina, Chile, Panama, Peru and Uruguay, between 9% and 34% (see table V.4). There is a high probability that young people who complete only eight years of schooling will reproduce the poverty of their household of origin. Inadequate educational capital is one of the main stumbling blocks in the efforts to reduce extreme poverty (see figure V.4).

Second, differences in the number of years of schooling are not the only source of inequality in educational capital. The quality of the education that young people receive also varies according to the social stratum from which they come. Measurements of the level of learning show significant differences between public and private schools. Delich (2002) states that while the average student in public schools scarcely learns 50% of the contents of the official curriculum, the graduates of private schools easily come close to 100%. In the same study, this author says that an analysis of reading and writing tests shows that two out of five pupils in the fourth or fifth grade do not understand what they read, and those two come precisely from families with a low socioeconomic level. Although the data from household surveys cannot be used to analyse the gap in educational quality, there are clear indications that those who manage to complete more years of education have generally received better-quality education.

Many governments in the region have carried out educational reforms focused on the curricula, institutional changes and the allocation of more financial resources. It is possible that such reforms may manage to bring the results and educational achievements of students from private and public establishments closer together, and thus reduce the educational inequalities between different socioeconomic strata.[3] It has not been sufficiently emphasized, however, that a very substantial proportion of the educational inequalities that are transmitted from one generation to another are still related to the number of years of schooling completed by young people from different social strata, independently of the quality of the education that they receive. Attempts to improve education may have little effect if they are not accompanied by policies

---

[3]   In the same study cited above (Delich, 2002, pp. 32 and 33), it is claimed that a review is also needed of the inequalities that have arisen in the educational system, which raise questions about education in general and which are greater in the public than in the private sector. There is a huge gap between a child who goes to school in Greater Buenos Aires, where he has three hours of classes in an overcrowded room for 50 days a year, and another child, also in a public school with a double-shift system who learns languages, computer studies and other subjects, as occurs in the capital. It is easy to imagine what this difference will mean, ten years later, in terms of income.

that extend the period for which young people in the middle and lower strata remain in the school system. A high proportion of these young people do not stay at school for the 12 years that are considered the minimum requirement.

Figure V.4
LATIN AMERICA: AVERAGE LABOUR INCOME AND PERCENTAGE OF POOR PEOPLE
AMONG EMPLOYED PERSONS AGED 20 TO 29 YEARS, URBAN AREAS, 1999
(Percentages)

Low group: Bolivia, El Salvador, Guatemala, Honduras, Paraguay and Venezuela

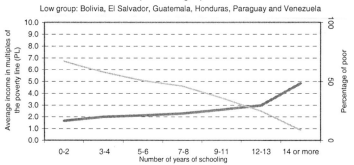

Intermediate group: Brazil, Colombia, Costa Rica, Ecuador, Mexico, Nicaragua and Dominican Republic

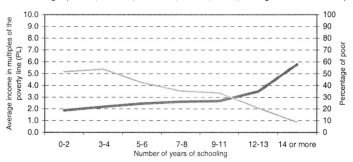

High group: Argentina, Chile, Panama, Peru and Uruguay

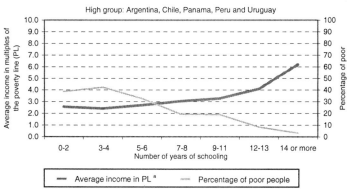

Source: ECLAC, on the basis of special tabulations of data from household surveys of the respective countries.

[a] PL: poverty lines.

3.   Educational capital and employment opportunities

The intergenerational transmission of opportunities for well-being, which begins in the household of origin and continues at school, links educational attainment with the occupations that are most likely to be accessible, and the income deriving from them. Those who complete 13 or more years of schooling (post-secondary education), will mainly be professionals, technicians or directors, who in urban areas amount to about 45% of this group (see table V.5).[4] The average monthly income for this group as a whole is between 4 and 18 poverty lines (see table V.6), with professionals and technicians earning an average of 6.5 poverty lines and directors receiving an average of 10.

In rural areas, 52% of those who have this level of educational attainment would work in the types of occupations mentioned (see table V.5). Unlike urban areas, where there is a relatively large supply of high qualifications and those who have them are therefore found in a greater variety of occupations, in rural areas there is a higher concentration of highly-qualified persons in professional, technical and upper management occupations. This higher concentration is clearly visible when the countries are grouped according to the level of gross secondary enrolment: in the lowest-level group (Bolivia, El Salvador, Guatemala and Honduras), the percentage of young people aged 20 to 29 years with post-secondary education who are in occupations of a professional or specialist nature or who reach upper management positions amounts to 75%; in the intermediate-level group (Brazil, Colombia, Costa Rica, Nicaragua, Mexico and the Dominican Republic) this percentage is around 42%, and in the group with the highest secondary enrolment ratios (Chile, Panama and Peru) it is no more than 35%.

The other occupations which are easily accessible with 13 or more years of schooling are those of administrative employee, accountant, salesperson or shop assistant: occupations which in most of the countries are exercised by between 35% and 45% of persons with that educational level in urban areas, with an average monthly income usually between 3.5 and 5.5 poverty lines.

---

[4]   In Brazil, Colombia, Costa Rica, Honduras, Nicaragua, Peru and Venezuela, the joint duration of the primary and secondary cycles is 11 years (see UIS, 2003). In these countries any education as from the twelfth year of schooling is considered to be post-secondary.

Table V.5

LATIN AMERICA (GROUPS OF COUNTRIES): PERCENTAGE DISTRIBUTION OF YOUNG PEOPLE AGED 20 TO 29 YEARS WHO WORK 20 OR MORE HOURS PER WEEK, BY OCCUPATION AND EDUCATIONAL LEVEL, URBAN AND RURAL AREAS, 1999[a]

URBAN AREAS

Group of countries [b]	Educational level	Total	Occupational category							
			Professionals and technicians	Management posts	Administrative employees and accountants	Salespersons and shop assistants	Industrial, transport and warehouse workers	Construction workers	Domestic employees, waiters and security staff	Agricultural workers
Low group	Total	100.0	11.3	3.7	15.9	16.5	33.6	7.1	9.2	2.7
	0-8	100.0	1.2	1.6	5.1	16.9	43.7	11.7	15.2	4.7
	9-12	100.0	8.0	3.0	20.5	19.5	34.9	5.2	7.3	1.7
	13 or more	100.0	38.1	9.2	27.1	10.1	11.2	1.0	2.3	1.0
Intermediate group	Total	100.0	10.3	2.5	14.5	19.5	32.3	4.8	11.5	4.5
	0-8	100.0	0.7	0.8	3.9	17.0	42.8	9.2	17.5	8.1
	9-12	100.0	4.9	2.1	18.9	24.4	33.5	3.5	10.3	2.4
	13 or more	100.0	37.4	6.8	25.6	16.7	9.7	0.4	3.0	0.4
High group	Total	100.0	13.9	2.5	16.2	16.4	30.9	5.4	11.6	3.2
	0-8	100.0	0.7	1.0	3.2	12.4	42.0	11.0	20.8	8.9
	9-12	100.0	3.8	1.9	17.3	20.5	36.3	5.1	12.5	2.7
	13 or more	100.0	41.5	5.0	25.6	11.5	11.2	1.0	3.5	0.7
Total countries	Total	100.0	11.6	2.9	15.4	17.6	32.4	5.7	10.8	3.5
	0-8	100.0	0.9	1.1	4.1	15.7	42.9	10.5	17.6	7.2
	9-12	100.0	5.6	2.3	19.0	21.7	34.7	4.5	9.9	2.2
	13 or more	100.0	38.8	7.1	26.1	13.0	10.6	0.7	2.9	0.7

RURAL AREAS

Group of countries [b]	Educational level	Total	Occupational category							
			Professionals and technicians	Management posts	Administrative employees and accountants	Salespersons and shop assistants	Industrial, transport and warehouse workers	Construction workers	Domestic employees, waiters and security staff	Agricultural workers
Low group	Total	100.0	4.7	1.8	1.6	7.3	18.2	12.7	4.7	49.1
	0-8	100.0	0.6	1.7	0.5	5.8	17.0	12.9	5.4	56.0
	9-12	100.0	11.4	1.1	6.7	15.2	24.9	9.4	2.9	28.6
	13 or more	100.0	73.3	1.6	6.2	5.5	4.8	1.3	0.9	6.4
Intermediate group	Total	100.0	3.5	1.0	3.6	10.6	24.6	4.6	7.9	44.3
	0-8	100.0	0.5	0.6	1.0	8.2	23.6	5.2	7.8	53.2
	9-12	100.0	6.0	1.3	9.4	19.7	29.4	3.5	8.9	21.7
	13 or more	100.0	37.2	5.0	15.6	16.0	11.4	4.0	4.1	6.7
High group	Total	100.0	4.1	1.6	4.0	8.0	23.0	3.6	7.5	48.3
	0-8	100.0	0.2	0.7	0.4	6.0	19.7	3.3	7.9	61.9
	9-12	100.0	4.2	2.2	6.1	10.9	30.1	5.0	7.4	34.1
	13 or more	100.0	29.4	3.7	15.2	9.5	18.2	0.9	5.7	17.4
Total countries	Total	100.0	4.1	1.4	3.0	8.9	21.9	7.3	6.7	46.9
	0-8	100.0	0.5	1.0	0.7	6.8	20.4	7.5	7.0	56.1
	9-12	100.0	7.6	1.4	7.7	16.2	27.9	5.9	6.4	26.8
	13 or more	100.0	48.4	3.5	12.2	10.9	10.5	2.4	3.3	8.9

Source: ECLAC, on the basis of special tabulations of data from household surveys of the respective countries.

[a] Simple averages of the country data.
[b] The countries are grouped according to the gross enrolment ratio for the secondary cycle in the mid-1990s, according to figures from the UNESCO Institute for Statistics (UIS). The low group consists of Bolivia, El Salvador, Guatemala, Honduras, Paraguay and Venezuela (only in the part of the table on urban areas); the intermediate group includes Brazil, Colombia, Costa Rica, Ecuador (urban areas), Mexico, Nicaragua and the Dominican Republic, and the high group consists of Argentina (urban areas), Chile, Panama, Peru and Uruguay (urban areas).

Table V.6
LATIN AMERICA (GROUPS OF COUNTRIES): AVERAGE INCOME OF YOUNG PEOPLE AGED 20 TO 29 YEARS WHO WORK 20 OR MORE HOURS PER WEEK, BY OCCUPATION AND EDUCATIONAL LEVEL, URBAN AND RURAL AREAS, 1999[a]
(Multiples of the per capita poverty line)

URBAN AREAS

Group of countries [b]	Educational level	Total	Professionals and technicians	Management posts	Administrative employees and accountants	Salespersons and shop assistants	Industrial, transport and warehouse workers	Construction workers	Domestic employees, waiters and security staff	Agricultural workers
Low group	Total	2.8	4.3	7.4	3.2	2.4	2.5	2.5	1.6	1.8
	0-8	2.1	2.5	5.4	2.1	2.0	2.2	2.4	1.5	1.7
	9-12	2.8	2.8	6.3	3.1	2.4	2.8	2.7	1.7	1.5
	13 or more	4.4	4.7	8.4	3.6	3.1	3.6	3.5	2.6	3.1
Intermediate group	Total	3.3	6.7	9.5	3.5	2.9	2.9	3.1	2.0	2.4
	0-8	2.4	2.7	4.4	2.8	2.4	2.6	2.6	1.7	2.3
	9-12	3.1	3.9	10.0	3.2	2.8	3.2	3.6	2.5	2.9
	13 or more	5.5	7.3	10.0	4.1	4.5	3.9	4.0	3.8	3.4
High group	Total	4.0	6.6	10.6	4.3	3.6	3.6	3.6	2.9	2.8
	0-8	2.9	4.1	5.4	2.9	2.8	3.0	3.2	2.6	2.4
	9-12	3.7	4.8	7.1	3.8	3.6	3.7	3.9	3.2	3.1
	13 or more	5.9	7.0	12.0	4.9	4.4	4.7	4.1	3.5	5.4
Total countries	Total	3.3	5.9	9.1	3.6	2.9	3.0	3.1	2.1	2.3
	0-8	2.4	2.9	5.1	2.6	2.4	2.6	2.7	1.9	2.1
	9-12	3.2	3.7	8.0	3.3	2.9	3.2	3.3	2.4	2.5
	13 or more	5.2	6.4	10.0	4.2	4.0	4.0	3.8	3.2	4.0

RURAL AREAS

Group of countries [b]	Educational level	Total	Professionals and technicians	Management posts	Administrative employees and accountants	Salespersons and shop assistants	Industrial, transport and warehouse workers	Construction workers	Domestic employees, waiters and security staff	Agricultural workers
Low group	Total	2.1	4.5	4.4	3.8	2.3	2.7	3.2	1.7	1.7
	0-8	1.8	3.0	3.8	2.9	2.0	2.6	2.9	1.8	1.7
	9-12	2.7	4.9	6.3	4.0	2.6	3.1	3.4	2.1	1.3
	13 or more	4.3	4.7	4.1	4.6	2.8	3.6	6.0	3.0	4.5
Intermediate group	Total	3.2	6.0	7.0	4.9	3.1	3.5	4.0	2.8	2.6
	0-8	2.8	3.4	4.5	4.3	2.8	3.3	3.9	2.4	2.5
	9-12	3.7	5.3	6.9	4.0	3.3	4.0	3.5	4.1	3.4
	13 or more	6.4	7.5	11.2	6.1	4.2	6.1	5.0	4.9	3.9
High group	Total	3.2	8.4	14.0	4.2	3.2	3.9	3.7	2.4	2.4
	0-8	2.5	3.0	4.8	5.1	2.6	3.8	3.4	2.1	2.2
	9-12	3.3	5.3	10.8	4.0	3.7	3.9	3.8	2.7	2.7
	13 or more	6.8	10.5	31.7	6.1	3.9	4.1	6.4	2.4	3.7
Total countries	Total	2.8	6.0	7.3	4.4	2.8	3.3	3.6	2.3	2.2
	0-8	2.4	3.2	4.3	3.9	2.5	3.2	3.4	2.1	2.2
	9-12	3.3	5.1	7.4	4.0	3.1	3.7	3.6	3.1	2.5
	13 or more	5.7	7.1	14.2	5.6	3.8	5.0	5.4	3.9	4.1

Source: ECLAC, on the basis of special tabulations of data from household surveys of the respective countries.

[a] Simple averages of the country data.
[b] The countries are grouped according to the gross enrolment ratio for the secondary cycle in the mid-1990s, according to figures from the UNESCO Institute for Statistics (UIS). The low group consists of Bolivia, El Salvador, Guatemala, Honduras, Paraguay and Venezuela (only in the part of the table on urban areas); the intermediate group includes Brazil, Colombia, Costa Rica, Ecuador (urban areas), Mexico, Nicaragua and the Dominican Republic, and the high group consists of Argentina (urban areas), Chile, Panama, Peru and Uruguay (urban areas).

Opportunities for individuals with an intermediate but inadequate level of education —between nine and eleven years of schooling— are usually concentrated in the lower half of the occupational structure. In urban areas, just over 40% manage to find work, at best, as administrative workers, accountants, salespersons or shop assistants, with an average monthly income that is usually equivalent to between 2.5 and 3.5 poverty lines. More than 50% (57%, on average, among the countries with higher levels of education) work as factory hands, labourers, caretakers, waiters or domestic employees, with an average monthly income of between 1.5 and 3.5 poverty lines.

In contrast, about 80% of urban workers with eight or less years of schooling usually work as labourers, security staff, waiters or domestic employees, with a monthly average income of between 2 and 2.5 poverty lines, which is insufficient to guarantee the well-being of a family (see tables V.5 and V.6). As the coverage of secondary education increases, the above percentage also increases, from 75% in the group with the lowest secondary coverage to 83% in the highest group, because when there is a larger supply of qualified workers, the least qualified workers tend to concentrate in occupations of lower status, quality and remuneration. Consequently, although there are different situations in the countries considered, there is basically a high degree of similarity in terms of the link between education, occupation and income which determines the socioeconomic stratification prevailing in the region.

Similarly, in rural areas, more than 90% of those who have eight or less years of schooling are employed as agricultural workers, labourers, watchmen, waiters or domestic employees, with an average monthly income that is usually between less than one and three poverty lines. It may be noted that agricultural workers account for approximately 60% of all those with this educational level, and their average monthly income is 2.2 poverty lines.

Figures V.5 and V.6 show the relationship between educational achievements and the probable type of employment and level of income corresponding to each educational level. It may be observed that young people aged 20 to 29 years with eight or fewer years of schooling are mostly employed in occupations that provide an inadequate degree of well-being, with an average monthly income of around 2.4 poverty lines. These occupations and, in second place, those which provide an intermediate level of well-being (with an average monthly wage of something over three poverty lines) represent the employment prospects for those who have between nine and eleven years of schooling, thus confirming the idea that this educational level is insufficient to ensure their well-being throughout their life.

Figure V.5
LATIN AMERICA: OCCUPATIONAL STRUCTURE AND AVERAGE INCOME OF YOUNG
PEOPLE AGED FROM 20 TO 29 YEARS BY COUNTRY GROUPS,
URBAN AREAS, 1999[a]

Low group: Bolivia, El Salvador, Guatemala, Honduras, Paraguay and Venezuela

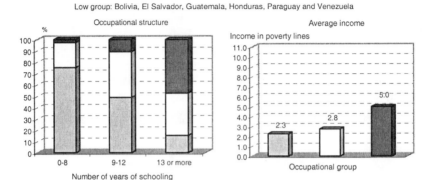

Intermediate group: Brazil, Colombia, Costa Rica, Ecuador, Mexico, Nicaragua and Dominican Republic

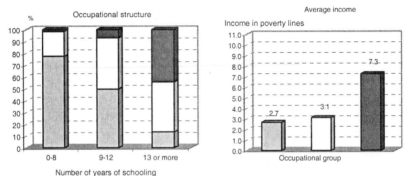

High group: Argentina, Chile, Panama, Peru and Uruguay

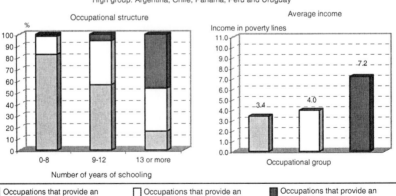

| Occupations that provide an inadequate degree of well-being | Occupations that provide an intermediate degree of well-being | Occupations that provide an adequate degree of well-being |

Source: ECLAC, on the basis of special tabulations of data from household surveys of the respective
countries.

[a] Ordered according to the gross secondary enrolment ratios.

Figure V.6
LATIN AMERICA: OCCUPATIONAL STRUCTURE AND AVERAGE INCOME OF YOUNG
PEOPLE AGED FROM 20 TO 29 YEARS BY COUNTRY GROUPS,
RURAL AREAS, 1999[a]

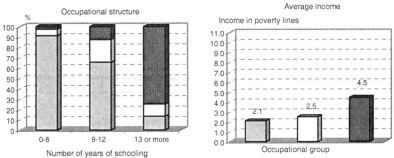

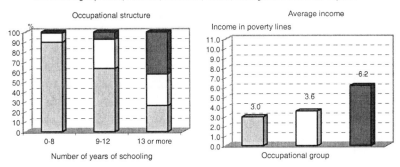

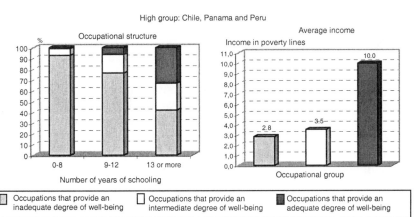

Source: ECLAC, on the basis of special tabulations of data from household surveys of the respective countries.

[a] Ordered according to the gross secondary enrolment ratios.

As may be seen from the above figures, young people who have completed between 9 and 11 years of schooling mainly have access only to occupations that provide an insufficient level of well-being. This fact also reflects the process of devaluation of education to which successive generations are exposed as secondary education coverage increases. At the same time, the significant concentration of individuals with 13 or more years of schooling in occupations that provide an adequate degree of well-being, with an average monthly income close to 7 poverty lines, once more shows the importance of this educational threshold and also confirms the significant determinism observed in this area.

The data also reveal another fact, which further emphasizes the importance of the differences deriving from the resources of the household of origin and the educational capital inherited. Thus, not only are very different possibilities of access to different occupational categories transmitted, but also very distinct possibilities of obtaining income within each of those categories. For example, salespersons and shop assistants with 12 or more years of schooling receive an average monthly income equivalent to 4 poverty lines, but that declines to 2.9 when they have between 9 and 11 years of schooling and to 2.4 when they have less than 9 years of schooling. A similar situation occurs in the case of administrative employees and accountants, and also in the case of industrial, transport and warehouse workers.

All of this shows more clearly how important it is to orient educational reforms towards improving educational equity for children and adolescents from the lower-income social strata, since education is the only form of capital that they have. Reforms of the school system, however, will not benefit those who are already aged 20 or more. As that group will represent more than two-thirds of the labour force in all the countries of the region in the next two decades, it is essential to define policies and programmes for adult training, so that distributional inequality does not increase further. This professional training for adults, as well as being closely linked to the changing demands of the labour market, must offer sideways routes to achieving better working and earning opportunities. The proper construction of such routes will determine to a large extent the possibility of curbing the trend towards distributional inequality, while at the same time raising the level of competitiveness.

4. Influence of family contacts

As from certain levels of education, the intergenerational transmission of opportunities for well-being is influenced by the social contacts associated with the household of origin. Thanks to the extensive network of contacts available to some households, their children can receive incomes that are, on average, 40% higher than those who do not have this advantage, even if they work in the same occupation groups and have a similar level of education.

In order to take this component into account in the set of factors that affect intergenerational transmission of opportunities for well-being, a brief review is given below of the situation of young people who have completed 12 or more years of schooling. An analysis is also made of the average monthly income received by young people who, although working in the same occupational groups, differ in terms of the scale of the resources available to their parents. In this analysis, young people are divided into those who have nine or less years of schooling and those with ten or more years of schooling, taking the educational capital of the parents into account in both cases.

In Brazil, for example, young people who work as administrative employees or accountants and whose parents have 10 or more years of schooling, receive an average monthly income of 4.2 poverty lines, but this goes down to 3.2 poverty lines for the same work in the case of young people whose parents have an educational capital of nine or less years of schooling. As there are no significant differences between the two groups of young people with regard to the average years of schooling, there should not be any differences with regard to average income, and so it seems reasonable to attribute the disparity observed to the effect of social contacts.

In Colombia, the gap is even greater in the case of salespersons and shop assistants, since although there are no great differences in their education, young people from households with little educational capital receive a monthly income equivalent to 2.3 poverty lines, in contrast to the 4 poverty lines received by young people from households with a higher educational level.[5] In Costa Rica, within the same occupational group, monthly income reaches 5.2 poverty lines in the case of young people who come from homes with a higher educational level, and 4.5 in the case of their less fortunate colleagues, although both groups have the same number of years of schooling (see table V.7 and figure V.7).

---

[5] In other words, the fact that young people from households with a higher level of educational capital have about one year more of schooling than those from homes with less educational capital is not sufficient to explain the large differences in income that are recorded for these groups.

Table V.7
LATIN AMERICA (18 COUNTRIES): AVERAGE INCOME AND AVERAGE YEARS OF
SCHOOLING OF YOUNG PEOPLE AGED 20 TO 29 YEARS WHO WORK FOR 20 OR
MORE HOURS PER WEEK AND HAVE COMPLETED 12 OR MORE YEARS OF
SCHOOLING, BY EDUCATIONAL LEVEL OF THEIR PARENTS,
URBAN AREAS, 1999

Country		Educational level	Employment category							
			Total		Professionals and technicians		Administrative employees and accountants		Salespersons and shop assistants	
			Average income	Average years of schooling	Average income	Average years of schooling	Average income	Average years of schooling	Average income	Average years of schooling
Argentina	1999	Total	4.7	13.8	6.0	15.7	4.2	13.2	4.0	12.6
		0-9	4.2	13.4	4.9	15.5	4.2	13.0	3.6	12.4
		10 or more	5.0	14.1	6.5	15.8	4.3	13.3	4.4	12.8
Bolivia	1999	Total	3.9	14.0	4.8	15.5	4.2	13.3	2.6	13.3
		0-9	2.5	13.8	2.7	15.3	2.9	13.2	2.0	13.2
		10 or more	5.3	14.2	6.4	15.6	5.8	13.5	3.4	13.4
Brazil	1999	Total	3.9	12.2	5.5	13.3	3.5	12.0	2.9	11.4
		0-9	3.4	11.9	4.4	12.7	3.2	11.8	2.7	11.3
		10 or more	5.4	13.1	7.2	14.2	4.2	12.4	3.7	12.1
Chile	2000	Total	4.9	13.6	7.1	15.0	3.9	12.9	3.5	12.6
		0-9	4.1	12.9	5.8	14.0	3.7	12.8	3.4	12.3
		10 or more	5.8	14.3	7.8	15.5	4.1	13.2	3.7	12.9
Colombia	1999	Total	3.5	13.1	5.1	14.9	3.0	12.4	2.6	12.0
		0-9	2.9	12.5	3.9	14.3	2.7	12.1	2.2	11.7
		10 or more	4.8	14.1	6.5	15.4	3.4	13.1	4.0	12.8
Costa Rica	1999	Total	5.9	13.4	7.0	14.7	5.1	12.5	4.8	12.3
		0-9	5.3	12.9	6.5	14.4	4.8	12.2	4.5	11.9
		10 or more	6.5	14.1	7.4	15.0	5.7	13.2	5.2	12.9
Ecuador	1999	Total	2.5	14.0	3.1	15.8	2.4	13.4	2.1	13.2
		0-9	2.1	13.5	2.6	15.2	2.1	13.1	1.7	12.9
		10 or more	3.1	14.8	3.5	16.4	2.9	13.9	3.0	13.9
El Salvador	1999	Total	3.9	13.5	4.9	15.1	4.1	12.9	2.9	12.4
		0-9	3.7	13.3	5.0	15.0	3.6	12.7	2.9	12.4
		10 or more	4.5	13.9	4.8	15.2	4.9	13.2	2.7	12.5
Guatemala	1998	Total	3.0	13.0	3.3	13.2	3.3	12.9	1.1	12.6
		0-9	2.6	12.8	2.8	12.9	3.3	12.8	0.7	12.4
		10 or more	3.9	13.6	4.7	14.1	3.3	13.0	1.1	13.4
Honduras	1999	Total	2.4	13.0	2.6	13.9	2.4	12.4	1.7	12.8
		0-9	2.0	12.5	2.2	13.1	2.2	12.2	1.1	12.2
		10 or more	3.5	14.6	3.7	15.9	3.2	13.3	3.6	14.4
Mexico	2000	Total	3.6	14.3	3.9	15.3	3.4	13.7	3.5	13.7
		0-9	3.1	13.8	3.3	14.9	2.9	13.5	3.2	12.9
		10 or more	4.2	14.8	4.4	15.7	4.2	14.0	3.8	14.5
Nicaragua	1998	Total	3.0	13.2	6.0	15.1	2.3	12.0	2.3	13.0
		0-9	2.5	13.0	3.5	14.6	1.5	12.0	2.3	13.0
		10 or more	6.7	14.4	11.8	16.3	2.4	12.1	2.6	13.0
Panama	1999	Total	6.1	14.6	7.6	15.8	5.5	14.1	5.0	13.7
		0-9	5.1	14.1	5.5	15.2	5.4	13.8	3.9	13.4
		10 or more	7.0	15.1	8.8	16.1	5.5	14.5	6.3	14.0
Paraguay	1999	Total	3.0	13.7	3.6	15.1	2.8	13.3	2.7	12.8
		0-9	2.8	13.5	3.3	15.0	2.8	13.1	2.4	12.6
		10 or more	3.3	14.1	4.3	15.6	2.9	13.7	3.7	13.4
Peru	1999	Total	3.4	13.4	3.4	14.7	4.6	13.2	2.5	11.9
		0-9	2.9	13.2	3.0	14.5	3.3	13.2	2.0	11.9
		10 or more	4.2	13.7	3,7	14.9	6.2	13.3	2.6	11.9
Dominican Rep.	1997	Total	4.7	14.3	7.2	16.0	3.7	13.8	3.8	13.5
		0-9	4.4	14.1	5.9	15.9	3.1	13.4	3.2	13.5
		10 or more	5.2	14.7	8.1	16.2	4.5	14.3	5.7	13.5
Uruguay	1999	Total	3.9	13.5	4.3	14.6	3.8	13.3	3.7	12.6
		0-9	3.5	13.0	3.8	13.9	3.5	12.8	3.3	12.5
		10 or more	4.3	13.9	4.7	15.0	4.1	13.6	4.3	12.9
Venezuela [a]	1999	Total	3.3	13.5	4.2	15.2	2.9	12.8	2.4	12.4
		0-9	3.0	13.1	3.5	14.7	2.8	12.5	2.3	12.1
		10 or more	3.8	14.3	5.1	15.8	3.1	13.4	2.6	13.3
Simple average of countries	1999	Total	3.9	13.6	5.0	14.9	3.6	13.0	3.0	12.7
		0-8	3.3	13.2	4.0	14.5	3.2	12.8	2.6	12.5
		9-12	4.8	14.2	6.1	15.5	4.2	13.4	3.7	13.2

Source: ECLAC, on the basis of special tabulations of data from household surveys of the respective countries.

[a] National total.

Figure V.7
LATIN AMERICA: EDUCATIONAL LEVEL AND LABOUR INCOME OF YOUNG PEOPLE
AGED 20 TO 29 YEARS WITH 12 OR MORE YEARS OF SCHOOLING, BY TYPE OF
OCCUPATION AND YEARS OF SCHOOLING OF PARENTS, URBAN AREAS, 1999
(Simple average of 18 countries)

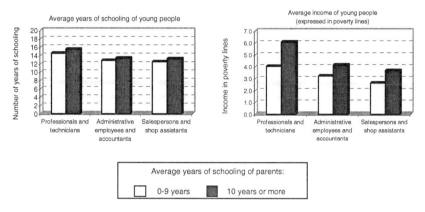

Source: ECLAC, on the basis of special tabulations of data from household surveys of the respective countries.

This trend is systematic. In all the countries there are differences in remuneration between young people in the same occupational group which cannot be attributed to their educational level alone. On average, young people who come from households with less educational capital receive around 70% of the income of those who come from households with more education. This gap is sustained in the three occupational groups analysed. As already noted, this is partly attributable to their greater potential for gaining access to better jobs, although it must also be taken into account they also have a higher level of cultural capital that can help them to perform the relevant tasks more effectively.

5.   The prospects with regard to inequality

A review of the link between income distribution and the general structure of occupations, in terms of remuneration and the capacity to provide well-being, shows that approximately 75% of employed persons from the 40% of households with the lowest incomes are factory hands, labourers, security staff, waiters or domestic employees, receiving an average monthly income equivalent to 2.1 poverty lines. In the 10% of households with the highest incomes, around half of those employed are professionals, technicians or hold upper management posts and receive a monthly income of around 17 poverty lines (see table V.8).

Table V.8
LATIN AMERICA (18 COUNTRIES): EMPLOYMENT AND INCOME OF PERSONS AGED
20 TO 59 YEARS EMPLOYED IN THE MOST FREQUENT OCCUPATIONS IN THE
FOUR LOWEST DECILES AND IN THE HIGHEST DECILE OF THE HOUSEHOLD
INCOME DISTRIBUTION, URBAN AREAS, 1999
(Percentages in each stratum of households)

Country	Year	Factory hands, labourers, waiters, security staff and domestic employees from the 40% of households with the lowest incomes		Professionals, technicians and managers from the 10% of households with the highest incomes	
		Percentage of employment in the four lowest deciles	Average income in terms of poverty lines	Percentage of employment in the highest decile	Average income in terms of poverty lines
Argentina	1999	75.3	3.2	58.3	21.2
Bolivia	1999	66.3	1.8	46.4	14.8
Brazil	1999	75.8	1.8	58.8	20.7
Chile	2000	75.3	2.8	74.5	33.2
Colombia	1999	64.8	1.6	55.5	12.6
Costa Rica	1999	69.9	3.1	60.2	16.7
Ecuador	1999	65.1	1.3	47.3	12.2
El Salvador	1999	77.1	2.1	49.8	13.9
Guatemala	1998	67.6	1.5	62.1	15.0
Honduras	1999	67.9	1.2	46.0	8.6
Mexico	2000	68.2	2.0	51.4	19.3
Nicaragua	1998	73.0	1.3	35.7	18.5
Panama	1999	74.0	2.7	58.1	19.7
Paraguay	1999	70.1	1.7	45.4	12.7
Peru	1999	69.3	1.6	48.8	14.0
Dominican Republic	1997	69.3	2.4	35.7	16.2
Uruguay	1999	74.5	3.3	53.2	17.5
Venezuela [a]	1999	55.4	1.9	44.1	11.3
Simple average of countries	1999	69.9	2.1	51.8	16.6

Source: ECLAC, on the basis of special tabulations of data from household surveys of the respective countries.

[a] National total.

As previously mentioned, there is also the fact that the occupational profile of the workforce, which will continue to define the structure of remunerations and their relationship to income distribution, is already largely fixed. About 80% of the currently employed population, whose characteristics are reflected in the figures mentioned above, will continue to be part of the employed population over the next 10 years.[6]

The close connection that exists between the profile of the occupational structure and the distribution of income —a connection that explains the rigidity of the latter— is apparent from the share in employment and income of the most frequent occupations in the different strata of the distribution pyramid. For example, employed persons aged 20 to 59 years whose remuneration brings them an inadequate degree of well-being —factory hands, labourers, security staff, waiters or domestic employees— and who belong to the 40% of households with the lowest income represent about 25% of total employment and receive about 11% of total income. In contrast, those who have an occupational category that provides them with a adequate degree of well-being —professionals, technicians and persons in upper management posts— and form part of the 10% of households with the highest incomes represent about 5.5% of total employment but receive 21% of total income (see table V.9).

The link between the location of individuals in the occupational structure and their situation in terms of household income distribution is so strong that in the majority of cases it prevails over the other factors that influence this situation, including the size and composition of the household and the amount of monetary income that does not come from employment. For example, if only heads of household are considered, we see that workers whose occupation brings them an inadequate degree of well-being and who come from households situated in the four lowest income deciles represent around 29% of total employment, but receive only a little more than 12% of total income. In contrast, heads of household whose occupation offers them a sufficient degree of well-being and who come from the highest income decile represent around 6% of those employed but receive on average 23% of total income (see table V.9).

---

[6]   This is because the new members joining the actively employed population and those leaving the group only change its composition at an annual rate of 2% to 3%.

Table V.9
LATIN AMERICA (18 COUNTRIES): EMPLOYMENT AND INCOME OF INDIVIDUALS AND HEADS OF HOUSEHOLD AGED 20 TO 59 YEARS EMPLOYED IN THE MOST FREQUENT OCCUPATIONS IN THE FOUR LOWEST DECILES AND IN THE HIGHEST DECILE OF THE HOUSEHOLD INCOME DISTRIBUTION, URBAN AREAS, 1999
(Percentages)

Country	Year	Factory hands, labourers, waiters, security staff and domestic employees from the 40% of households with the lowest incomes				Professionals, technicians and managers from the 10% of households with the highest incomes			
		Percentage of total employment		Percentage of income		Percentage of total employment		Percentage of income	
		Individuals	Heads of household	Individuals	Heads of household	Individuals	Heads of household	Individuals	Heads of household
Argentina	1999	25.8	30.5	12.9	14.2	6.8	7.8	22.2	24.9
Bolivia	1999	24.2	30.7	11.3	14.0	4.6	5.2	18.0	19.1
Brazil	1999	27.5	31.7	10.0	11.0	5.9	6.3	25.1	26.6
Chile	2000	27.4	32.6	10.2	10.5	8.3	9.4	37.1	42.6
Colombia	1999	21.9	27.3	10.0	11.8	5.2	5.5	18.5	20.2
Costa Rica	1999	21.7	25.6	10.8	12.3	6.7	6.9	18.0	19.4
Ecuador	1999	21.2	25.3	8.5	9.2	5.5	6.4	21.2	24.6
El Salvador	1999	25.8	29.1	12.2	13.2	5.7	6.1	17.6	19.3
Guatemala	1998	25.1	29.4	10.9	11.6	6.9	7.9	29.1	31.9
Honduras	1999	27.0	30.0	12.3	12.6	4.0	4.0	12.9	13.8
Mexico	2000	25.6	29.8	11.5	12.0	4.7	5.3	20.8	23.7
Nicaragua	1998	22.6	26.2	8.4	8.6	4.1	4.9	21.1	24.9
Panama	1999	23.5	29.3	10.6	13.0	6.7	7.4	21.9	24.8
Paraguay	1999	23.6	28.3	11.4	13.7	5.5	5.5	19.3	20.1
Peru	1999	24.9	30.4	12.1	14.3	4.7	5.4	19.4	22.9
Dominican Republic	1997	20.2	25.5	10.6	12.0	4.4	4.6	15.4	16.5
Uruguay	1999	31.6	35.5	18.6	20.1	4.8	5.6	15.0	17.0
Venezuela[a]	1999	16.3	20.2	8.6	9.7	5.3	5.2	16.3	17.6
Simple average of countries	1999	24.2	28.7	11.2	12.4	5.5	6.1	20.5	22.8

Source: ECLAC, on the basis of special tabulations of data from household surveys of the respective countries.

[a] National total.

Methodological annex

(a) Determination of the minimum educational capital in terms of well-being

An analysis of the earned income of those who join the labour market shows that at present, in order to attain well-being, they must have completed the secondary cycle as a minimum, which is 11 or 12 years depending on the country. As may be inferred from the data for 18 countries in the region, reaching that educational threshold results in an income that gives a reasonable probability of escaping poverty, i.e., a probability higher than the average for urban employed persons aged 20 to 29 years in the respective country who work 20 or more hours per week (see table V.10). The data on the remuneration for such workers, expressed in per capita poverty lines, clearly shows that for those who did not reach the educational threshold, even additional years of schooling beyond the initial number will not give them much advantage in terms of income, since those years have a lower yield, from the income point of view, than in the case of persons who did complete the secondary cycle. In other words, for a person who enters the labour market without having completed secondary school, the fact of completing a few additional years (but still not completing the secondary cycle) does not have much influence on the remuneration received. The result, in most cases, is that such persons receive practically the same as employees with six years of schooling and thus have little possibility of escaping poverty. In contrast, income increases sharply when individuals who have already completed the secondary cycle of 11 or 12 years, depending on the country, subsequently add a few additional years of schooling (see table V.10).

(b) Labour income thresholds for attaining well-being

The first identifiable income threshold with regard to the possibility of attaining well-being is an income of 2.5 poverty lines. This minimum level allows the person who receives such an income to keep a family of

Table V.10
LATIN AMERICA: NUMBER OF YEARS OF SCHOOLING REQUIRED TO HAVE A
PROBABILITY OF AVOIDING POVERTY EQUAL TO OR GREATER THAN THE
AVERAGE IN EACH COUNTRY AMONG EMPLOYED PERSONS
AGED 20 TO 29 YEARS
(Percentages and multiples of the poverty line)

Country	Average poverty level of employed persons (%)	Minimum number of years of schooling	Average labour income (poverty lines)
Argentina, 1999	11.5	11	3.7
Bolivia, 1999	38.7	13	3.4
Brazil, 1999	22.5	8	3.0
Chile, 2000	10.1	12	4.1
Colombia, 1999	33.8	11	2.7
Costa Rica, 1999	7.5	10	4.4
Ecuador, 1999	51.4	12	2.4
El Salvador, 1999	25.6	10	2.9
Guatemala, 1998	34.0	9	1.9
Honduras, 1999	58.9	9	2.7
Mexico, 2000	22.5	10	3.3
Nicaragua, 1998	52.8	11	2.9
Panama, 1999	10.8	11	3.5
Paraguay, 1999	28.5	12	2.9
Peru, 1999	22.3	11	2.5
Dominican Republic, 1997	15.6	11	3.6
Uruguay, 1999	5.8	9	3.8
Venezuela, 1999 [a]	32.8	11	3.1

Source: ECLAC, on the basis of special tabulations of data from household surveys of the respective countries.

[a] National total.

two persons out of poverty. If both the head of household and his/her spouse are working, they can keep a family of up to four persons (i.e., with two dependants) out of poverty. If there is a third child, however, they will be on the verge of poverty or even below the poverty line.

An income equivalent to four poverty lines allows a greater degree of well-being. If there is only one breadwinner, a family of three dependent members can be kept out of poverty, and if both the head of household and his/her spouse work, they can support the costs of up to four persons who are not working.

(c)   Factors which affect the transmission of educational capital: the educational climate of the home

In order to analyse the educational opportunities of young people and the way in which they are transmitted from parents to children, a variable must be defined that measures the educational capital of the household of origin. This variable should reflect all the factors that affect the quality of the education and the number of years of schooling that individuals manage to accumulate, including the availability of economic resources and material infrastructure, the support received, the preparation for school, and the importance attached in that household to education as such and as a means of training.

There are various variables that make it possible to measure the educational capital of the household of origin. In the present study, a variable was selected which, in addition to reflecting the economic capacity of the household, is a good indicator of the educational climate. This was defined as the average number of years of schooling of the head of household and his/her spouse. In the case of households where the head does not have a spouse, the number of years declared by that person was used as the indicator. This indicator has the advantage of remaining relatively invariable throughout the period in which the children acquire their educational capital. It is also closely linked to the monetary income of the household, which makes it possible to take into account both the differences in educational assets between households of different social strata, as well as their differences in terms of economic resources (see table V.11).

On the basis of the average years of schooling of the parents, in households with children aged 20 to 24 years, four types of educational climate were distinguished, as shown in table V.11: very low (less than 6 years), low (from 6 to 10 years), medium (10 to 12) and high (13 or more years of schooling).

Table V.11
LATIN AMERICA: DISTRIBUTION OF HOUSEHOLDS WITH CHILDREN AGED 20 TO 24,
BY AVERAGE YEARS OF SCHOOLING OF THE PARENTS AND HOUSEHOLD INCOME
QUARTILES, BY GROUPS OF COUNTRIES [a]
(Percentages)

Simple average of urban households in Bolivia, El Salvador, Guatemala, Honduras,
Paraguay and Venezuela

Average years of schooling of the parents	Total	Income quartiles [b]			
		Quartile 1 (poorest)	Quartile 2	Quartile 3	Quartile 4 (richest)
0 to 5	50.6	74.1	62.1	46.8	19.5
6 to 9	28.6	20.6	28.2	34.2	29.4
10 to 12	9.3	4.4	5.5	10.7	18.3
13 or more	11.6	2.9	4.2	8.3	32.9
Total	100.0	100.0	100.0	100.0	100.0

Simple average of urban households in Brazil, Colombia, Costa Rica, Ecuador, Mexico,
Nicaragua and the Dominican Republic

Average years of schooling of the parents	Total	Income quartiles [b]			
		Quartile 1 (poorest)	Quartile 2	Quartile 3	Quartile 4 (richest)
0 to 5	45.8	65.1	56.3	44.2	18.4
6 to 9	29.8	29.0	31.3	33.9	24.5
10 to 12	11.5	4.4	8.8	13.7	18.3
13 or more	13.0	1.7	3.6	8.2	38.8
Total	100.0	100.0	100.0	100.0	100.0

Simple average of urban households in Argentina, Chile, Panama, Peru and Uruguay

Average years of schooling of the parents	Total	Income quartiles [b]			
		Quartile 1 (poorest)	Quartile 2	Quartile 3	Quartile 4 (richest)
0 to 5	24.5	41.4	28.8	19.0	7.0
6 to 9	39.7	46.4	47.2	42.7	17.4
10 to 12	20.5	9.6	18.8	25.3	29.7
13 or more	15.3	2.5	5.2	13.0	45.9
Total	100.0	100.0	100.0	100.0	100.0

Source: ECLAC, on the basis of special tabulations of data from household surveys of the respective
countries.

[a] The countries are grouped according to the gross enrolment ratio for the secondary cycle in the mid-
1990s.
[b] Per capita income of households.

(d)   Household surveys as tools for intergenerational analysis and selection of the appropriate age group for study

In order to examine the ways in which educational capital is transmitted from one generation to another, a link must to be established between the level of education of the children and that of their parents or other characteristics of their household. Household surveys offer this possibility, but the population group most appropriate for analysis must be selected. As it is a matter of examining the total number of years of schooling that young people of the current generation complete in relation to their social strata, it is important to select an age group that consists mostly of persons who have finished studying and therefore have completed the stock of educational capital that they will bring to their working life. As the age of the selected cohort increases, however, the proportion of young people who no longer live in the paternal home increases, and consequently this reduces the number of cases in which the education of the children can be compared with that of their parents. Of the three age groups in which the population aged 15 to 29 is divided, the cohort of 20 to 24 years is the most appropriate for analysis, since it includes a high proportion of young people who live in the paternal home and a low percentage of young people who are still in the educational system. Table V.12 summarizes the information on these three groups in the urban areas of 18 countries.

Young people who stay longer in the paternal home have more opportunities to increase their educational capital. In the group aged 20 to 24 years, the rate of school attendance is higher among young people who live with their parents (37%) than among other young people (18%). This last group stops studying earlier and, on average, accumulates fewer years of education. This circumstance introduces a selection bias in the analysis, as, generally speaking, young people who stay longer in the paternal home attain a higher level of education than the others, amounting to a difference of one to two years. This bias, however, does not change the conclusions with regard to the intergenerational transmission of inequality of opportunities. Apart from the fact that young people who do not live with their parents are a smaller fraction of the total cohort (around 41%), leaving the home early is more frequent in households with a lower level of education (see table V.13).

Table V.12
LATIN AMERICA (18 COUNTRIES): YOUNG PEOPLE WHO LIVE IN THE PATERNAL
HOME AND YOUNG PEOPLE WHO STUDY, URBAN AREAS
(Percentages)

	Young people who live in the paternal home					Young people who study			
	Total	Age groups				Total	Age groups		
		15-19 years	20-24 years	25-29 years				15-19 years	20-24 years	25-29 years
Minimum value	51	69	50	25	Minimum value	26	47	14	8
Average [a]	59	78	59	36	Average [a]	37	64	29	13
Maximum value	67	90	69	45	Maximum value	51	77	43	24

Source: ECLAC, on the basis of special tabulations of data from household surveys of the respective countries.

[a] Simple average of 18 countries.

Table V.13
LATIN AMERICA: YOUNG PEOPLE AGED 20 TO 24 YEARS WHO ARE STUDYING AND
THEIR AVERAGE NUMBER OF YEARS OF SCHOOLING

	Percentage of young people aged 20 to 24 years who are studying				Average number of years of schooling of young people aged 20 to 24 years		
	Total	Residence			Total	Residence	
		In the paternal home	Not in the paternal home			In the paternal home	Not in the paternal home
Minimum value	14	17	9	Minimum value	8.1	8.5	7.2
Average [a]	29	37	18	Average [a]	9.9	10.5	9
Maximum value	43	54	33	Maximum value	11.7	12	11.1

Source: ECLAC, on the basis of special tabulations of data from household surveys of the respective countries.

[a] Simple average of 18 countries.

(e)   A methodological approach to intergenerational educational betterment

The term "intergenerational educational betterment" refers to the situation of young people who surpass the average level of education of their parents, taking into account the devaluation of education. The average educational level of the parents is calculated on the basis of the number of years of schooling completed by the head of household and his/her spouse. In single-parent households, the average corresponds to the educational level of the head of household.

The concept of the devaluation of education takes into account the fact that as educational coverage increases, more years of schooling are needed in order to command the same type of job and the same level of income. The devaluation of education over the 25 to 30 years which, on average, separate one generation from another has been calculated on the basis of the functions linking occupational categories and the corresponding incomes with different levels of education among employed persons in 1990 and 1999. It was concluded that the rate of devaluation was lower at higher educational levels, so that the higher the educational level of the parents, the fewer the years of additional schooling required to surpass their income level.

The foregoing means that there is intergenerational educational betterment in the case of young people aged 20 to 24 years who, on leaving school, have surpassed the average educational level of their parents by:

(i)   7 or more years when the parents had less than 3 years of schooling;

(ii) 6 or more years when the parents had from 3 to 5 years of schooling;

(iii) 5 or more years when the parents had from 5 to 7 years of schooling;

(iv) 4 or more years when the parents had from 7 to 10 years of schooling;

(v)   3 or more years when the parents had from 10 to 11 years of schooling;

(vi) 2 or more years when the parents had from 11 to 13 years of schooling;

(vii) 1 or more years when the parents had 13 or more years of schooling.

In the case of young people who continued studying, two groups were distinguished: young people aged 20 to 22 years and young people aged 23 and 24 years. On the basis of the observations made, it was estimated for the first group that if the parents had less than 10 years of education, their children would complete another year, and if they had ten years or more of education, the young people would add another two. In the second group it was estimated that young people would add only one more year in all cases.

In short, if the young person was not studying, the years of schooling completed were considered, while if the person was studying, one or two years would be added according to his age and the education of the parents. It was considered that there was no intergenerational educational betterment in the case of young people who did not surpass the average educational level of their parents, taking educational devaluation into account.

The situations of educational betterment or non-betterment in comparison with the parents were classified in turn according to whether the young person did or did not have 12 or more years of schooling, which is the basic educational capital required to have a good chance of access to well-paid occupations.

(f)   Occupational category and well-being opportunities

The grouping of occupations into eight categories gives a general picture of the occupational structure and a good classification of the different levels of well-being associated with that structure. In this case, the occupational classification adopted was that used by each country for the household surveys, which in general is a variation of the International Standard Classification of Occupations (ISCO). Initially, the categories corresponding to the two- or three-digit level of ISCO were considered.

The "professionals and technicians" group includes all university and technical professions, whether of higher or intermediate level. The "managers" group includes both political posts and entrepreneurs in the public and private sector, as well as department heads, area managers and others. The "administrative employees and accountants" category also covers secretarial activities. "Salespersons and shop assistants" is for all occupations related to sales, both in the commercial sector and in services. The "industrial, transport and warehouse workers" category includes factory hands and labourers in the relevant sectors. Construction workers form a special group. The "domestic employees, waiters and security staff" category includes all occupations in the services sector that require little or no training. "Agricultural workers" includes all occupations that depend on the agricultural sector.

The "occupations that provide an adequate level of well-being" category groups together "professionals and technicians" and "managers", whose average monthly income, in the majority of the countries analysed, is between five and ten poverty lines, in both urban and rural areas. The average monthly income of the second group, "occupations that provide an intermediate level of well-being", is from 2.5 to 5.5 poverty lines. This group includes the categories "administrative employees and accountants" and "salespersons and shop assistants". The third group, which covers all the remaining categories, is "occupations that provide an inadequate level of well-being", as the corresponding average monthly income in the majority of the countries studied is between 1.5 and 4 poverty lines.

Chapter VI

Social expenditure in Latin America

1.   Trends in public social spending during the 1990s

Social spending rose considerably during the 1990s. In most of the countries, the per capita amount of resources allocated to the social sectors increased as a result of economic reactivation, increased budgetary pressure and the higher fiscal priority assigned to social expenditure (percentage of total public spending devoted to the social sectors), which in turn raised its macroeconomic priority (percentage of GDP earmarked for social sector spending).[1] In fact, in the 17 countries of the region as a whole, per capita public spending between the 1990-1991 and 1998-1999 bienniums rose on average by about 50%. Thus, from an average of US$ 360 per capita at the start of the decade, social expenditure climbed to US$ 540 per capita per annum by the end of it.[2]

Social expenditure increased throughout the region, falling in real terms in only two countries, Honduras and Venezuela (see table A.16 of the statistical annex). The increases were not uniform throughout the region, however, and tended to be greater in countries with moderate or low levels of per capita social expenditure. Thus it rose by over 100% in Colombia, Guatemala, Paraguay, Peru and the Dominican Republic,

---

[1]   In the analysis of public expenditure, "social sectors" does not refer to social classes or groups but rather to health, welfare, social security, housing, etc.

[2]   Refers to the simple average of the figures for all countries. Per capita social expenditure is expressed in 1997 dollars.

whereas in countries with relatively high levels of spending (Argentina, Brazil, Costa Rica and Panama), the increases were somewhat smaller, amounting to between 20% and 40% compared with the start of the decade.

In most of the countries, social spending rose more steeply during the first half of the decade and, although it continued to climb in the second half, it did so more slowly. Between 1990-1991 and 1994-1995, per capita expenditure in Latin America as a whole rose by 30%, whereas the increase between 1994-1995 and 1998-1999 was only 16%. This trend was closely related to economic growth trends in the region during the 1990s, since the annual growth rate of Latin America was 4.1% of GDP up to 1995 but then dropped to 2.5% in the second half of the decade. This indicates the existence of a strong linkage between the amount of resources that each country is able to allocate to social sectors and the level and growth rate of its GDP (see figures VI.1 and VI.2).

Figure VI.1
LATIN AMERICA (17 COUNTRIES): PUBLIC SOCIAL EXPENDITURE PER CAPITA IN
THE TWO-YEAR PERIODS 1990-1991 AND 1998-1999
(1997 dollars)

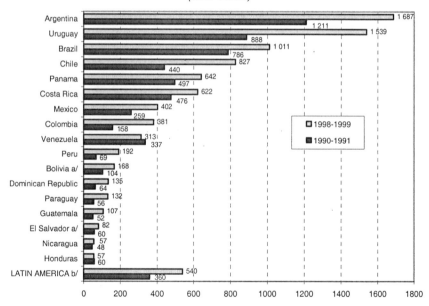

Source: ECLAC, Social Development Division, social expenditure database.
[a] First figure corresponds to average for two-year period 1994-1995.
[b] Simple average of the countries, excluding Bolivia and El Salvador.

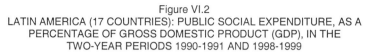

Figure VI.2
LATIN AMERICA (17 COUNTRIES): PUBLIC SOCIAL EXPENDITURE, AS A
PERCENTAGE OF GROSS DOMESTIC PRODUCT (GDP), IN THE
TWO-YEAR PERIODS 1990-1991 AND 1998-1999

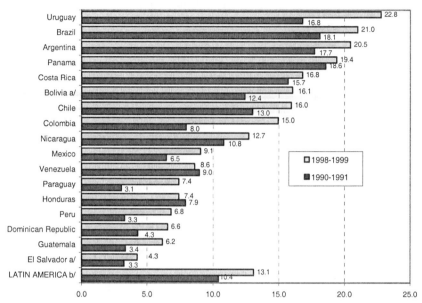

Source: ECLAC, Social Development Division, social expenditure database.

[a] First figure corresponds to average for two-year period 1994-1995.
[b] Simple average of the countries, excluding Bolivia and El Salvador.

The increase in social spending in the 1990s was not only due to economic growth, however. It was also associated with an increasing effort on the part of these countries to raise spending levels by boosting government revenues and allocating a larger portion of them to the social sectors. The fiscal priority of social spending in the region as a whole thus climbed from nearly 42% to almost 48% of total public expenditure. This trend was general throughout the region; the share of public spending earmarked for social purposes fell only in Honduras and, to a lesser extent, in Panama.

The combined effect of these two factors, i.e., the increased budgetary pressure (the percentage of GDP represented by public spending) and the decision to assign greater fiscal priority to social expenditure (the percentage of total public expenditure allocated to the social sectors) was reflected in a substantial increase in the share of GDP allocated to public social spending (macroeconomic priority). In the region as a whole, this share rose from 10.4% to 13.1% between 1990-1991 and 1998-1999 (se table A.17 of the statistical annex). It should be noted that between 1996-1997 and 1998-1999, the share of social spending continued to climb in most countries of the region, thanks to their efforts to keep up their pre-crisis levels of social expenditure. However, that trend can also be explained by the delayed effect of budgetary adjustments made necessary by declines in the product and, hence, in public revenues.

Although 12 countries substantially increased the macroeconomic priority of social expenditure, and several of them had low spending levels, the differences between the 17 countries analysed did not diminish very much, and the considerable disparities that existed in this respect at the start of the decade persisted. These differences are due to two factors: On the one hand, the social security component of spending is considered a higher good, and its relative weight increases as a country's per capita income rises (see figure VI.3a), owing to the extension of coverage provided by social security systems, which is associated with the relative size of the older adult population. The other factor is that a very high percentage of the meagre revenues received by the State in some countries is used for general purposes (government, defence and justice) and to meet the country's basic economic needs.

As shown in figure VI.3b, there was no significant change in the regional situation as regards the countries' efforts to allocate resources to the social sectors as a function of their per capita income levels. Thus, one group of countries, which includes those with the highest per capita social expenditure levels (Argentina, Brazil, Costa Rica, Panama and Uruguay), continued to allocate a larger percentage of their GDP to social sectors than would be expected from the regional pattern. Only Bolivia and Nicaragua spent more than would be expected given their income levels. The group of countries with low or very low levels of per capita social expenditure tend to devote a much smaller share of their GDP to social sectors than the regional average. The exception is Colombia, which more than doubled its per capita social expenditure between 1992-1993 and 1996-1997, thereby greatly increasing its macroeconomic priority and progressing from being one of the countries with spending levels far below the regional average to one of the countries that exceeds it.

Figure VI.3a
LATIN AMERICA: SOCIAL EXPENDITURE ON SOCIAL SECURITY,[a] (AS A PERCENTAGE OF GROSS DOMESTIC PRODUCT (GDP)), AS A FUNCTION OF PER CAPITA GDP

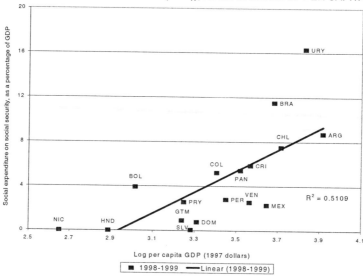

Source: ECLAC, Social Development Division, social expenditure database.

[a] Corresponds to fiscal contribution to this sector and not to the total resources administered by the public social security system.

Figure VI.3b
LATIN AMERICA: SOCIAL EXPENDITURE (AS A PERCENTAGE OF GROSS DOMESTIC PRODUCT (GDP)), AS A FUNCTION OF PER CAPITA GDP

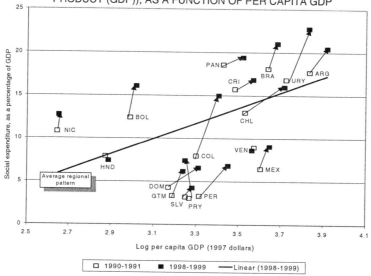

Source: ECLAC, Social Development Division, social expenditure database.

Even though social expenditure rose considerably during the decade, the per capita levels of resources earmarked for social spending are still very low compared with international levels, so most countries therefore still have a great deal of room for expanding their public revenue base and redirecting expenditure to social purposes Around the mid-1990s, public spending as a share of GDP in the Latin American countries was around nine percentage points below the level corresponding to their GDP level, thus limiting the ability of States to promote redistributive policies through social expenditure.[3] It appears that for all the countries in the region there is room to raise expenditure from 3.5 to 4.5 percentage points of GDP simply by increasing public resources, since social expenditure typically represents between 40% and 50% of total public spending.

Bearing in mind the factors that account for the growth of per capita social expenditure (GDP growth, increased budgetary pressure and greater priority assigned to social sectors in the fiscal budget), it may be concluded that during the decade there was an increase in the macroeconomic priority of social expenditure with respect to GDP growth (see figure VI.4). Of the total increase in per capita social spending of around US$ 196 between 1990 and 1999, US$ 81 was attributable to economic growth, US$ 42 to higher budgetary pressure and US$ 73 to increased fiscal priority.

In order to overcome poverty and inequality in the region, the countries will need to give high priority to social expenditure, which must be viewed in all its complexity as an important component of public spending to which explicit criteria aimed at achieving greater equity must be applied. Thus, priority areas of social investment must be identified with a view to breaking the cycles that perpetuate inequality.

---

[3]   See IDB, 1998, p. 200. The low level of public spending in relation to GDP is in turn associated with the fact that the taxation levels of several countries in the region are also below international standards and even well below those applying to the English-speaking Caribbean. According to estimates by ECLAC (1998b), which concur with those of other organizations such as the Inter-American Development Bank (IDB), tax revenue as a percentage of GDP is some 6 percentage points below the level that should apply according to the countries' standard of development.

Figure VI.4
LATIN AMERICA: FACTORS IN GROWTH OF PUBLIC SOCIAL EXPENDITURE
PER CAPITA, 1990-1999

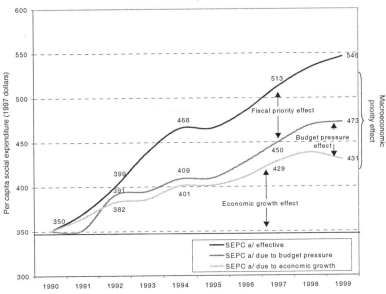

Source: ECLAC, Social Development Division, social expenditure database.

[a] SEPC: social expenditure per capita.

2.   Impact of the crisis on social expenditure

When economic growth was strong, most of the Latin American countries managed to increase social expenditure, both as a share of the public budget and as a percentage of GDP. Likewise, thanks to the measures taken by a number of countries to protect it, social expenditure did not decline as a result of the economic slowdown of the late 1990s or the subsequent period of reduced flexibility of the public budget.

Analyses of trends in the allocation of resources to the social sectors have often focused on variations in social expenditure with respect to fluctuations in the government budget. Since the total amount of public resources tends to vary in line with countries' GDP levels, social expenditure in the Latin American countries has usually followed trends in the macroeconomic cycle, falling during slowdowns and rising during upturns in economic growth. This behaviour is termed procyclical, as opposed to countercyclical behaviour, when social expenditure is increased in years of economic recession and lower government revenues in order to counter the decline in the living conditions of the population, especially its most vulnerable sectors.

(a) Patterns of public social spending in situations of highly unstable growth

The increasingly unstable nature of economic growth makes it even more important to ensure the financing of social protection networks (ECLAC, 1998b). The region was indeed marked by macroeconomic vulnerability during the 1990s as sizeable current-account deficits were often financed with volatile capital. This was reflected in short cycles of growth and of adjustment, in line with the behaviour of that capital.[4] In addition, there was the impact of the various international crises on the economies, and especially on the public finances.

Figures VI.5a to VI.5d show the sequence of episodes of variation in the social expenditure, public spending and gross domestic product of 17 Latin American countries during the 1990s.

Figure VI.5a shows how public spending tended to co-vary closely with GDP: the vast majority of the episodes of economic growth were accompanied by an increase in budgetary resources, and those increases were usually greater than the increases in the product. Nevertheless, during the decade there were also episodes of moderate increases in the product which were accompanied by absolute reductions in public sector financial resources, and in some cases, those reductions were greater than the relevant increases in GDP. At the same time, there were also situations where moderate drops in the product were not accompanied by a decline in public spending.

The question arises as to whether, in cases where total public resources rose, the situations that tended to predominate were those in which social expenditure was maintained or increased, i.e., whether or not there was a propensity to give higher priority to the social components. As shown in figure VI.5b, not only did social expenditure rise when the government budget increased, but also, in a very high percentage of cases, the resources allocated to social components rose at a higher rate. This indicates that there was indeed a tendency to prioritize social expenditure. In many countries, justification by the government of the need to raise social expenditure was enough to gain acceptance for increased budgetary pressure. It is interesting to note that this also occurs even when social security is excluded from social expenditure; thus, the

---

[4]   One indication of the increasing volatility of economic growth in the region may be seen from a comparison of the variability coefficients of annual GDP growth rates: this coefficient was 0.71 during the 1990-1997 period but 1.1 between 1990 and 1999 (ECLAC, 2000c).

higher priority given to social expenditure seems to have worked more to the benefit of the middle- and low-income sectors, even though social security was the spending component that grew most during the past decade, as we shall see in section 3 below.

Figure VI.5a
LATIN AMERICA (17 COUNTRIES): PERCENTAGE VARIATIONS IN TOTAL
PUBLIC EXPENDITURE AND THE GROSS DOMESTIC PRODUCT
OVER THE 1990-1999 PERIOD

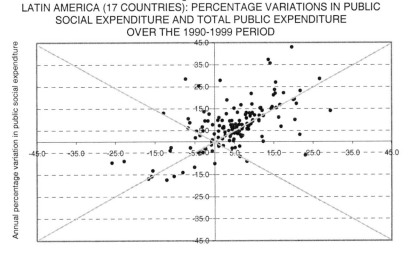

Annual percentage variation in gross domestic product

Source: ECLAC, Social Development Division, social expenditure database.

Figure VI.5b
LATIN AMERICA (17 COUNTRIES): PERCENTAGE VARIATIONS IN PUBLIC
SOCIAL EXPENDITURE AND TOTAL PUBLIC EXPENDITURE
OVER THE 1990-1999 PERIOD

Annual percentage variation in total public expenditure

Source: ECLAC, Social Development Division, social expenditure database.

Figure VI.5c
LATIN AMERICA (17 COUNTRIES): PERCENTAGE VARIATIONS IN PUBLIC
SOCIAL EXPENDITURE (EXCLUDING SOCIAL SECURITY) AND TOTAL
PUBLIC EXPENDITURE OVER THE 1990-1999 PERIOD

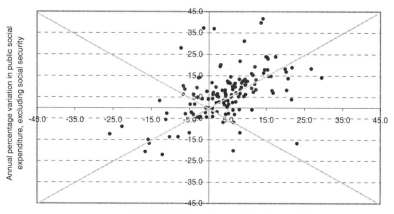

Annual percentage variation in total public expenditure

Source: ECLAC, Social Development Division, social expenditure database.

Figure VI.5d
LATIN AMERICA (17 COUNTRIES): PERCENTAGE VARIATIONS IN PUBLIC
SOCIAL EXPENDITURE AND THE GROSS DOMESTIC PRODUCT
OVER THE 1990-1999 PERIOD

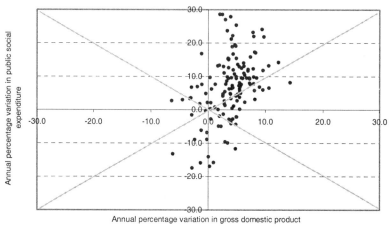

Annual percentage variation in gross domestic product

Source: ECLAC, Social Development Division, social expenditure database.

In short, in a decade when episodes of economic growth prevailed, social expenditure rose, and it usually did so faster than GDP (see figure VI.5d). This tendency to give greater priority to the social sectors is not sufficient in itself, however, to give a full idea of the redistributive effect of social expenditure.

(b) Patterns of social expenditure during the recession of the late 1990s

In order to analyse the behaviour of social expenditure in relation to trends in total public spending during the late-1990s recession, six countries in which GDP contracted in 1999 were selected, namely, Argentina, Chile, Colombia, Honduras, Uruguay and Venezuela. In all these countries, the fall in the product followed a period of growth, making them suitable subjects for an analysis of the behaviour and vulnerability of social expenditure.

Analysis of the trends in total public spending and public social expenditure in a context of declining GDP in those countries shows that allocations to social sectors were shielded, partly because of the inertia of many of the current expenditure items within social expenditure, such as fiscal contributions to social security, which had been increasing,. This offset the procyclical tendency of expenditure items which were more dependent on the volume of budgetary resources (see figure VI.6). In all of these countries except Venezuela, total public spending rose in 1998-1999 despite the decrease in GDP.

Argentina, Chile and Uruguay clearly decided to reallocate resources to benefit the social sectors, albeit with some important differences in each case. In Argentina, although more resources were allocated to social sectors, this measure worked more to the benefit of the poorest strata in the 1998-1999 biennium, whereas in the following period (1999-2000), the greatest increase was in the social security component, which is the largest element in social spending in the country. In consolidated national expenditure (including the national public administration, Buenos Aires and provincial governments, and local governments), the increased priority assigned to the social components prevented the decline in GDP from being reflected in a fall in per capita social expenditure. In Chile, both total social expenditure and social expenditure excluding social security rose at similar rates, although the rates of increase were slightly lower during the budget year 2000 compared with the previous year. In Uruguay, up to 1999 there was clear protection of social expenditure, both including and excluding social security, since both aggregates showed similar levels of increase in the 1998-1999 biennium, despite a context of zero growth in public spending.

Figure VI.6
LATIN AMERICA: EVOLUTION OF THE GROSS DOMESTIC PRODUCT, TOTAL
PUBLIC EXPENDITURE, PUBLIC SOCIAL EXPENDITURE, AND PUBLIC
SOCIAL EXPENDITURE EXCLUDING SOCIAL SECURITY
OVER THE 1996-2000 PERIOD
(Percentages; indexes: 1996 = 100)

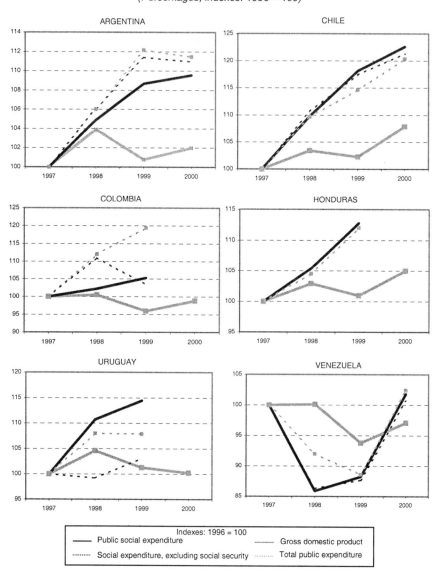

Source: ECLAC, Social Development Division, social expenditure database.

Note: The sectoral information available in Honduras does not record expenditure on social security.

The case of Colombia is a special one, since the fall in expenditure (excluding social security) nevertheless did not mean that fewer resources were allocated to the components that mostly benefit the middle- and low-income strata, which usually suffer the most during periods of slower growth. This was due to the extension of social security coverage and of the health and welfare benefits included in it, which are areas that mainly benefit poor strata. Social security spending was the component that grew the most in real terms between 1998 and 1999, so that social expenditure overall rose at a much higher rate than that of total public spending, despite the fall in GDP in those two years.

Honduras is an example of spending patterns in countries that allocate a relatively small share of their resources to the social sectors. In this country, social expenditure —which does not have a significant social security component there —and public spending rose at relatively high rates before and during the 1999 recession. However, that inertia was due not so much to an explicit policy of protection as to the impact of resources from international aid that are channeled through the government budget.

Finally, what stands out in the case of Venezuela is the instability of its growth and hence of the volume of public resources, including those that are allocated to social sectors. The substantial rise in public spending and social expenditure in 1996 and 1997, both including and excluding social security, stems from the reactivation brought about by the growth of the product following the sharp downturn of 1996. Nevertheless, the pattern of social expenditure in 1998-1999 indicates that an effort was definitely made to protect the resources earmarked for social purposes, since during that same period, total budgetary resources fell as a result of the contraction of GDP. In 1999 and 2000, however, all the components of public spending began to rise again at virtually the same rate (around 15%).

3.   Sectoral trends in social expenditure and their impact on income distribution

During the 1990s, increases in social expenditure had a relatively greater redistributive effect in countries with lower per capita income levels, because of the relatively greater increase in public spending on education and health. In contrast, the redistributive effect was less pronounced in countries with higher per capita income levels, because approximately 50% of the increase in public social expenditure went to social security: its least progressive component in terms of redistribution.

This section provides some background on the impact that public social expenditure has had on the distribution of income of Latin American households. For that purpose, a summary is first given of the results of a series of studies on eight countries in order to assess the impact of public spending on the social sectors on different population strata. Secondly, sectoral trends during the decade are analysed in order to determine whether or not the increase in public social spending has had a leveling-out effect on income distribution.

(a) The redistributive effect of the various social expenditure components

The available data show marked differences in the distributive progressiveness of the different components of public social expenditure. The data on the share of expenditure received by households in each income distribution quintile are summarized in table A.18 of the statistical annex.[5] As may be seen from the table, the most progressive types of expenditure —those that provide relatively greater benefits to the poorest households— are spending on primary and secondary education, followed by spending on health care and nutrition and then by spending on housing and basic services (water and sanitation). These data confirm that expenditure on primary education continues to be the most progressive item and has the greatest levelling-out effect on income distribution (see figure VI.7). It should be noted that, in contrast to the findings of similar studies conducted in the 1970s and early 1980s, expenditure on secondary education seems to have a fairly strong progressive impact, similar to that of spending on health and nutrition. This difference may be accounted for by the notable expansion in the coverage of secondary education since that time (ECLAC, 2000d, Chapter V), especially over the last twenty years. That led to very significant increases in secondary-school enrolment ratios, which have been of proportionally more benefit to young people from middle- and low-income strata.

Expenditures on social security and university education are the least progressive components of public spending, especially the latter. This reflects the fact that medium- and low-income strata still have difficulty in gaining access to this level of education.

---

[5]   Two indices of the progressiveness of this expenditure are also shown: the Gini coefficient and an index comparing the share of total expenditure on each item that goes to households in the 40% lowest-income bracket with the share of primary income they obtain (see section (c) of the methodological annex).

Figure VI.7
LATIN AMERICA: DISTRIBUTION OF PRIMARY INCOME AND OF EXPENDITURE ON
PRIMARY, SECONDARY AND TERTIARY EDUCATION,
BY HOUSEHOLD QUINTILES [a]

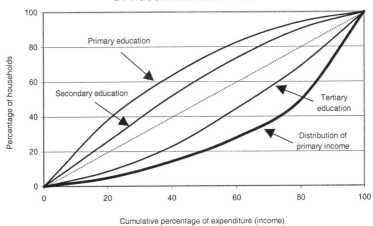

Cumulative percentage of expenditure (income)

Source: ECLAC, on the basis of country studies.

[a] Simple average of the data for eight countries: Argentina, Bolivia, Brazil, Chile, Colombia, Costa Rica, Ecuador and Uruguay.

Expenditures on housing, which show an intermediate degree of progressiveness, follow a rather uneven pattern in the countries examined. This is due to the marked differences among programmes and in the extent to which households in the 40% lowest-income category have access to them.

Taken as a whole, social expenditure was highly redistributive in all the countries and even more so if spending on social security is excluded from the figures (see figure VI.8). If social security is excluded, then the 20% of households having the lowest incomes receive 28% of total public revenues, while the richest 20% of households only receive 12% of those resources. These differences are evident when these figures are compared with those relating to the distribution of households' primary income, i.e., income not including monetary transfers from the State and social expenditure benefits. This means that —not counting expenditure on social security— the poorest 20% of households receive, on average, a portion of the funds devoted to social expenditure that is six times greater than their share of primary income (28.2% of funds devoted to social expenditure, versus 4.8% of total primary income). For the richest 20% of households, this ratio is inverted, with the percentage of social expenditure they receive representing just only a quarter of their share in total income (12.4% of social expenditure versus 50.7% of total primary income).

Figure VI.8
LATIN AMERICA: DISTRIBUTION OF PRIMARY INCOME, TOTAL INCOME AND
SOCIAL EXPENDITURE, BY HOUSEHOLD QUINTILES [a]

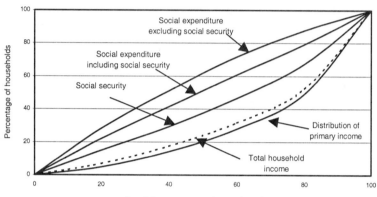

Cumulative percentage of expenditure (income)

Source: ECLAC, on the basis of country studies.

[a] Simple average of the data for eight countries: Argentina, Bolivia, Brazil, Chile, Colombia, Costa Rica, Ecuador and Uruguay.

The same pattern in terms of the progressiveness of spending may be observed from the Gini coefficient values. With few exceptions, the Gini coefficient for spending on tertiary education and social security, unlike the other spending components, shows positive values in all the countries, albeit lower than the coefficient for primary income distribution (see table A.18 of the statistical annex). The fact that the Gini coefficient for certain specific items of expenditure is greater than zero does not mean that the expenditure has a net regressive impact on the final distribution of household income, however. For its effect to be progressive, the value of the Gini coefficient must be lower than that for the distribution of autonomous income. As shown in figure VI.8, all the components of social expenditure are progressive in relation to primary income distribution, albeit to different degrees.

The countries analysed differ considerably in terms of their targeting of social expenditure (other than social security). Chile and Colombia have been making efforts to concentrate the benefits of social programmes in the lower-income strata. Both countries show the highest degree of targeting of expenditure on the poorest 40% of households in comparison with the share of income they receive, the indices being 4.9 for Chile and 4.2 for Colombia (see table A.18 of the statistical annex). Costa Rica and Uruguay have the lowest levels of relative targeting, with indices of 2.6 and 2.9 respectively. Policies in both countries have been focused on greater distribution of primary income and the implementation of social programmes that benefit a high percentage of all households to similar degrees. Argentina, Bolivia and Ecuador show intermediate levels of progressiveness of social expenditure, with targeting indices for the poorest 40% of 3.7, 3.8 and 3.5, respectively.

The net redistributive effect of public social expenditure is shown in figure VI.9, where estimates of the sectoral distribution of subsidies are combined with data on the size of the subsidies to determine how much of total household income in each stratum corresponds to monetary transfers and the transfer of goods and services free of charge or at subsidized prices. Figure VI.9 shows that this percentage is much higher in the lower-income strata, where it amounts to 43%, whereas in the upper-income sectors (the fourth and fifth quintiles) the figures are 13% and 7% respectively. If social security (mainly retirement and other pensions) is deducted, the reduction in the effect of social expenditure is much smaller in the case of the poorest strata; in the highest stratum, more than 60% of the transfers correspond to social security, whereas in the poorest quintile they represent only about 25% of the total. It should be noted that, despite the low impact of social expenditure on the incomes of the richest stratum, the actual sums that those households receive are quite high. In fact, in several of the countries analysed, these transfers are close to or even greater than the amount that goes to the poorest households. This is due to the substantial size of social security transfers. It should be emphasized that the aforementioned figures do not represent the net redistributive action of the State, since they do not take into account the funding of social expenditure from tax revenues.

The significant redistributive effect of all items of social expenditure, excluding social security, is clearly shown in figure VI.8, in which the Lorenz curves for spending, with and without social security, are compared with the curve for primary income distribution and the curve for total household income. In all of the eight countries on which information is available, the expenditure and income-distribution curves follow the same pattern.

Figure VI.9
**LATIN AMERICA (8 COUNTRIES): REDISTRIBUTIVE IMPACT OF SOCIAL
EXPENDITURE (EXCLUDING SOCIAL SECURITY) AND OF SOCIAL
SECURITY ON HOUSEHOLD INCOME**
(Total amount of income = 100)

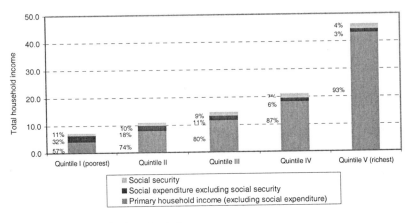

Source: ECLAC, on the basis of country studies.

(b)   Sectoral trends in social expenditure between 1990 and 1999

In considering the different redistributive effects of individual components of public social expenditure in the countries, it is important to ascertain whether or not the substantial increase in per capita social expenditure during the 1990s was directed towards its more progressive components. For the region as a whole, approximately 44% of the growth in spending went to education and health (28% and 16% respectively); 51% to social security, mainly retirement and other pensions; and the remaining 9% to other expenditures, such as housing, drinking water and sanitation. These variations seem to indicate that, in the region as a whole, the increase in spending was accounted for to similar degrees by the most and the least progressive social sectors.

The effect on equity was not uniform in all the countries. In countries with lower per capita income levels, spending increases were relatively greater in the more progressive components (education and health), which accounted for 56% of the total, while social security represented only 20%. In countries where expenditure was highest, in contrast, social security accounted for around half of the total increase.

The substantial increase in spending on education was linked to the implementation of reform programmes, especially at the primary and secondary levels, designed to improve quality and equity in education.

These reforms included teacher training and salary increases, the cost of which had a significant impact on the sector's budget. The rise in current and capital expenditure items also contributed to this increase, especially in those countries which decided to improve their physical and technological infrastructure, update teaching methods and materials and establish systems for measuring educational output.

As regards trends in expenditure on health, the greatest progress was registered in Argentina, Chile and Colombia, where the increase was between US$ 76 and US$ 109 per capita: i.e., much higher than the US$ 28 by which the regional average rose.

Finally, the biggest increases in spending on social security occurred precisely in those countries where that component already receives a higher share of public resources (Argentina, Brazil, Chile and Uruguay). In Argentina, Brazil and Chile, the increase ranged between US$ 150 and US$ 200 per capita, while in Uruguay it was just over US$ 500. These increases stem from adjustments in retirement and other pensions, especially in Uruguay, where four-monthly adjustments were introduced in accordance with a constitutional amendment adopted in 1989. Other factors involved in these increases were the acknowledgement and amortization of liabilities accumulated by the system and increases in the coverage and amount of benefits provided.

The trends discussed above indicate that the increased efforts of the countries which allocate a lower share of GDP to the social sectors had a positive effect on the distribution of well-being, which was more marked in these countries than in those with the highest per capita social expenditure levels, in which social security, which mostly benefits the middle- and high-income strata, accounts for a much larger share of public resources.

In conclusion: bearing in mind the importance of the distributive effect of social expenditure, there is a need to: (i) intensify efforts to increase social expenditure, given that its level is quite low in the majority of the countries of the region; (ii) stabilize its financing, in order to forestall the serious adverse effects of spending cuts during economic downturns, and (iii) target public social expenditure more accurately, especially in the case of programmes aimed at vulnerable or poor groups, by reallocating the available funds to those components which have the most impact. In short, efforts should be made to maintain or increase resources, manage them more efficiently, and ensure that the programmes they finance have the desired effect on the population they are intended to benefit.

Methodological annex

(a)   Sources of statistics on total public spending and social expenditure

The methodologies used, and especially the coverage of statistical series on total public spending and on social expenditure, vary throughout the region. The main differences in methodology have to do with how expenditure is recorded in the accounts and how social expenditure is defined. As regards coverage, the disparities have to do with the different characteristics of public institutions and whether or not spending by local governments is included.

Public spending can be broken down into different levels according to the different entities that implement it. A first distinction is between public spending by the financial public sector (FPS), i.e. the Central Bank and other State-owned financial institutions, and public expenditure by the non-financial public sector (NFPS), which is made up of the central government (CG), public enterprises (PE) and local government (LG).

In 11 of the 17 countries analysed, the series refer to central government expenditure. Within this category, a distinction may be made between entities that manage their own budgets (autonomous entities (AE)) and entities that are funded directly by the Treasury (central government budget (CGB)). In one country, coverage relates to general government expenditure (GG), which comprises CG and LG.

The following is a classification of countries according to the institutions covered by social expenditure series:

Institutions covered	Countries
NFPS = CG + PE + LG	Argentina, Brazil, Colombia, Costa Rica, Panama
GG = CG + LG	Bolivia
CG = CGB + AE	Chile, El Salvador, Guatemala, Honduras, Peru, Dominican Republic, Uruguay and Venezuela
CGB	Mexico, Nicaragua and Paraguay

Bearing in mind the accounting definitions applied to the series for these 17 countries and the way in which social expenditure is funded and executed in each of them, the figures can be regarded as reasonably comparable for 16 of the countries. In the case of Mexico, however, the fact that social expenditure at the local level is not included and that there is a degree of decentralization in its funding leads to some degree of underestimation of public social spending, and this limits the comparability of the figures with those for the other countries.

The indicators of priority (social expenditure/GDP and social expenditure/total public spending) are ratios calculated using the current-price figures for each year. Per capita social expenditure in 1997 dollars was estimated on the basis of total social expenditure at current prices. To express it in constant 1997 dollars, the implicit GDP deflator and the average exchange rate for that year were used.

The data in current prices on total public spending and social expenditure, as well as the sectoral breakdown of social expenditure, are official figures provided by the relevant public institutions of each country. GDP at current prices and the implicit GDP deflator are also official figures obtained from the ECLAC Annual Statistics Data Bank (BADEANU). The exchange rate used corresponds to the 1997 average of the "rf" series, taken from International Financial Statistics, published by the International Monetary Fund (IMF). The population figures are derived from projections prepared by the Population Division of the Latin American and Caribbean Demographic Centre (CELADE) and published in its Demographic Bulletin.

(b)   A model for analysing the behaviour of public social spending

One way of summarizing the behaviour of social expenditure in different macroeconomic scenarios is to estimate the elasticity of social expenditure in relation to GDP, i.e., the extent to which social expenditure increases or decreases with a rise or fall in GDP. This parameter (ε) can be estimated by taking as reference points the different episodes shown as dots on figure VI.10 below, which represent variations, in consecutive years, in the total government budget and total social expenditure for each of the 17 countries and for bienniums for which data were available.

The parameter ε can be estimated with the following formula:

$$\frac{SE_{t+1}}{SE_t} = \alpha \left(\frac{GDP_{t+1}}{GDP_t} \right)^{\varepsilon}$$

where SE_{t+1} and SE_t represent social expenditure in consecutive years, and GDP_{t+1} and GDP_t represent the gross domestic product.

With logarithms, the following equation is obtained:

$$\log SE_{t+1} - \log SE_t = \alpha' + \varepsilon(\log GDP_{t+1} - \log GDP_t) + e_t$$

where α' is the logarithm of α, ε is the elasticity of social expenditure in relation to GDP, and e is the estimation error.[6]

Estimation of ε for the 141 episodes observed between 1990 and 2000 produced a value of $\varepsilon = 1.147$, a highly significant parameter ($t = 6.16$), with a value of adjusted $R^2 = 0.206$ and $\alpha' = 0.0175$ (with an antilogarithm of 1.018). The estimation of this elasticity for the episodes in which public spending rose —the most frequent situation during the decade (121 out of 141 episodes)— gives a social expenditure/gross domestic product elasticity value closer to one ($\varepsilon = 1.1189$, with a value of $t = 4.38$, $R^2 = 0.137$ and $\alpha = 1.020$). This demonstrates the procyclical nature of social expenditure, since its growth was in most instances similar to the rate of increase of GDP. This tallies with the fact that throughout the decade, the macroeconomic priority of social expenditure rose for all the countries of the region (see figure VI.2).

This is the case both for total social expenditure and for social expenditure excluding the amounts allocated by the countries to social security. In this latter case, the average elasticity for all the episodes in question (139) shows a value of $\varepsilon = 1.313$ ($t = 6.709$) and $\alpha = 1.002$, i.e., an elasticity higher than that estimated for overall spending on the social sectors. This shows, by counterposition, that the main inertial component of public social expenditure is social security.

An alternative application of this model is to consider that patterns of variation in public social expenditure are due to variations in GDP, but with a certain delay or lag time. This may be expressed as:

$$\frac{SE_{t+2}}{SE_{t+1}} = \alpha\left(\frac{GDP_{t+1}}{GDP_t}\right)^{\varepsilon}$$

For the purposes of this study, various regressions were applied in which the lag was taken into account, but no proof of a significant relationship was found: for the 126 episodes observed between 1999 and 2000, ε was estimated at a non-significant 0.285, with $t = 1.204$ and adjusted $R^2 = 0.0035$.

---

[6]   For an extended application of the model in the case of Argentina, see Ravallion (2000).

Figure VI.10
LATIN AMERICA: VARIATIONS IN PUBLIC SOCIAL EXPENDITURE AND THE GROSS
DOMESTIC PRODUCT (GDP)[a]

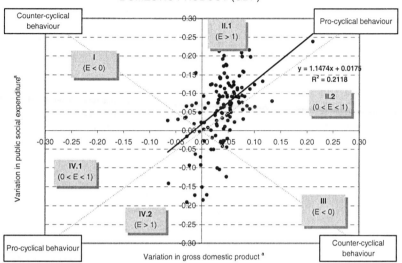

Source: ECLAC, Social Development Division, social expenditure database.

[a] Corresponds to the differences, in consecutive years, between the logarithms for public social expenditure and GDP.

(c) Progressiveness of social expenditure by sector

In order to analyse the degree of distributive progressiveness of social expenditure in each sector (education, health, housing and social security), a synthetic index based on the share of expenditure received by households in each income-distribution quintile was used.

The index was calculated on the basis of the following equation:

$$I_G = \frac{N+1}{N} - \frac{2}{N} * \sum_{i=1}^{N} Q_i$$

where N represents the number of segments into which the population was divided (5 segments) and Q_i represents the cumulative percentage of expenditure received by the population in each of the quintiles based on the distribution of autonomous household income.

Depending on how progressive expenditure is, this index can take the following values:

If $-1 \le I_c < 0$ then the distribution of expenditure is progressive, i.e., low-income households receive a proportionally higher share of the expenditure than middle- and high-income households.

If $0 < I_c \le 1$ then the distribution of expenditure is regressive, i.e., low-income households receive a proportionally lower share of the expenditure than middle- and high-income households.

(d)   Decentralization and public social expenditure

It should be noted that is difficult to carry out analyses of this type in countries where the financing of public expenditure and public social expenditure is decentralized to a considerable degree. In such cases, consolidated national totals must be used when making a comparative regional analysis of total public spending and social expenditure over time. This makes it possible to avoid the considerable underestimation of expenditure levels that occurs when only central government spending is recorded.

The case of Brazil —where a high percentage of public revenues and social expenditure is obtained and administered on a decentralized basis— illustrates this problem, as well as the differences that occur in the various social expenditure indicators when all levels of public administration are taken into consideration. In Brazil, for example, if only federal expenditure is analysed, the per capita social expenditure figure for 1998 comes to US$ 613 (in 1997 dollars), and the real increase for the period 1990-1998 comes to 20.7%. However, if the source of the resources is taken into account, and total spending by the three spheres of government (federal, state and municipal) is consolidated, per capita social expenditure in 1998 rises to US$ 1,011, which is about 65% higher than the federal expenditure figure, with the variation being 21.5% over the same period.

The decentralization of social expenditure in Brazil displays major differences between sectors (health, education, social security and others), and this means that the differences in spending levels and the corresponding variations from year to year become more significant. Thus, for example, the gradual marked decentralization of educational funding caused federal government spending in this area to fall from 34% of expenditure in 1989 to 26.1% in 1996.

No systematic compilation of consolidated data for expenditure levels in the three spheres of government is available, however. The consolidated information therefore had to be estimated on the basis of three studies, thanks to which it was possible to calculate federal expenditure growth coefficients by sector in order to estimate spending in each of the three spheres of government.[7] This made it possible to obtain the data on consolidated social expenditure between 1990 and 1998 that are used in this chapter. This structure of coefficients was extrapolated to the nearest years, on the assumption that the coefficients remained constant.

That assumption is based on the studies in question, which show that the coefficients do not vary significantly from year to year and indicate a gradual process of decentralization of social expenditure in Brazil, as evidenced by the coefficients of the growth of federal expenditure calculated to estimate consolidated expenditure: in the early 1980s, the coefficients were around 1.50; between 1984 and 1989, they varied between 1.60 and 1.65, and during the 1990s, they ranged around 1.70.

---

[7]   The sources of information used were: 1990-1993, Médici (1994); 1994-1996, IPEA (1995), and for 1997-1998, IPEA (1996).

Chapter VII

Concluding observations

Social development in the 1990s can be seen from two different viewpoints: an objective one involving the analysis of data, estimates and indicators (obtained basically from household surveys), as exemplified by the foregoing chapters of this book, and another which seeks to sound out people's subjective reactions to and perceptions of economic and social changes, together with their assessment of the social system as a whole, the prevailing economic model and the central actors in these processes. This information is derived from public opinion polls.

The issues included on Latin America's new social development agenda emerged both from the challenges posed by those objective factors and from the population's ambivalent response to the changes that have taken place.

In the first few years of the decade the primary concern of many Latin Americans was to stop the inflationary processes that were eroding their income. To achieve this, they voted for governments that had been successful in the stabilization process (Mora and Araujo, 1992), staking their future on the hope that, in time, some of the fruits of growth would filter down to them.

Only a few sectors reacted negatively —in particular, public employees affected by the privatization of State-owned companies or public spending cuts—, as indicated in the *Social Panorama of Latin America, 1995* (ECLAC, 1996).

By contrast, towards the end of the 1990s, amid the uncertainty created by international financial crises and economic stagnation, a malaise emerged and became widespread, as shown by public opinion polls. Of the individuals surveyed in 16 countries of the region, 67% felt that the distribution of wealth was unfair, while 61% said that their country was not developing.

Clearly, such opinions were strongly influenced by the survey respondents' personal experiences with the changes that had occurred.

The answers were also strongly marked by generational differences. Members of the present generation feel that they have fewer opportunities than the preceding generation and the one that will follow (Latinobarómetro, 2000). Young people commonly express dissatisfaction at the difficulties they face in finding a job that meets their expectations.

Even in Chile —where economic reforms have matured more than in other countries and where high levels of growth have been achieved over a long period— inequality has become a growing cause of concern and has taken precedence over poverty, defined as a lack of resources. It seems that the country's very success in meeting a priority need —poverty reduction— has brought new concerns to the fore: as Manzi-Catalán (1998) points out, the population is now focusing on the different speeds with which the benefits of economic progress reach different sectors of society. Low- and middle-income respondents say that current levels of poverty and inequality are not consistent with the level of growth achieved. They think that this inconsistency arises from the dynamics of the system itself and from the policies of social decision-makers, whom they criticize as insensitive. They also complain about what they regard as the State's failure to change this state of affairs (Manzi-Catalán, 1998).

In processes of economic and social change, even those involving growth and major social advances, signs of dissatisfaction usually emerge, in part because the process of change itself triggers new aspirations. Maslow (1954) showed that once certain primary needs are met, they are immediately replaced by new ones that are strongly felt and are usually hard to satisfy in the short term.

This discrepancy between aspirations and achievements usually prompts people to criticize politics and distance themselves from political activity. The survey respondents' tendency to belittle politics may be due to a number of factors. Certainly, the decisive changes observed in political life have had an impact. Today the communications media, especially television, play a central role in election campaigns. At the same time, rallies and face-to-face rapport between candidates and their constituents are on the decline. This also reduces the role of the political volunteers and organizers who were once the lifeblood of political parties. On the other hand, the media, which are, as López Pintor (1999) puts it, among the institutions that are undermining traditional forms of authority throughout the world, have taken on tasks such as reporting instances of arbitrariness, corruption and abuse of power and are also helping to solve the problems of individuals and communities that have no other way of making themselves heard, thereby replacing politicians and parties. Nevertheless, it must be admitted that the media are sometimes used to wage campaigns designed to discredit public figures and that this is another way in which they erode the prestige of politicians and politics.

The citizenry's estrangement from politics may also reflect the transition from a period of intense popular participation, generated by the weight that the State apparatus had at that time, to a stage where strong political involvement is no longer necessary (Huneeus, 1997). This may also reflect the fact that extreme positions have disappeared from the ideological spectrum and have been replaced by a focus on political consensus-building, which enables citizens to devote more time to other aspects of life.

Surveys show that there is even an increasing loss of enthusiasm for democracy, which is supported by only 37% of the respondents (Latinobarómetro, 2000). An optimistic interpretation is that this critical view is related to the performance of specific administrations, especially in the economic sphere, and not to political institutions themselves; this assessment is confirmed by the respondents' general tendency to strongly reject authoritarianism (Huneeus, 1997). They also express an interest in staying informed and in discussing politics. In addition, in most of the countries voter turnout in presidential and legislative elections has not declined, which may be interpreted as a sign of support for the democratic system. Most of the respondents affirm their faith that elections can bring change, except in those countries where no reasonable person could believe such a thing.

Nevertheless, it is clear that the State's legitimacy is based not only on how its authorities came to power, but also on economic efficiency and the capacity to do things well and solve problems. On average, 64% of the survey respondents were somewhat or completely dissatisfied in this regard. In addition, in seven countries 60% of the respondents said they did not trust State institutions, while a slightly smaller proportion did not trust civil-society institutions. The least distrusted institutions are the armed forces (46%) and the Catholic Church (27%), while the most distrusted are political parties (72%), trade unions (65%) and business associations (63%).

In view of these findings, the fundamental challenge facing the Latin American agenda, in addition to that of further reducing poverty and indigence, is to take these perceptions into account, since they affect the basic pillars of social organization and of the State's functioning. Citizens must understand that they have a vital role to play in making democracy and democratic political systems work and that it is important for them to participate in public life, not only to defend their own interests but also to help create a healthy society.

To advance towards the achievement of these aims, the countries must carry out economic and social reforms simultaneously and must intensify political reforms, on the understanding that these different kinds of reform are mutually reinforcing. The main tasks in this regard are the following:

- To begin with, the countries must improve the functioning of democracy by consolidating the rule of law and equality before the law. This involves moving beyond outdated ways of practising politics, such as patronage and corporatism, which are closely tied to the gaping inequalities found in the region; these, in turn, are perpetuated by the persistence of social structures left over from the days of colonialism and slavery. While most of the region's countries have undergone transformations that have helped to dilute —although without eradicating completely— these traditional forms of social control, especially those prevailing in rural areas, and have thus paved the way for the development of modern democracies, much remains to be done in this regard.

- In addition, the reduction of poverty and indigence must be accompanied by an increase in the population's incorporation into the consumer society. In an atmosphere that stresses the problems of consumerism, little attention has been paid to the weakness of consumer society in Latin America. Most households do not have sufficient income to enjoy a minimum level of mass consumption. This is a matter not only of material well-being, but also of social prestige and integration, on which society increasingly places a premium. In general, only two to three out of every 10 urban households currently have enough per capita income to take part in consumer society at a level consistent with the degree of development attained in Latin America.[1] Uruguay is an exception, since about half of the country's households had already reached this level by the 1990s; in other countries this proportion amounts to only a third, and very few of the countries in this second group can expect that as many as half of their households will attain that level of consumption in the next few years (Gerstenfeld, 1998).

• Social mobility plays a crucial role in an open, modern society that seeks to enhance social equity. One way to ensure that people perform well in their social roles is to give them opportunities and incentives to move up to better-paid or more socially prestigious positions. In traditional societies, on the other hand, people generally acquire their positions by assignment rather than merit.

In the early stages of development, a type of "structural" mobility takes place in which new and better positions are rapidly created and are filled without regard to people's qualifications to carry out the functions concerned. In more advanced stages, mobility becomes "circular" in the sense that fewer positions are created and changes can be made only through rotation; that is, through vacancies that arise —owing to retirement, death or dismissal— in higher positions, enabling duly qualified candidates to be promoted to fill them (Pastore and Silva, 2000).

Studies have shown that, in the region, only two out of every four young people in urban areas, and one out of every four in rural areas, have access to educational mobility. As a result, the likelihood of social mobility has remained virtually unchanged since 1980 (ECLAC, 1998a). The educational system is the key to changing this pattern.

A meritocracy —that is, a society in which positions are filled by individuals possessing certain capacities— can only function if there is social mobility and if non-merit-based criteria for assigning social positions become less and less important. However, it should also be stressed that, in a

---

[1] To be considered part of consumer society, a household must have per capita income higher than three times the poverty line. At that income level, the distribution shows a clear jump in the level of expenditure. It should be recalled that the poverty line is, precisely, the income level at which people are considered to be poor; incomes of less than twice the poverty line are a sign of vulnerability and of an increased risk of becoming poor at some point in life.

society of this type, individuals who do not meet the requirements for occupying well-paid, more socially prestigious positions can be plunged into poverty. Therefore, a concern for equity is vital in a modern society, and calls for the incorporation of elements that make up for these shortcomings and ensure that the whole population has a decent minimum standard of living.

- Undoubtedly, the key instrument for addressing many of the aforementioned issues on the regional agenda is public policy. It should be borne in mind that a sound economic policy has positive effects on social development by generating conditions conducive to job creation and high wages. Even if the only employment created is in low-productivity, low-paying jobs, as has tended to be the case in recent years, this enables more members of poor households to obtain employment, thereby increasing the employment density and, consequently, the per capita income of households. Economic growth also makes it possible to increase public spending and to finance programmes that can help to enhance equity and reduce poverty.

- It should be understood from the outset that social policies cannot single-handedly bring about social equity. Responsibility for social development is not the exclusive preserve of social policy; rather, it is shared with economic policy. That being said, social policies do have a direct and indirect impact on poverty reduction and the improvement of living conditions, through their three basic functions: investment in human capital, provision of social protection and enhancement of social integration or cohesiveness.

- Investment in human capital is made fundamentally through education, which must break the mechanism whereby opportunities for achieving well-being are determined by intergenerational transmission (ECLAC, 1998a); that is, the characteristics of individuals' households of origin determine the quantity and quality of their education, and hence the type of work they will perform and, ultimately, the degree of well-being they can achieve in the course of their lifetime. In this situation, the future of new generations is decided at an early stage, and a distinction is made between those who are excluded (those with too little education to obtain well-paid jobs) and those who are socially integrated.

Every individual should have access to education and the opportunity to reach the education threshold, defined as the number of years of schooling which, at any given time, affords people access to jobs that will give them a good chance of staying above the poverty line for the rest of their lives. In Latin America the education threshold is now about 12 years of formal schooling (ECLAC, 1999b), and it is reached by only a third of young people in urban areas and a tenth in rural areas.

Hence, it is important to reduce repetition and drop-out rates and to improve the quality of education. These efforts are not sufficient in themselves, however, considering that school performance is strongly influenced by factors external to the educational system. It is also necessary to offset the differences stemming from the different characteristics of students' households of origin.

- To combat poverty and indigence, policies to build human capital must be complemented by social safety nets, or sets of compensatory measures for increasing income and other assets through targeted transfers designed to sustain or increase the well-being of poor or vulnerable groups in times of crisis, economic transition or disaster (Graham, 1994). Such safety nets must be stable and permanent and must have specialized staff, clearly defined eligibility mechanisms, project portfolios and established practices for evaluating them, among other elements. Otherwise they will not be able to respond promptly to the needs that arise in times of crisis (Cornia, 1999).

Since the 1980s the protection of poor groups in times of crisis has been based on emergency job programmes, anti-poverty programmes and social emergency or social investment funds, which are intended to complement traditional social assistance programmes. Also useful in this regard are measures to keep people employed, such as bringing forward scheduled investments in infrastructure or promoting public works in communities hit by natural disasters or adverse economic conditions (Iglesias, 2001). The basic approach of these programmes should be countercyclical; that is, their coverage and benefits should expand as the economy contracts. It is important, therefore, to identify items of expenditure that should be maintained or expanded during crisis periods.

- An integrated society is one in which the population follows socially accepted patterns of conduct and there is a good match between cultural goals, the structure of opportunities for achieving them and the acquisition of individual skills for seizing such opportunities. Of course, there are always instances of deviant behaviour, which can either enhance or break down social cohesiveness and which are usually linked to various forms of exclusion, or circumstances in which society does not give people appropriate means (opportunities) of achieving the goals imposed by their culture (ECLAC, 1997).

   Cohesiveness does not mean homogenization, inasmuch as modern societies value diversity and the creative contributions that each cultural group can make. Rather, it refers to a set of common overall goals and rules that leave room for aims specific to certain individuals and groups. This is especially important in multi-ethnic, multicultural societies.

- The region's long-standing problems of poor social integration (poverty, ethnic discrimination, social segmentation, residential segregation) have been compounded by more recent phenomena such as violence in various forms, an erosion of public safety, drug trafficking and corruption.

   Feelings of insecurity increase faster than the violence or criminal behaviour that engenders them. Violence has an intimidating effect that grows as it spreads and as it receives high-profile coverage in the media. This effect is also intensified by the public perception that many of the culprits go unpunished. This creates a climate of fear and gives the population a strong sense of vulnerability.

   Acts of violence and perceptions such as these alter the way people live. They tend to spend less time in public places, take refuge indoors and seek recreation in private places. There is accordingly less interaction between people of different social backgrounds, and spontaneous socializing is discouraged. People isolate themselves with their peers, and feelings of suspicion emerge towards others or towards those who are "different". Urban design also changes as gated communities and condominiums proliferate and many people opt to live in apartments instead of houses. Higher amounts are spent on theft insurance, private security services and self-defence items.

- In summary, strengthening social integration involves rebuilding channels for social mobility that reflect the transformations under way, implementing a development model whose fruits reach all members of society, creating a public sphere that recognizes and values diversity and fosters the strengthening of civil society and consolidating a political system in which the demands and interests of all stakeholders are represented and negotiated.

The region's future agenda will reflect the aspiration to build more inclusive, egalitarian societies in which disadvantaged population groups are increasingly incorporated into consumer society and processes of upward social mobility.

It is also necessary to stress the importance of democracy and its quality, as a basic ingredient of a healthy society. Exclusionary societies can easily lead to patronage and populism, breed violence and insecurity and end up impairing the functioning of democracy.

An issue currently being debated in Europe is the emergence of "two-thirds societies", or societies in which only two out of every three people are socially integrated. Most of the Latin American countries now have "one-third societies". The challenge before them, then, is to expand the means of inclusion. Societies cannot become genuinely competitive unless they achieve human development at the same time.

As Dahrendorf (1996) has noted, achieving growth, social cohesiveness and freedom all at the same time is difficult and may even be tantamount to squaring the circle. It is never possible to do this perfectly, of course, but it is always possible to come close.

Bibliography

Bajraj, Reynaldo and Juan Chackiel (1995), "La población en América Latina y el Caribe: tendencias y percepciones", Pensamiento iberoamericano, No. 62, July-December.

Bravo, Jorge and Jorge Rodríguez (1993), "América Latina y el Caribe: dinámica de población y desarrollo. Un perfil sintético", Notas de población, year 21, No. 8 (LC/DEM/G.137), Santiago, Chile, Latin American Demographic Centre (CELADE), December.

Bucheli, Marisa and Magdalena Furtado (2001), Impacto del desempleo sobre el salario: una estimación de la pérdida salarial para Uruguay (LC/MVD/R.188/Rev.1), Montevideo, ECLAC office in Montevideo, June.

Cardoso, Fernando H. (2003), "Retos de la política social para la promoción de la equidad en América Latina", document presented at the fifth Social Equity Forum, (Washington, D.C., 27 February), Inter-American Development Bank (IDB).

___ (1998), "O Presidente segundo o sociólogo", interview of Fernando Henrique Cardoso to Roberto Pompeu de Toledo, São Paulo, Companhia das Letras.

Chackiel, Juan (1999), "Las tendencias de la población de América Latina hacia el final de la transición demográfica. Un análisis orientado al sector salud", Las consecuencias de las transiciones demográficas y epidemiológicas en América Latina, Ken Hill, José Morelos and Rebeca Wong (coords.), Mexico City, El Colegio de México/Johns Hopkins University Press.

Cohen, Ernesto (1996), "Presentación", Educación, eficiencia y equidad, Ernesto Cohen (coord.), Santiago, Chile, Economic Commission for Latin America and the Caribbean (ECLAC)/Organization of American States (OAS)/Sur.

Cohen, Ernesto and Rolando Franco (1992), Evaluación de proyectos sociales, Mexico City, Siglo XXI editores.

Cornia, Giovanni Andrea (1999), Liberalization, Globalization and Income Distribution, Working Paper, No. 157, Helsinski, World Institute for Development Economics Research (WIDER)/The United Nations University.

Dahrendorf, Ralf (1996), La cuadratura del círculo. Bienestar económico, cohesión social y libertad política, Mexico City, Fondo de Cultura Económica.

Delich, Francisco (2002), "La declinación argentina", Archivos del presente, year 7, No. 27, Buenos Aires, Fundación Foro del Sur, October-November-December.

ECLAC (Economic Commission for Latin America and the Caribbean) (2002a), Globalización y desarrollo (LC/G.2157(SES.29/3)), document prepared to Twenty-ninth session of the Economic Commission for Latin America and the Caribbean (ECLAC) (Brasilia, 6-10 May), Santiago, Chile.

___ (2002b), Panorama social de América Latina, 2001-2002 (LC/G.2183-P), Santiago, Chile, October. United Nations publication, Sales No.: S.02.II.G.65.

___ (2001a), Panorama social de América Latina, 2000-2001 (LC/G.2138-P), Santiago, Chile. United Nations publication, Sales No.: S.01.II.G.141.

___ (2001b), Una década de luces y sombras. América Latina y el Caribe en los años noventa, Bogotá, D.C., CEPAL/Alfaomega.

___ (2000a), Juventud, población y desarrollo: problemas, posibilidades y desafíos (LC/L.1424-P), Santiago, Chile. United Nations publication, Sales No.: S.00.II.G.98.

___ (2000b), La brecha de la equidad: una segunda evaluación (LC/G.2096), Santiago, Chile.

___ (2000c), Equidad, desarrollo y ciudadanía (LC/G.2071/Rev.1-P), Santiago, Chile, August. United Nations publication, Sales No.: S.00.II.G.81.

___ (2000d), Panorama social de América Latina, 1999-2000 (LC/G.2068-P), Santiago, Chile. United Nations publication, Sales No.: S.00.II.G.18.

___ (1999a), "América Latina: proyecciones de población urbana y rural 1970-2025", Boletín demográfico, año 32, No. 63 (LC/G.2052; LC/DEM/G.183), Santiago, Chile, Population Division of ECLAC - Latin American and Caribbean Demographic Centre (CELADE), January.

___ (1999b), La crisis financiera internacional: una visión desde la CEPAL (LC/G.2040), Santiago, Chile, October.

___ (1999c), Panorama Social de América Latina, 1998 (LC/G.2050-P), Santiago, Chile, May. United Nations publication, Sales No.: S.99.II.G.4.

___ (1998a), Panorama social de América Latina, 1997 (LC/G.1982-P), Santiago, Chile. United Nations publication, Sales No.: S.98.II.G.3.

___ (1998b), El pacto fiscal: fortalezas, debilidades, desafíos (LC/G.1997/Rev.1), Santiago, Chile, April.

___ (1997), La brecha de la equidad. América Latina, el Caribe y la Cumbre Social, Libros de la CEPAL series, No. 44 (LC/G.1954/Rev.1-P), Santiago, Chile. United Nations publication, Sales No.: S.97.II.G.11.

___ (1996), Panorama Social de América Latina, 1996 (LC/G. 1946-P), Santiago, Chile. United Nations publication, Sales No.: S.97.II.G.4.

___ (1995), Panorama Social de América Latina, 1995 (LC/G. 1886-P), Santiago, Chile. United Nations publication, Sales No.: S.95.II.G.17.

___ (1994), Panorama Social de América Latina, 1994 (LC/G. 1844), Santiago, Chile.

___ (1993), Panorama Social de América Latina, 1993 (LC/G.1768), Santiago, Chile.

___ (1991), Panorama Social de América Latina, 1991 (LC/G.1688), Santiago, Chile.

ECLAC/CELADE/IDB (Economic Commission for Latin America and the Caribbean/Latin American Demographic Centre/Inter-American Development Bank) (1996), Impacto de las tendencias demográficas sobre los sectores sociales en América Latina (LC/DEM/161), Santiago, Chile.

ECLAC/GTZ (Economic Commission for Latin America and the Caribbean/German Agency for Technical Cooperation) (2003), "Funcionamiento del mercado de tierras en América Latina", Santiago, Chile, forhtcoming.

ECLAC/UNESCO (Economic Commission for Latin America and the Caribbean/United Nations Educational, Scientific and Cultural Organization) (1992), Educación y conocimiento: eje de la transformación productiva con equidad (LC/G.1702/Rev.2-P), Santiago, Chile, April. United Nations publication, Sales No.: S.92.II.G.6.

ECLAC/FAO/IDB/RIMISP (Economic Commission for Latin America and the Caribbean/Food and Agriculture Organization of the United Nations/Inter-American Development Bank/International Network for Farming Systems Research Methodology) (2003), "Rural non Farm Employment and Income in Latin America", forthcoming.

Foster, James, Joel Greer and Erik Thorbecke (1984), "A class of decomposable poverty measures", Econometrica, vol. 52, No. 3, May.

Franco, Rolando and Ernesto Espíndola (2002), "La educación media, clave del crecimiento y la equidad", Alternativas de reforma de la educación secundaria en América Latina y el Caribe, Germán Rama (ed.), Washington, D.C., Inter-American Development Bank (IDB), October.

Gerstenfeld, Pascual (1998), "Oportunidades de bienestar y movilidad social en América Latina. Percepciones y realidades", Revista paraguaya de sociología, No. 101, Montevideo.

Gerstenfeld, Pascual and others (1995), "Variables extrapedagógicas y equidad en la educación media: hogar, subjetividad y cultura escolar", Políticas sociales series, No. 9 (LC/L.924), Santiago, Chile, Economic Commission for Latin America and the Caribbean (ECLAC).

Graham, Carol (1994), Safety Nets, Politics and the Poor, Washington, D.C., The Brookings Institution.

Hardy, C. (2000), "Repensar la agenda progresista", Revista Rocinante, Santiago, Chile, October.

Huneeus, Carlos (1997), "La difícil política en América Latina. Reflexiones a la luz del Latinobarómetro", Partidos políticos y gestión estratégica, Santiago, Chile, Latin American and Caribbean Institute for Economic and Social Planning (ILPES).

IDB (Inter-American Development Bank) (1998), América Latina frente a la desigualdad. Informe de progreso económico y social en América Latina, 1998-1999 edition, Washington, D.C.

Iglesias, E. V. (2001), "La crisis, el desempleo y las redes de protección social. Explorando nuevas fronteras", Sociología del desarrollo, políticas sociales y democracia, Rolando Franco (ed.), Mexico City, CEPAL/Siglo XXI editores.

IPEA (Institute of Applied Economic Research) (1996), Gastos sociais das tres esferas de governo - 1996, Brasilia.

___ (1995), Gastos sociais das tres esferas de governo - 1995, Brasilia.

Kaztman, Rubén (coord.) (1999), Activos y estructuras de oportunidades: estudios sobre las raíces de la vulnerabilidad social en el Uruguay (LC/MVD/R.180), Montevideo, ECLAC office in Montevideo.

Latinobarómetro (2000), "Informe de prensa Latinobarómetro 1999-2000", Santiago, Chile, Corporación Latinobarómetro.

López Pintor, Rafael (1999), Votos contra balas, Barcelona, Editorial Planeta.

Manzi, Jorge and Carlos Catalán (1998), "Los cambios en la opinión pública", Chile en los noventa, Cristián Toloza and Eugenio Lahera (eds.), Santiago, Chile, Dolmen.

Maslow, Abraham H. (1954), Motivation and Personality, New York, Harper & Bros.

Médici, André A. (1994), A dinámica do gasto social no Brasil nas tres esferas do governo: una análise do período 1980-1992, São Paulo, Foundation for Administrative Development (FUNDAP)/Institute of Public Sector Economics (IESP), June.

MIDEPLAN (Ministry of Planning and Cooperation) (1999), "Resultados de la VII Encuesta de Caracterización Socioeconómica Nacional (Casen 1998)", Working paper, No. 12, Santiago, Chile.

Molinas, José (1999), "El mercado de tierras rurales en Paraguay: situación actual y perspectivas", document prepared for ECLAC/GTZ joint project "Policy options to promote the development of rural land markets", Santiago, Chile.

Mora y Araujo, Manuel (1992), Ensayo y error, Buenos Aires, Sudamericana.

Muñoz, Jorge (1999), "Los mercados de tierra rurales en Bolivia", document prepared for ECLAC/GTZ joint project "Policy options to promote the development of rural land markets", Santiago, Chile.

Ocampo, José Antonio (2000), "Nuestra Agenda", presentación del Secretario Ejecutivo en el Foro Conmemorativo del Quincuagésimo Aniversario de la CEPAL (Santiago, Chile, 26 October 1998), La CEPAL en sus 50 años. Notas de un seminario conmemorativo, Libros de la CEPAL series, No. 54 (LC/G.2103.P), Santiago, Chile, Economic Commission for Latin America and the Caribbean (ECLAC). United Nations publication, Sales No.: S.00.II.G.57.

Pastore, José and Nelson do Valle Silva (2000), Mobilidade social no Brasil, São Paulo, Makron Books.

Ramos, J. (2003), "¿Ha sido efectivo en Chile el chorreo?", El Mercurio, Santiago, Chile, 20 May.

Ravallion, Martin (2000), Are the Poor Protected from Budget Cuts? Theory and Evidence for Argentina, Washington, D.C., World Bank/Université Toulouse 1 Sciences Sociales.

Reardon, Thomas, María Elena Cruz and Julio Berdegué (1999), "Los pobres en el desarrollo del empleo rural no-agrícola en América Latina: paradojas y desafíos", paper presented at the Seminar on decentralization and rural poverty within the framework of investment projects (Temuco, 25-26 October).

Sen, Amartya (1992), "Conceptos de pobreza y pobreza: identificación y agregación", América Latina: el reto de la pobreza. Conceptos, métodos, magnitud, características y evolución, Luis Alberto Beccaria and others (eds.), Bogotá, D.C., United Nations Development Programme (UNDP).

Solari, Aldo E. (1994), "La desigualdad educativa: problemas y políticas", Políticas sociales series, No. 4 (LC/L.851), Santiago, Chile, Economic Commission for Latin America and the Caribbean (ECLAC).

Stallings, Barbara and Jürgen Weller (2001), "El empleo en América Latina, base fundamental de la política social", CEPAL Review, No. 75 (LC/G.2150-P), Santiago, Chile, December.

Tejada, Ángela and Soraya Peralta (1999), "Mercados de tierras rurales en la República Dominicana", document prepared for ECLAC/GTZ joint project "Policy options to promote the development of rural land markets", Santiago, Chile.

UIS (UNESCO Institute for Statistics) (2003), "Education and Literacy Database" (http://www.uis.unesco.org/en/stats/stats0.htm).

UNDP (United Nations Development Programme) (2002), Desarrollo humano en el Uruguay, 2001, Montevideo, March.

World Bank (2001), Informe sobre el desarrollo mundial 2000-2001: lucha contra la pobreza, New York, Oxford University Press, September.

Statistical annex

Table A.1
LATIN AMERICA (18 COUNTRIES): POVERTY INDICATORS, 1990-1999
(Percentages)

| Country | Year | Households and population below the poverty line [a] | | | | | |
| | | Country total | | Urban areas | | Rural areas | |
		Households	Population	Households	Population	Households	Population
Argentina [b]	1990	-	-	16.2	21.2	-	-
	1994	-	-	10.2	13.2	-	-
	1997	-	-	13.1	17.8	-	-
	1999	-	-	13.1	19.7	-	-
Bolivia	1989 [c]	-	-	49.4	53.1	-	-
	1994 [c]	-	-	45.6	51.6	-	-
	1997	56.7	62.1	46.8	52.3	72.0	78.5
	1999	54.7	60.6	42.3	48.7	75.6	80.7
Brazil	1990	41.4	48.0	35.6	41.2	63.9	70.6
	1993	37.1	45.3	33.3	40.3	52.9	63.0
	1996	28.6	35.8	24.6	30.6	45.6	55.6
	1999	29.9	37.5	26.4	32.9	45.2	55.3
Chile	1990	33.3	38.6	33.3	38.4	33.5	39.5
	1994	23.2	27.5	22.8	26.9	25.5	30.9
	1998	17.8	21.7	17.0	20.7	22.7	27.6
	2000	16.6	20.6	16.2	20.1	19.2	23.8
Colombia	1991	50.5	56.1	47.1	52.7	55.4	60.7
	1994	47.3	52.5	40.6	45.4	57.4	62.4
	1997	44.9	50.9	39.5	45.0	54.0	60.1
	1999	48.7	54.9	44.6	50.6	55.8	61.8
Costa Rica	1990	23.7	26.2	22.2	24.8	24.9	27.3
	1994	20.8	23.1	18.1	20.7	23.1	25.0
	1997	20.3	22.5	17.1	19.3	22.9	24.8
	1999	18.2	20.3	15.7	18.1	20.5	22.3
Ecuador	1990	-	-	55.8	62.1	-	-
	1994	-	-	52.3	57.9	-	-
	1997	-	-	49.8	56.2	-	-
	1999	-	-	58.0	63.6	-	-
El Salvador	1995	47.6	54.2	40.0	45.8	58.2	64.4
	1997	48.0	55.5	38.6	44.4	61.6	69.2
	1999	43.5	49.8	34.0	38.7	59.0	65.1
Guatemala	1989	63.0	69.1	48.2	53.1	72.1	77.7
	1998	53.5	60.5	38.8	46.0	64.7	70.0
Honduras	1990	75.2	80.5	64.5	69.8	83.5	88.0
	1994	73.1	77.9	69.6	74.5	76.1	80.5
	1997	73.8	79.1	67.0	72.6	79.9	84.2
	1999	74.3	79.7	65.6	71.7	82.3	86.3
Mexico	1989	39.0	47.8	33.9	42.1	48.4	57.0
	1994	35.8	45.1	29.0	36.8	46.5	56.5
	1996	43.4	52.1	37.5	45.1	53.4	62.5
	1998	38.0	46.9	31.1	38.9	49.3	58.5
	2000	33.3	41.1	26.5	32.3	45.1	54.7
Nicaragua	1993	68.1	73.6	60.3	66.3	78.7	82.7
	1998	65.1	69.9	59.3	64.0	72.7	77.0

(Continued)

Table A.1 (concluded)

Country	Year	Households and population below the poverty line [a]					
		Country total		Urban areas		Rural areas	
		Households	Population	Households	Population	Households	Population
Panama	1991	36.3	42.8	33.6	40.9	42.5	50.6
	1994	29.7	36.1	25.2	30.8	40.6	49.2
	1997	27.3	33.2	24.6	29.7	33.5	41.9
	1999	24.2	30.2	20.8	25.7	32.6	41.5
Paraguay	1990 [d]	-	-	36.8	42.2	-	-
	1994	-	-	42.4	49.9	-	-
	1996	-	-	39.6	46.3	-	-
	1999	51.7	60.6	41.4	49.0	65.2	73.9
Peru	1997	40.5	47.6	28.0	33.7	65.6	72.7
	1999	42.3	48.6	30.9	36.1	66.8	72.5
Dominican Republic	1997	32.4	37.2	31.6	35.6	33.6	39.4
	1998	25.7	30.2	21.2	25.4	33.6	38.4
Uruguay	1990	-	-	11.8	17.8	-	-
	1994	-	-	5.8	9.7	-	-
	1997	-	-	5.7	9.5	-	-
	1999	-	-	5.6	9.4	-	-
Venezuela	1990	34.2	40.0	33.4	38.8	38.4	46.5
	1994	42.1	48.7	40.9	47.1	47.7	55.6
	1997	42.3	48.1	-	-	-	-
	1999	44.0	49.4	-	-	-	-
Latin America [e]	1990	41.0	48.3	35.0	41.4	58.2	65.4
	1994	37.5	45.7	31.8	38.7	56.1	65.1
	1997	35.5	43.5	29.7	36.5	54.0	63.0
	1999	35.3	43.8	29.8	37.1	54.3	63.7

Source: ECLAC, based on special tabulations of household survey data from the countries concerned. For definitions of the indicators, see ECLAC, *Social Panorama of Latin America, 2000-2001* (LC/G.2138-P), Santiago, Chile, March 2002. United Nations publication, Sales No. E.01.II.G.141, box I.2.

[a] Includes households (persons) living in indigence or extreme poverty.
[b] Greater Buenos Aires.
[c] Eight departmental capitals plus the city of El Alto.
[d] Metropolitan area of Asunción.
[e] Estimate for 18 countries of the region.

Table A.2
LATIN AMERICA (18 COUNTRIES): INDIGENCE INDICATORS, 1990-1999
(Percentages)

Country	Year	Households and population below the indigence line					
		Country total		Urban areas		Rural areas	
		Households	Population	Households	Population	Households	Population
Argentina [a]	1990	-	-	3.5	5.2	-	-
	1994	-	-	1.5	2.6	-	-
	1997	-	-	3.3	4.8	-	-
	1999	-	-	3.1	4.8	-	-
Bolivia	1989 [b]	-	-	22.1	23.3	-	-
	1994 [b]	-	-	16.8	19.8	-	-
	1997	32.7	37.2	19.2	22.6	53.8	61.5
	1999	32.6	36.5	16.4	19.8	59.6	64.7
Brazil	1990	18.3	23.4	13.3	16.7	37.9	46.1
	1993	15.3	20.2	11.6	15.0	30.2	38.8
	1996	10.5	13.9	7.6	9.6	23.1	30.2
	1999	9.6	12.9	7.1	9.3	20.5	27.1
Chile	1990	10.6	12.9	10.2	12.4	12.1	15.2
	1994	6.2	7.6	5.9	7.1	7.9	9.8
	1998	4.7	5.6	4.3	5.1	6.9	8.7
	2000	4.6	5.7	4.2	5.3	6.7	8.3
Colombia	1991	22.6	26.1	17.2	20.0	30.6	34.3
	1994	25.0	28.5	16.2	18.6	38.2	42.5
	1997	20.1	23.5	14.6	17.2	29.3	33.4
	1999	23.2	26.8	18.7	21.9	31.1	34.6
Costa Rica	1990	9.8	9.8	6.9	6.4	12.3	12.5
	1994	7.7	8.0	5.6	5.7	9.5	9.7
	1997	7.4	7.8	5.2	5.5	9.1	9.6
	1999	7.5	7.8	5.4	5.4	9.4	9.8
Ecuador	1990	-	-	22.6	26.2	-	-
	1994	-	-	22.4	25.5	-	-
	1997	-	-	18.6	22.2	-	-
	1999	-	-	27.2	31.3	-	-
El Salvador	1995	18.2	21.7	12.4	14.9	26.5	29.9
	1997	18.5	23.3	12.0	14.8	27.9	33.7
	1999	18.3	21.9	11.1	13.0	29.3	34.3
Guatemala	1989	36.7	41.8	22.9	26.2	45.2	50.1
	1998	28.0	34.1	12.9	17.2	39.6	45.2
Honduras	1990						
	1994	54.0	60.6	38.0	43.2	66.4	72.8
	1997	48.5	53.9	40.8	46.0	54.9	59.8
	1999	48.3	54.4	36.8	41.5	58.7	64.0
Mexico	1989	50.6	56.8	37.1	42.9	63.2	68.0
	1994	14.0	18.8	9.3	13.1	22.4	27.9
	1996	11.8	16.8	6.2	9.0	20.4	27.5
	1998	15.6	21.3	10.0	13.8	25.0	32.4
	2000	13.2	18.5	6.9	9.7	23.5	31.1
Nicaragua	1993	10.7	15.2	4.7	6.6	21.2	28.5
	1998	43.2	48.4	32.2	36.8	58.3	62.8

(Continued)

Table A.2 (concluded)

Country	Year	Households and population below the indigence line [a]					
		Country total		Urban areas		Rural areas	
		Households	Population	Households	Population	Households	Population
Panama	1991	16.0	19.2	13.9	16.0	21.1	26.7
	1994	12.0	15.7	8.7	11.4	19.8	26.2
	1997	10.2	13.0	8.6	10.7	14.1	18.8
	1999	8.3	10.7	6.6	8.1	12.6	17.2
Paraguay	1990 [c]	-	-	10.4	12.7	-	-
	1994	-	-	14.8	18.8	-	-
	1996	-	-	13.0	16.3	-	-
	1999	26.0	33.9	13.9	17.4	42.0	52.8
Peru	1997	20.4	25.1	7.9	9.9	45.5	52.7
	1999	18.7	22.4	7.6	9.3	42.6	47.3
Dominican Republic	1997	12.8	14.4	11.0	11.8	15.2	17.9
	1998	5.8	6.8	3.7	4.4	9.4	10.9
Uruguay	1990	-	-	2.0	3.4	-	-
	1994	-	-	1.1	1.9	-	-
	1997	-	-	0.9	1.7	-	-
	1999	-	-	0.9	1.8	-	-
Venezuela	1990	11.8	14.6	10.9	13.3	16.5	21.7
	1994	15.1	19.2	13.5	17.1	22.9	28.3
	1997	17.1	20.5	-	-	-	-
	1999	19.4	21.7	-	-	-	-
Latin America [d]	1990	17.7	22.5	12.0	15.3	34.1	40.4
	1994	15.9	20.8	10.5	13.6	33.5	40.8
	1997	14.4	19.0	9.5	12.3	30.2	37.6
	1999	13.9	18.5	9.1	11.9	30.7	38.3

Source: ECLAC, based on special tabulations of household survey data from the countries concerned. For definitions of the indicators, see ECLAC, *Social Panorama of Latin America, 2000-2001* (LC/G.2138-P), Santiago, Chile, March 2002. United Nations publication, Sales No. E.01.II.G.141, box I.1.

[a] Greater Buenos Aires.
[b] Eight departmental capitals plus the city of El Alto.
[c] Metropolitan area of Asunción.
[d] Estimate for 18 countries of the region.

Table A.3
LATIN AMERICA (16 COUNTRIES): DISTRIBUTION OF THE EMPLOYED
ECONOMICALLY ACTIVE POPULATION, BY OCCUPATIONAL CATEGORY,
RURAL AREAS, 1990-2000
(Percentages)

Country	Year	Total	Employers	Wage earners			Own-account workers and unpaid family workers	
				Total	Public sector	Private sector [a]	Total	Agriculture
Bolivia	1997	100.0	3.3	8.9	2.4	6.5	87.8	79.9
	1999	100.0	1.2	9.2	2.3	6.9	89.6	82.1
	2000	100.0	0.5	8.6	2.8	5.8	90.9	83.0
Brazil	1990	100.0	3.0	44.3	...	44.3	52.7	44.3
	1993	100.0	1.9	33.6	5.1	28.5	64.5	58.4
	1996	100.0	1.8	34.3	4.4	29.9	63.8	57.2
	1999	100.0	2.0	34.3	5.2	29.1	63.7	56.4
Chile [b]	1990	100.0	2.8	64.9	...	64.9	32.3	25.0
	1994	100.0	2.6	66.6	...	66.6	30.8	21.5
	1996	100.0	2.4	64.2	3.6	60.6	33.3	26.6
	1998	100.0	2.8	64.5	...	64.5	32.7	24.4
	2000	100.0	2.5	65.1	4.9	60.2	32.5	24.3
Colombia	1991	100.0	6.3	48.6	...	48.6	45.0	25.5
	1994	100.0	4.5	54.2	...	54.2	41.3	22.4
	1997	100.0	4.2	50.6	...	50.6	45.1	25.0
	1999	100.0	3.7	47.2	3.7	43.5	49.2	27.9
Costa Rica	1990	100.0	5.1	66.2	10.5	55.7	28.7	16.8
	1994	100.0	6.8	69.0	9.6	59.4	24.2	11.1
	1997	100.0	7.1	67.8	9.0	58.8	25.2	11.3
	1999	100.0	8.2	69.2	8.9	60.3	22.7	9.5
	2000	99.9	5.8	66.9	9.6	57.3	27.3	12.3
Ecuador	2000	100.0	3.2	42.4	3.9	38.5	54.3	40.7
El Salvador	1995	100.0	6.0	49.6	3.2	46.4	44.3	26.8
	1997	100.0	4.0	50.9	3.1	47.8	45.1	28.1
	1999	100.0	4.1	50.8	3.9	46.9	45.2	26.3
	2000	100.0	4.6	47.2	3.9	43.3	48.1	26.7
Guatemala	1989	100.0	0.6	38.7	2.9	35.8	60.7	47.5
	1998	100.0	2.0	42.9	1.7	41.2	55.1	34.8
Honduras	1990	100.0	0.6	34.9	4.0	30.9	64.6	47.6
	1994	100.0	1.7	37.0	4.8	32.2	61.4	43.5
	1997	100.0	2.6	34.8	3.4	31.4	62.6	41.6
	1999	100.0	3.1	33.4	3.7	29.7	63.5	41.3
Mexico [c]	1989	100.0	2.5	50.2	...	50.2	47.3	34.6
	1994	100.0	4.0	48.6	5.5	43.1	47.4	30.8
	1996	100.0	5.1	48.1	6.4	41.7	46.7	28.6
	1998	100.0	4.5	45.6	6.0	39.6	49.9	29.2
	2000	100.0	5.0	51.0	6.6	44.4	44.0	25.1
Nicaragua	1993	100.0	0.2	38.4	6.6	31.8	61.3	45.8
	1998	100.0	3.3	43.7	...	43.7	53.0	39.7

(Continued)

Table A.3 (concluded)

Country	Year	Total	Employers	Wage earners			Own-account workers and unpaid family workers	
				Total	Public sector	Private sector [a]	Total	Agriculture
Panama	1991	100.0	2.9	39.1	12.5	26.6	58.0	45.5
	1994	100.0	3.3	47.0	11.8	35.2	49.7	34.4
	1997	100.0	2.2	46.1	10.1	36.0	51.6	33.4
	1999	100.0	3.2	44.9	10.1	34.8	51.9	31.6
Paraguay	1997	100.0	2.3	24.8	3.2	21.6	72.8	57.3
	1999	100.0	3.4	27.0	3.4	23.6	69.7	54.0
Peru	1997	100.0	5.3	19.8	3.6	16.2	74.8	61.0
	1999	100.0	6.3	19.9	2.3	17.6	73.9	61.9
Dominican Republic	1992	100.0	4.0	52.4	13.2	39.2	43.7	21.6
	1995	100.0	2.1	56.1	11.5	44.6	41.9	15.7
	1997	100.0	3.4	45.6	10.3	35.3	51.0	28.5
	2000	100.0	1.8	40.3	8.1	32.2	57.8	32.6
Venezuela	1990	100.0	6.9	46.6	8.3	38.3	46.5	33.3
	1994	100.0	7.6	47.6	7.4	40.2	44.8	29.7
	1997	100.0	5.4	49.6	5.4	44.2	44.9	33.1

Source: ECLAC, based on special tabulations of household survey data from the countries concerned.

[a] Includes domestic employees. For Brazil (1990), Chile (1990, 1994 and 1998), Mexico (1989) and Nicaragua (1998), public-sector wage earners are included.
[b] Information from national socio-economic surveys (CASEN).
[c] Information from National Survey of Household Income and Expenditure (ENIGH).

Table A.4
LATIN AMERICA: COMPOSITION OF THE WORKING-AGE POPULATION,
BY SEX, URBAN AND RURAL AREAS,[a] 1990-1999
(Millions of persons and percentages)

Description	National total				Urban areas				Rural areas			
	1990	1994	1997	1999	1990	1994	1997	1999	1990	1994	1997	1999
	(Millions of persons)											
Working-age population	274.6	302.9	324.7	339.7	202.5	228.4	248.5	262.4	72.2	74.5	76.2	77.3
Males	134.9	148.5	159.0	166.3	97.1	109.5	119.2	125.9	37.8	38.9	39.8	40.4
Females	139.7	154.4	165.7	173.4	105.3	118.8	129.3	136.5	34.4	35.6	36.4	36.9
Economically active population	167.5	186.4	201.4	211.8	120.7	138.1	152.0	161.6	46.8	48.3	49.4	50.2
Males	114.5	125.1	133.3	139.0	79.1	89.0	96.7	102.0	35.4	36.1	36.7	37.0
Females	53.0	61.3	68.1	72.8	41.6	49.1	55.3	59.6	11.4	12.2	12.8	13.2
Employed	159.8	175.6	187.8	193.7	114.1	128.0	139.1	144.2	45.8	47.6	48.7	49.5
Males	109.5	118.7	125.7	129.0	74.8	83.1	89.5	92.5	34.7	35.5	36.1	36.5
Females	50.3	57.0	62.2	64.7	39.3	44.8	49.6	51.7	11.1	12.1	12.6	13.0
Unemployed	7.6	10.8	13.6	18.1	6.6	10.1	12.9	17.5	1.0	0.7	0.7	0.7
Males	4.9	6.4	7.7	10.0	4.2	5.8	7.2	9.5	0.7	0.6	0.5	0.4
Females	2.7	4.4	5.9	8.1	2.4	4.3	5.7	7.9	0.3	0.1	0.2	0.2
	(Percentages)											
Participation rate [b]	61.0	61.6	62.0	62.4	59.6	60.5	61.2	61.6	64.8	64.9	64.9	64.9
Males	84.9	84.3	83.8	83.6	81.4	81.2	81.1	81.0	93.7	92.8	92.0	91.5
Females	37.9	39.7	41.1	42.0	39.5	41.4	42.8	43.7	33.1	34.3	35.2	35.8
Employment rate [c]	58.2	58.0	57.8	57.0	56.4	56.0	56.0	55.0	63.4	64.0	63.9	64.0
Males	81.2	79.9	79.0	77.6	77.1	75.9	75.1	73.5	91.8	91.3	90.7	90.4
Females	36.0	36.9	37.5	37.3	37.3	37.7	38.3	37.9	32.2	34.1	34.6	35.2
Unemployment rate	4.6	5.8	6.7	8.6	5.5	7.3	8.5	10.8	2.2	1.5	1.5	1.3
Males	4.3	5.1	5.7	7.2	5.4	6.5	7.4	9.4	2.0	1.7	1.4	1.2
Females	5.1	7.2	8.7	11.2	5.7	8.7	10.3	13.3	2.9	0.8	1.6	1.6

Source: ECLAC, based on estimates by the Population Division-Latin American and Caribbean Demographic Centre (CELADE) and special tabulations of household survey data from the countries concerned.

[a] Aged 15 years and over.
[b] Economically active population as a percentage of the working-age population.
[c] Employed population as a percentage of the working-age population.

Table A.5
LATIN AMERICA: SELECTED CHARACTERISTICS OF THE
EMPLOYED POPULATION,[a] 1990-1999
(Thousands of persons and percentages)

Description	Persons (thousands)				Percentage breakdown			
	1990	1994	1997	1999	1990	1994	1997	1999
Employed persons								
Age (in years)	159 841	175 632	187 824	193 714	100.0	100.0	100.0	100.0
15 to 24	42 741	44 706	45 450	45 275	26.7	25.5	24.2	23.4
25 to 44	79 612	87 609	94 515	96 042	49.8	49.9	50.3	49.6
45 to 59	27 724	31 051	34 712	38 216	17.3	17.7	18.5	19.7
60 and over	9 764	12 266	13 147	14 181	6.1	7.0	7.0	7.3
Years of schooling	159 841	175 632	187 824	193 714	100.0	100.0	100.0	100.0
0 to 5	73 387	75 771	74 746	72 505	45.9	43.1	39.8	37.4
6 to 9	41 366	47 910	56 557	59 066	25.9	27.3	30.1	30.5
10 to 12	22 046	26 314	34 095	37 783	13.8	15.0	18.2	19.5
13 and over	23 043	25 636	22 426	24 361	14.4	14.6	11.9	12.6
Branch of activity	159 841	175 632	187 824	193 714	100.0	100.0	100.0	100.0
Agriculture	37 227	39 540	39 424	39 789	23.3	22.5	21.0	20.5
Industry	26 911	28 738	29 564	29 065	16.8	16.4	15.7	15.0
Construction	9 499	12 119	12 057	12 284	5.9	6.9	6.4	6.3
Transport and communications	7 159	8 129	9 337	9 839	4.5	4.6	5.0	5.1
Commerce	27 747	31 211	34 824	36 968	17.4	17.8	18.5	19.1
Finance	4 581	7 359	8 273	8 932	2.9	4.2	4.4	4.6
Social Services	30 325	31 042	35 084	36 695	19.0	17.7	18.7	18.9
Personal services	8 131	8 546	9 572	9 960	5.1	4.9	5.1	5.1
Domestic service	7 886	8 552	9 273	9 754	4.9	4.9	4.9	5.0
Unclassified	374	395	418	429	0.2	0.2	0.2	0.2
Size of establishment [b] (employers and employees)	100 116	104 779	110 889	113 051	100.0	100.0	100.0	100.0
1 to 5	26 538	27 849	33 495	34 621	30.7	30.2	31.9	32.3
6 to 10	9 242	9 163	11 479	11 687	10.7	9.9	10.9	10.9
11 to 49	28 267	29 972	31 121	31 572	32.7	32.5	29.6	29.4
50 and over	22 514	25 321	29 029	29 352	26.0	27.4	27.6	27.4
Unclassified	13 554	12 474	5 764	5 818	-	-	-	-
Secondary employed persons [c]	71 404	75 031	80 626	82 393	44.7	42.7	42.9	42.5

Source: ECLAC, based on estimates by the ECLAC Population Division-Latin American and Caribbean Demographic Centre (CELADE) and special tabulations of household survey data from the countries concerned.

[a] Aged 15 years and over.
[b] By number of persons employed. Percentage breakdown does not include unclassified workers.
[c] Refers to employed persons whose incomes are lower than that of their households' main breadwinner.

Table A.6

LATIN AMERICA: DISTRIBUTION OF THE EMPLOYED POPULATION IN URBAN AREAS, BY LABOUR MARKET SEGMENT, 1990-1999

(Percentage of total urban employment)

Country	Year	Formal sector						Informal sector					
		Total formal sector	Public sector	Private sector				Total informal sector	Employment in microenterprise [a]	Domestic employment	Unskilled own-account workers		
				Employers and self-employed professionals and specialist workers	Wage earners						Total [b]	Industry and construction	Commerce and services
					Total wage earners	Professionals and specialist workers	Neither professionals nor specialist workers						
Argentina [c]	1990	55.5	...	4.2	51.3	6.5	44.8	44.4	15.8	5.7	22.9	6.9	16.0
	1999	59.0	11.6	5.9	41.5	9.4	32.1	40.4	18.1	5.3	17.0	5.1	11.9
Bolivia	1989	41.5	17.9	3.9	19.7	3.4	16.3	58.5	11.6	5.8	41.1	9.8	30.0
	1999	35.7	10.3	4.0	21.4	6.3	15.1	64.3	15.3	3.1	45.9	12.1	31.1
Brazil	1990	59.2	15.5	4.2	39.5	3.4	36.1	40.7	13.1	6.2	21.4	3.5	15.8
	1999	52.6	13.0	4.6	35.0	9.3	25.7	47.3	12.3	8.5	26.5	5.2	16.4
Chile	1990	61.3	...	3.6	57.7	12.0	45.7	38.8	11.1	7.0	20.7	5.7	14.0
	1998	65.6	...	6.2	59.4	16.0	43.4	34.4	13.3	5.9	15.2	4.1	10.2
Colombia [d]	1991	67.1	11.6	6.5	49.0	4.9	44.1	32.9	...	5.6	27.3	6.4	20.0
	1999	59.1	8.7	6.9	43.5	5.7	37.8	40.9	...	5.2	35.7	7.5	26.7
Costa Rica	1990	63.0	25.0	3.2	34.8	5.3	29.5	36.9	14.9	4.4	17.6	6.4	10.1
	1999	58.4	17.2	4.0	37.2	7.5	29.7	41.6	19.2	5.1	17.3	4.5	11.9
Ecuador	1990	45.5	17.5	3.0	25.0	3.9	21.1	54.5	15.5	4.5	34.5	7.8	24.4
	1999	41.0	10.7	2.4	27.9	5.4	22.5	58.9	22.0	5.4	31.5	5.6	23.8
El Salvador	1990	44.3	13.8	1.1	29.4	3.1	26.3	55.6	16.3	6.1	33.2	8.7	21.8
	1999	47.9	12.3	1.6	34.0	8.3	25.7	52.2	18.7	4.3	29.2	6.7	20.0
Guatemala	1989	45.4	14.4	2.8	28.2	5.4	22.8	54.6	16.7	7.0	30.9	7.4	14.9
	1998	45.0	8.2	12.2	24.6	6.3	18.3	55.1	24.1	6.7	24.3	7.3	11.6
Honduras	1990	46.7	14.4	1.8	30.5	4.2	26.3	53.3	14.9	6.7	31.7	8.9	18.7
	1999	44.8	9.7	1.6	33.5	6.5	27.0	55.2	17.3	4.8	33.1	7.4	22.0
Mexico	1989	59.3	17.1	1.9	40.3	5.2	35.1	40.7	19.1	2.7	18.9	3.0	12.5
	1998	55.7	14.2	2.8	38.7	5.6	33.1	44.3	19.8	4.1	20.4	3.2	16.4
Nicaragua	1993	50.7	20.3	9.4	21.0	5.0	16.0	49.2	13.8	6.2	29.2	7.7	17.5
	1998	39.4	...	2.2	37.2	11.8	25.4	60.6	19.2	6.4	35.0	4.3	26.4

(Continued)

Table A.6 (concluded)

Country	Year	Formal sector						Informal sector					
		Total formal sector	Public sector	Private sector				Total informal sector	Employment in microenterprise [a]	Domestic employment	Unskilled own-account workers		
				Employers and self-employed professionals and specialist workers	Wage earners						Total [b]	Industry and construction	Commerce and services
					Total wage earners	Professionals and specialist workers	Neither professionals nor specialist workers						
Panama	1991	62.2	26.6	1.8	33.8	6.8	27.0	37.9	8.4	7.0	22.5	4.3	11.2
	1999	62.7	19.4	1.8	41.5	10.1	31.4	37.3	9.3	6.1	21.9	4.6	13.5
Paraguay [c]	1990	44.8	11.9	3.6	29.3	4.4	24.9	55.5	23.8	10.5	21.2	5.2	15.5
	1999	48.0	12.7	4.3	31.0	5.6	25.4	51.9	19.6	9.1	23.2	5.7	19.2
Dominican Republic	1992	64.0	14.3	5.3	44.4	8.7	35.7	36.0	...	3.2	32.8	5.6	23.0
	1997	53.1	11.9	4.1	37.1	6.0	31.1	47.0	11.2	4.4	31.4	6.8	21.3
Uruguay	1990	60.9	21.8	4.2	34.9	4.8	30.1	39.2	13.3	6.9	19.0	5.6	12.0
	1999	58.5	16.2	4.6	37.7	5.9	31.8	41.5	13.4	7.5	20.6	7.0	12.7
Venezuela	1990	60.7	21.4	3.7	35.6	5.6	30.0	39.2	11.6	6.3	21.3	4.1	15.3
	1999 [f]	46.1	14.9	2.8	28.4	4.4	24.0	53.7	16.5	2.0	35.2	6.7	23.7
Weighted average [g]	1990	58.9	16.0	3.8	40.6	4.7	35.9	41.0	14.7	5.4	22.3	4.3	15.8
	1999	53.6	12.9	4.3	36.9	7.8	29.1	46.3	15.5	6.3	25.8	5.2	17.7

Source: ECLAC, based on special tabulations of household survey data from the countries concerned.

[a] Includes employers and wage earners in enterprises with five employees or fewer.
[b] Includes workers in agriculture, forestry, hunting and fishing.
[c] Greater Buenos Aires.
[d] The formal sector includes employment in microenterprise.
[e] Asunción and Central Department.
[f] National total.
[g] The "public sector" subtotal excludes Argentina, Chile and Nicaragua, and the "microenterprise" subtotal excludes Colombia and the Dominican Republic, in 1990 and 1999.

Table A.7
LATIN AMERICA: CONTRIBUTION OF INDIVIDUAL OCCUPATIONAL CATEGORIES IN URBAN AREAS, 1990-1999
(Thousands of employed persons and percentages of total urban employed)

Country	Total	Formal sector						Informal sector					
		Total formal sector	Public sector	Private sector				Total informal sector	Employment in microenterprise [a]	Domestic employment	Unskilled own-account workers		
				Employers and self-employed professionals and specialist workers	Wage earners						Total [b]	Industry and construction	Commerce and services
					Total wage earners	Professional and specialist workers	Neither professionals nor specialist workers						
Argentina [c]	100.0	87.9	…	18.9	68.9	31.6	37.4	12.1	36.2	2.5	-26.6	-8.2	-18.4
1990-1999	781.3	686.5	…	147.9	538.6	246.8	291.8	94.8	282.5	19.8	-207.5	-64.0	-143.5
Bolivia	100.0	26.5	-1.7	4.2	24.1	10.9	13.2	73.5	21.1	-1.2	53.5	15.7	32.8
1989-1999	671.4	178.2	-11.4	27.9	161.7	73.1	88.7	493.2	142.0	-7.8	359.1	105.6	220.5
Brazil	100.0	20.7	0.9	6.5	13.2	37.9	-24.7	79.3	8.4	19.7	51.3	13.4	19.3
1990-1999	9 368.4	1 935.2	83.7	613.0	1 238.5	3 551.7	-2 313.2	7 433.1	790.1	1 841.7	4 801.3	1 259.7	1 810.4
Chile	100.0	84.3	…	17.3	66.9	33.2	33.7	15.7	22.8	1.2	-8.3	-2.7	-6.0
1990-1998	820.3	691.2	…	142.3	549.0	272.1	276.8	129.0	186.7	10.0	-67.7	-22.4	-49.3
Colombia [d]	100.0	19.5	-5.7	8.9	16.3	9.7	6.6	80.5	…	3.2	77.3	12.9	59.9
1991-1999	1 673.5	326.5	-94.6	148.6	272.5	161.6	110.8	1 347.0	…	53.9	1 293.1	216.6	1001.7
Costa Rica	100.0	48.9	1.3	5.6	42.0	12.0	30.0	51.1	27.9	6.5	16.7	0.6	15.5
1990-1999	247.4	121.0	3.3	13.9	103.9	29.6	74.3	126.3	69.0	16.1	41.2	1.6	38.4
Ecuador	100.0	29.1	-7.4	0.8	35.7	9.4	26.3	70.9	39.4	7.8	23.6	-0.3	22.3
1990-1999	725.0	211.2	-53.8	5.8	259.2	68.3	190.8	513.8	285.9	56.7	171.1	-1.8	161.6
El Salvador	100.0	55.5	9.0	2.7	43.9	19.6	24.3	44.5	23.8	0.3	20.3	2.3	16.0
1990-1999	404.7	224.6	36.3	10.9	177.5	79.3	98.1	180.1	96.5	1.4	82.2	9.3	64.6
Guatemala	100.0	43.9	-6.7	34.7	15.9	8.4	7.4	56.1	41.8	6.0	8.4	7.0	3.6
1989-1998	421.6	185.0	-28.2	146.3	67.0	35.6	31.4	236.5	176.1	25.1	35.4	29.7	15.4
Honduras	100.0	41.7	2.1	1.3	38.4	10.2	28.1	58.3	21.2	1.7	35.4	5.0	27.4
1990-1999	430.8	179.7	9.0	5.5	165.3	44.1	121.2	251.1	91.3	7.4	152.4	21.4	117.8
Mexico	100.0	46.0	6.4	5.2	34.4	6.7	27.7	54.0	21.7	7.9	24.4	3.7	26.9
1989-1998	7 752.6	3 568.9	497.3	404.4	2 667.2	517.4	2 149.8	4 183.7	1 680.7	609.2	1 893.7	289.7	2 083.1
Nicaragua	100.0	-11.7	…	-30.3	18.5	42.4	-23.9	111.7	43.5	7.3	61.0	-11.1	66.4
1993-1998	157.5	-18.5	…	-47.7	29.2	66.8	-37.6	176.0	68.4	11.5	96.1	-17.4	104.6
Panama	100.0	64.1	1.7	1.8	60.6	18.3	42.3	35.9	11.5	3.9	20.5	5.4	19.2
1991-1999	170.6	109.3	2.8	3.1	103.4	31.2	72.2	61.3	19.7	6.6	34.9	9.1	32.8

(Continued)

Table A.7 (concluded)

Country	Total	Formal sector		Private sector				Informal sector			Unskilled own-account workers		
		Total formal sector	Public sector	Employers and self-employed professionals and specialist workers	Wage earners			Total informal sector	Employment in microenterprise [a]	Domestic employment	Total [b]	Industry and construction	Commerce and services
					Total wage earners	Professionals and specialist workers	Neither professionals nor specialist workers						
Paraguay [e]	100.0	55.9	14.7	6.0	35.3	8.5	26.8	44.1	10.0	5.9	28.1	6.9	28.0
1990-1999	325.5	182.1	47.8	19.4	114.8	27.5	87.3	143.4	32.6	19.3	91.5	22.5	91.2
Dominican Republic	100.0	64.9	5.4	8.6	50.9	-1.3	52.2	35.1	...	7.6	27.5	10.0	16.6
1992-1997	526.0	341.2	28.4	45.2	267.6	-6.8	274.5	184.8	...	40.1	144.7	52.6	87.5
Uruguay	100.0	36.7	-35.7	8.4	64.1	16.2	47.9	63.3	14.5	13.1	35.7	20.1	19.3
1990-1999	119.4	43.9	-42.6	10.0	76.5	19.3	57.2	75.6	17.3	15.7	42.6	24.0	23.1
Venezuela	100.0	-2.1	-6.6	-0.2	4.7	0.4	4.2	102.1	32.8	-12.2	81.5	15.4	51.7
1990-1999 [f]	1 620.7	-33.5	-106.5	-2.7	75.8	7.2	68.6	1 654.2	532.2	-198.5	1 320.5	248.9	837.6
Simple average	100.0	41.9	-2.5	5.9	37.3	16.1	21.2	58.1	25.4	4.8	31.2	5.7	23.6
	100.0	34.1	2.1	6.5	25.5	20.1	5.4	65.9	18.2	9.4	38.3	8.1	24.2
Weighted average	26 216	8 933	551	1 703	6 679	5 260	1 419	17 284	4 784	2 466	10 034	2 131	6 344

Source: ECLAC, based on special tabulations of household survey data from the countries concerned.

[a] Includes employers and wage earners in enterprises with five employees or fewer.
[b] Includes workers in agriculture, forestry, hunting and fishing.
[c] Greater Buenos Aires.
[d] The formal sector includes employment in microenterprise.
[e] Asunción and Central Department.
[f] National total.

Table A.8

LATIN AMERICA (18 COUNTRIES): INTERGENERATIONAL EDUCATIONAL ATTAINMENT OF YOUNG PEOPLE AGED BETWEEN 20 AND 24 YEARS, BY SEX, URBAN AND RURAL AREAS, 2000

(Percentages)

Country	Sex	Total	Urban areas — Educational attainment				Total	Rural areas — Educational attainment			
			Young people surpassing their parents' educational level		Young people failing to surpass their parents' educational level			Young people surpassing their parents' educational level		Young people failing to surpass their parents' educational level	
			And obtaining a basic educational capital	And failing to obtain a basic stock of educational capital	And obtaining a basic educational capital	And failing to obtain a basic stock of educational capital		And obtaining a basic educational capital	And failing to obtain a basic stock of educational capital	And obtaining a basic educational capital	And failing to obtain a basic stock of educational capital
Argentina	Both sexes	100	40	4	21	34	...	...	...	...	...
	Males	100	31	4	21	44	...	...	...	...	...
	Females	100	50	4	22	25	...	...	...	...	...
Bolivia	Both sexes	100	56	10	16	18	100	18	13	...	68
	Males	100	55	12	14	19	100	23	17	...	60
	Females	100	57	9	18	16	100	12	8	...	80
Brazil	Both sexes	100	30	12	14	44	100	12	11	3	74
	Males	100	23	12	13	52	100	9	9	2	80
	Females	100	38	12	16	34	100	18	16	4	62
Chile	Both sexes	100	49	5	27	19	100	36	13	5	47
	Males	100	48	6	26	21	100	29	14	4	53
	Females	100	50	5	28	17	100	45	12	5	38
Colombia	Both sexes	100	52	4	20	24	100	28	10	6	56
	Males	100	46	5	20	29	100	22	10	5	63
	Females	100	59	4	20	18	100	38	12	8	42
Costa Rica	Both sexes	100	34	4	20	41	100	23	4	4	69
	Males	100	32	4	18	46	100	19	3	4	74
	Females	100	37	4	23	36	100	28	6	4	62
Ecuador	Both sexes	100	48	8	16	28	100	21	8	2	70
	Males	100	44	7	18	32	100	19	7	2	72
	Females	100	52	10	14	23	100	23	10	1	67
El Salvador	Both sexes	100	48	13	13	27	100	18	19	...	63
	Males	100	44	12	15	28	100	17	20	1	63
	Females	100	53	13	10	25	100	19	18	...	63
Guatemala	Both sexes	100	33	12	6	48	100	5	6	...	89
	Males	100	32	13	6	50	100	6	6	...	88
	Females	100	34	12	7	47	100	4	6	...	90
Honduras	Both sexes	100	30	7	13	50	100	8	4	1	87
	Males	100	25	7	10	57	100	6	3	1	90
	Females	100	35	8	15	42	100	13	5	...	83
Mexico	Both sexes	100	43	13	12	33	100	18	18	3	61
	Males	100	36	15	11	38	100	17	19	4	60
	Females	100	50	10	13	27	100	19	17	2	62
Nicaragua	Both sexes	100	29	12	7	52	100	11	17	1	72
	Males	100	24	11	6	60	100	7	13	1	79
	Females	100	34	14	9	44	100	16	22	1	61
Panama	Both sexes	100	44	4	20	32	100	30	8	4	59
	Males	100	35	4	21	40	100	22	8	4	66
	Females	100	55	4	19	22	100	42	9	3	45
Paraguay	Both sexes	100	44	7	11	38	100	14	10	...	75
	Males	100	38	5	13	44	100	12	10	...	77
	Females	100	54	11	8	29	100	18	10	1	71
Peru	Both sexes	100	37	18	11	34	100	13	30	...	57
	Males	100	30	20	12	38	100	9	35	1	56
	Females	100	43	16	10	31	100	18	24	...	58
Dominican Republic	Both sexes	100	46	12	9	34	100	22	22	2	55
	Males	100	35	12	8	46	100	19	19	2	60
	Females	100	59	12	10	20	100	27	26	3	44
Uruguay	Both sexes	100	29	8	10	53	...	...	...	...	...
	Males	100	19	7	10	64	...	...	...	...	...
	Females	100	40	8	11	41	...	...	...	...	...
Venezuela[a]	Both sexes	100	35	7	15	44	...	...	...	...	...
	Males	100	25	6	14	54	...	...	...	...	...
	Females	100	47	7	16	30	...	...	...	...	...

Source: ECLAC, based on special tabulations of household survey data from the countries concerned.

[a] National total.

Table A.9

LATIN AMERICA (18 COUNTRIES): YOUNG PEOPLE BETWEEN 20 AND 24
YEARS OF AGE WHO DO NOT SURPASS THEIR PARENTS' EDUCATIONAL LEVEL
AND COMPLETED LESS THAN 12 YEARS OF SCHOOLING,
BY SEX AND EDUCATIONAL LEVEL OF THEIR PARENTS,
URBAN AND RURAL AREAS, 2000

(Percentages)

Country	Sex	Urban areas						Rural areas					
		Total	Educational level of parents					Total	Educational level of parents				
			0-2 years	3-5 years	6-9 years	10-12 years	13-15 years		0-2 years	3-5 years	6-9 years	10-12 years	13-15 years
Argentina	Both sexes	34	59	64	42	18	12	...	...	...	...	...	...
	Males	44	65	75	52	24	19	...	...	...	...	...	...
	Females	25	52	51	31	13	6	...	...	...	...	...	...
Bolivia	Both sexes	18	20	27	15	17	8	68	76	55	58	...	...
	Males	19	22	23	16	23	10	60	72	37	56	...	...
	Females	16	19	30	14	9	7	80	82	78	62	...	...
Brazil	Both sexes	44	56	50	39	24	13	74	82	66	45	26	8
	Males	52	63	59	47	28	17	80	86	73	57	20	7
	Females	34	46	38	30	18	7	62	72	52	26	33	9
Chile	Both sexes	19	31	32	27	15	4	47	53	54	39	22	2
	Males	21	35	36	30	15	5	53	58	61	45	26	3
	Females	17	26	28	24	15	3	38	45	44	30	18	1
Colombia	Both sexes	24	44	33	18	8	5	56	70	51	31	12	6
	Males	29	49	38	24	12	5	63	76	57	41	27	...
	Females	18	38	27	11	5	5	42	58	39	14	...	38
Costa Rica	Both sexes	41	66	66	46	32	14	69	85	78	60	26	10
	Males	46	61	67	53	31	11	74	87	82	66	35	15
	Females	36	74	64	37	35	17	62	82	71	54	15	3
Ecuador	Both sexes	28	50	42	30	13	4	70	80	72	60	19	15
	Males	32	60	46	36	12	3	72	82	76	61	22	31
	Females	23	40	38	23	14	6	67	77	66	58	15	...
El Salvador	Both sexes	27	42	34	24	14	2	63	66	61	43	27	...
	Males	28	44	37	27	15	...	63	65	61	48	...	...
	Females	25	39	30	21	13	5	63	66	60	36	50	...
Guatemala	Both sexes	48	67	49	29	31	10	89	90	84	62	...	...
	Males	50	67	61	24	37	18	88	89	86	74	...	...
	Females	47	68	40	37	26	3	90	94	80	57	...	...
Honduras	Both sexes	50	69	58	48	34	16	87	92	84	59	...	82
	Males	57	73	69	50	43	19	90	94	89	72	...	63
	Females	42	65	44	45	17	14	83	90	77	41	...	90
Mexico	Both sexes	33	45	45	39	16	4	61	70	55	57	29	...
	Males	38	47	51	42	26	6	60	67	53	73	28	...
	Females	27	41	38	37	5	3	62	74	60	34	31	...
Nicaragua	Both sexes	52	65	57	42	55	6	72	79	60	43	...	...
	Males	60	75	56	49	70	...	79	85	69	52	...	...
	Females	44	53	58	33	40	9	61	69	45	33	...	...
Panama	Both sexes	32	53	49	41	18	6	59	77	66	49	25	27
	Males	40	64	65	50	28	8	66	83	77	54	31	21
	Females	22	35	26	31	8	4	45	65	47	42	17	30
Paraguay	Both sexes	38	69	63	25	6	13	75	83	75	65	40	...
	Males	44	76	70	30	4	14	77	80	80	67	56	...
	Females	29	50	52	17	8	11	71	89	66	63	...	...
Peru	Both sexes	34	27	34	48	32	22	57	60	50	51	55	85
	Males	38	32	38	59	25	14	56	56	55	47	87	90
	Females	31	21	29	37	37	29	58	65	43	55	...	80
Dominican Republic	Both sexes	34	39	43	34	20	31	55	64	54	44	25	23
	Males	46	59	50	47	30	46	60	69	62	44	11	50
	Females	20	15	31	22	11	21	44	51	39	44	48	...
Uruguay	Both sexes	53	56	68	62	37	25	...	...	...	...	...	...
	Males	64	62	78	72	48	40	...	...	...	...	...	...
	Females	41	46	56	50	25	12	...	...	...	...	...	...
Venezuela [a]	Both sexes	44	65	60	43	26	11	...	...	...	...	...	...
	Males	54	75	70	54	31	18	...	...	...	...	...	...
	Females	30	48	46	29	20	4	...	...	...	...	...	...

Source: ECLAC, based on special tabulations of household survey data from the countries concerned.

[a] National total.

Table A.10
LATIN AMERICA (18 COUNTRIES): DISTRIBUTION OF YOUNG PEOPLE BETWEEN 20
AND 24 YEARS OF AGE, BY EDUCATIONAL LEVEL OF THEIR PARENTS,
URBAN AND RURAL AREAS
(Percentages)

| Country | Year | Total | Urban areas | | | | Total | Rural areas | | | |
| | | | Educational level of parents | | | | | Educational level of parents | | | |
			0-5	6-9	10-12	13 and over		0-5	6-9	10-12	13 and over
Argentina	2000	100.0	16.4	43.5	21.3	18.9	...	...	...	...	...
Bolivia	2000	100.0	38.8	21.5	22.4	17.2	100.0	91.8	7.0	0.7	0.5
Brazil	1999	100.0	63.3	19.1	8.0	9.6	100.0	92.6	4.4	1.9	1.2
Chile	2000	100.0	16.8	32.5	33.0	17.6	100.0	63.0	28.9	6.5	1.5
Colombia	1999	100.0	48.8	23.6	14.3	13.4	100.0	85.4	9.0	3.7	1.8
Costa Rica	2000	100.0	23.4	43.1	11.9	21.6	100.0	57.6	34.5	4.0	3.9
Ecuador	2000	100.0	27.0	42.5	14.1	16.4	100.0	68.1	28.6	2.7	0.5
El Salvador	2000	100.0	46.9	26.8	13.9	12.4	100.0	93.8	5.9	0.3	0.1
Guatemala	1998	100.0	65.5	19.4	8.8	6.3	100.0	97.3	2.6	0.0	0.1
Honduras	1999	100.0	53.6	28.1	2.9	15.3	100.0	90.2	8.6	0.0	1.2
Mexico	2000	100.0	37.1	33.6	12.9	16.4	100.0	78.8	16.3	2.3	2.5
Nicaragua	1998	100.0	61.7	25.5	5.2	7.6	100.0	94.1	5.4	0.2	0.3
Panama	1999	100.0	17.8	44.9	19.9	17.4	100.0	55.4	34.7	6.5	3.5
Paraguay	1999	100.0	41.6	39.6	9.7	9.1	100.0	79.1	19.4	0.8	0.6
Peru	1997	100.0	45.3	25.6	14.5	14.6	100.0	92.8	5.2	1.2	0.8
Dominican Republic	2000	100.0	47.1	30.0	14.0	8.9	100.0	80.0	14.6	3.9	1.5
Uruguay	2000	100.0	18.6	51.3	18.2	11.9	...	...	...	...	...
Venezuela [a]	2000	100.0	35.3	42.9	9.8	12.0	...	...	...	...	...
Simple average for the countries	2000	100.0	39.2	33.0	14.2	13.7	100.0	81.3	15.0	2.3	1.3

Source: ECLAC, based on special tabulations of household survey data from the countries concerned.

[a] National total.

Table A.11
LATIN AMERICA (18 COUNTRIES): PERCENTAGE DISTRIBUTION OF YOUNG PEOPLE
BETWEEN 20 AND 24 YEARS OF AGE WHO COMPLETED AT LEAST 12 YEARS OF
SCHOOLING, BY EDUCATIONAL LEVEL OF THEIR PARENTS, URBAN AREAS
(13 years and over = 100)

Country	Year	Total	Educational level of parents			
			0-5	6-9	10-12	13 and over
Argentina	1990	53	18	55	79	100
(Greater Buenos Aires)	2000	69	27	61	87	100
Bolivia	1989	73	58	76	93	100
	2000	78	62	81	85	100
Brazil	1990	38	27	66	80	100
	1999	49	33	62	84	100
Chile	1990	69	48	67	88	100
	2000	77	53	69	85	100
Colombia	1991	55	42	68	94	100
	1999	75	58	84	95	100
Costa Rica	1990	56	33	62	93	100
	2000	61	28	55	74	100
Ecuador	1990	63	43	65	91	100
	2000	69	39	67	94	100
El Salvador	1995	54	36	70	96	100
	2000	63	41	70	88	100
Guatemala	1989	41	27	67	80	100
	1998	46	27	75	79	100
Honduras	1990	42	26	59	92	100
	1999	49	30	53	72	100
Mexico	1989	40	27	52	75	100
	2000	57	28	57	88	100
Nicaragua	1993	33	25	46	79	100
	1998	39	24	56	50	100
Panama	1991	62	34	64	82	100
	1999	67	38	59	85	100
Paraguay	1994	54	33	61	95	100
	1999	62	27	79	105	100
Peru	1997	61	42	61	81	100
Dominican Republic	1997	49	36	55	71	100
Uruguay	1990	45	18	41	74	100
	2000	50	25	38	78	100
Venezuela	1990	32	13	33	69	100
	2000	54	27	57	79	100
Simple average for the	1990	51	32	60	85	100
countries	2000	59	35	63	84	100

Source: ECLAC, based on special tabulations of household survey data from the countries concerned.

Table A.12
LATIN AMERICA (18 COUNTRIES): PERCENTAGE DISTRIBUTION OF YOUNG PEOPLE BETWEEN 20 AND 29 YEARS OF AGE WHO WORK 20 OR MORE HOURS PER WEEK, BY OCCUPATIONAL CATEGORY AND EDUCATIONAL LEVEL, URBAN AREAS

Country	Year	Educational level	Total	Occupation							
				Professionals and specialist workers	Managers	Administrative employees and accountants	Salespersons and shop assistants	Industrial, transport and warehouse labourers	Construction workers	Domestic employees, waiters and guards	Agricultural workers
Argentina	1999	Total	100.0	12.8	2.6	17.4	15.5	25.9	7.9	17.4	0.4
		0 - 8	100.0	...	0.5	1.9	14.3	37.8	21.3	23.2	1.0
		9 - 12	100.0	...	2.7	21.2	20.2	30.4	4.8	20.4	0.3
		13 and over	100.0	46.5	4.4	25.9	8.9	7.3	0.3	6.7	0.1
Bolivia	1999	Total	100.0	9.1	2.4	9.0	21.1	37.1	9.8	8.4	3.1
		0 - 8	100.0	...	0.7	1.0	22.3	39.7	15.4	15.1	5.7
		9 - 12	100.0	1.1	0.9	9.7	21.9	48.6	10.4	4.5	2.9
		13 and over	100.0	33.0	6.9	17.1	18.4	15.0	2.1	6.9	0.5
Brazil	1999	Total	100.0	9.6	5.4	13.1	16.3	29.9	0.3	19.8	5.5
		0 - 8	100.0	1.1	2.8	3.9	14.7	41.0	0.1	26.4	10.0
		9 - 11	100.0	10.5	6.6	21.7	21.0	22.8	0.5	15.7	1.2
		12 and over	100.0	41.1	12.4	25.3	9.5	6.1	0.5	5.0	0.2
Chile	2000	Total	100.0	18.6	2.2	15.5	15.5	25.3	6.7	10.3	5.8
		0 - 8	100.0	1.1	0.9	2.0	9.2	30.9	14.8	20.6	20.5
		9 - 12	100.0	7.3	1.6	16.4	19.8	31.0	7.7	11.0	5.4
		13 and over	100.0	46.8	3.7	19.4	10.1	12.5	1.6	4.9	0.9
Colombia	1999	Total	100.0	11.7	1.2	17.5	22.1	26.1	4.7	13.9	2.9
		0 - 8	100.0	0.7	0.1	4.0	20.7	35.8	9.5	22.9	6.2
		9 - 11	100.0	4.2	0.4	21.7	27.5	28.5	3.3	12.9	1.6
		12 and over	100.0	41.7	4.2	29.6	14.0	7.3	0.1	2.7	0.4
Costa Rica	1999	Total	100.0	14.1	5.1	16.4	17.5	31.5	4.6	7.6	3.1
		0 - 8	100.0	0.8	1.6	4.3	19.5	45.3	11.0	11.3	6.2
		9 - 11	100.0	4.6	3.3	23.1	22.4	35.4	1.4	7.5	2.3
		12 and over	100.0	39.4	11.2	24.8	10.4	10.8	...	3.3	0.1
Ecuador	1999	Total	100.0	11.0	2.1	14.6	22.6	27.2	6.3	10.1	6.0
		0 - 8	100.0	0.7	0.3	3.3	19.6	34.5	11.8	17.8	12.1
		9 - 12	100.0	4.9	1.1	16.5	27.4	31.2	5.3	9.1	4.6
		13 and over	100.0	37.4	6.5	25.9	16.8	9.3	1.1	2.0	0.9
El Salvador	1999	Total	100.0	10.5	1.6	12.1	21.4	39.9	5.2	6.0	3.2
		0 - 8	100.0	0.2	...	1.9	15.4	53.8	8.9	12.3	7.5
		9 - 12	100.0	1.1	1.0	16.2	30.2	42.1	4.3	3.7	1.3
		13 and over	100.0	52.5	6.1	19.7	10.1	9.5	0.8	0.8	0.5
Guatemala	1998	Total	100.0	18.1	8.2	12.6	13.9	28.4	9.6	6.8	2.3
		0 - 8	100.0	4.2	6.9	3.7	12.4	39.4	17.7	11.9	3.8
		9 - 12	100.0	27.7	8.0	21.5	17.9	19.5	2.3	2.4	0.6
		13 and over	100.0	44.4	14.6	20.0	6.7	11.5	0.1	0.4	2.2
Honduras	1999	Total	100.0	10.5	4.1	11.6	15.6	39.4	5.5	8.3	5.0
		0 - 8	100.0	1.8	1.1	2.0	15.0	52.5	8.7	12.2	6.7
		9 - 11	100.0	8.6	3.3	12.5	22.7	38.0	3.1	8.6	3.3
		12 and over	100.0	27.1	10.1	28.9	13.9	15.9	0.6	0.9	2.6
Mexico	2000	Total	100.0	14.6	1.8	21.7	14.8	31.9	6.2	7.7	1.2
		0 - 8	100.0	1.5	...	6.8	11.3	47.0	15.5	15.3	2.5
		9 - 12	100.0	8.6	0.8	23.7	17.7	36.6	4.7	6.9	1.0
		13 and over	100.0	42.5	6.1	32.6	11.4	5.4	0.1	1.7	0.2
Nicaragua	1998	Total	100.0	3.3	1.9	5.7	23.4	37.0	7.6	12.9	8.4
		0 - 8	100.0	...	0.8	2.2	16.4	43.3	9.6	14.8	12.9
		9 - 11	100.0	...	2.3	10.4	31.2	34.0	6.8	12.4	2.9
		12 and over	100.0	24.6	5.8	11.4	37.6	15.1	...	5.6	...

(Continued)

Table A.12 (concluded)

Country	Year	Educational level	Total	Professionals and specialist workers	Managers	Administrative employees and accountants	Salespersons and shop assistants	Industrial, transport and warehouse labourers	Construction workers	Domestic employees, waiters and guards	Agricultural workers
						Occupation					
Panama	1999	Total	100.0	12.9	5.1	18.8	13.9	35.2	3.7	7.7	2.7
		0 - 8	100.0	1.6	2.4	4.2	11.4	50.1	5.3	15.8	9.2
		9 - 12	100.0	4.3	2.8	18.2	16.4	43.9	4.7	8.3	1.4
		13 and over	100.0	34.7	10.8	30.1	11.7	10.6	1.1	1.0	0.1
Paraguay	1999	Total	100.0	10.0	3.1	19.4	17.0	27.5	4.5	16.2	2.3
		0 - 8	100.0	0.4	0.2	4.1	15.3	41.1	7.1	27.4	4.3
		9 - 12	100.0	4.4	2.5	23.6	21.7	27.9	4.3	14.1	1.7
		13 and over	100.0	36.8	9.2	35.9	10.2	4.7	0.7	2.2	0.3
Peru	1999	Total	100.0	15.7	0.5	9.0	21.9	35.0	3.2	11.3	3.4
		0 - 8	100.0	...	...	1.7	15.0	45.1	4.2	27.0	7.0
		9 - 11	100.0	1.7	...	7.3	27.2	43.4	4.0	12.7	3.8
		12 and over	100.0	42.9	1.5	14.8	17.0	18.5	1.5	2.6	1.4
Dominican Republic	1997	Total	100.0	7.6	0.3	12.7	19.6	42.6	4.1	8.7	4.3
		0 - 8	100.0	0.4	...	2.6	17.1	52.6	6.8	13.7	6.8
		9 - 12	100.0	1.5	0.2	15.3	23.9	45.8	2.8	7.4	3.1
		13 and over	100.0	35.4	1.3	29.7	16.9	14.1	0.9	0.5	1.3
Uruguay	1999	Total	100.0	9.3	2.2	20.1	15.1	33.0	5.4	11.2	3.8
		0 - 8	100.0	1.0	1.0	6.3	12.1	46.2	9.3	17.4	6.7
		9 - 12	100.0	5.8	2.2	23.4	18.9	32.8	4.3	9.9	2.7
		13 and over	100.0	36.8	4.8	37.9	9.6	7.1	0.3	2.5	0.9
Venezuela [a]	1999	Total	100.0	9.3	2.6	30.6	10.1	29.5	8.1	9.7	0.1
		0 - 8	100.0	0.8	0.4	17.9	20.8	35.5	12.3	12.2	0.2
		9 - 11	100.0	4.9	2.0	39.3	2.8	33.5	6.8	10.7	0.1
		12 and over	100.0	34.6	8.3	41.0	1.3	10.3	1.6	2.8	...

Source: ECLAC, based on special tabulations of household survey data from the countries concerned.

[a] National total.

Table A.13
LATIN AMERICA (14 COUNTRIES): PERCENTAGE DISTRIBUTION OF YOUNG PEOPLE
BETWEEN 20 AND 29 YEARS OF AGE WHO WORK 20 OR MORE HOURS PER WEEK,
BY OCCUPATIONAL CATEGORY AND EDUCATIONAL LEVEL, RURAL AREAS

Country	Year	Educational level	Total	Occupation							
				Professionals and specialist workers	Managers	Administrative employees and accountants	Salespersons and shop assistants	Industrial, transport and warehouse labourers	Construction workers	Domestic employees, waiters and guards	Agricultural workers
Bolivia	1999	Total	100.0	5.3	...	0.5	4.9	8.5	4.2	1.2	75.6
		0 - 8	100.0	...	...	0.2	3.6	5.6	2.4	1.2	87.0
		9 - 12	100.0	4.9	...	...	10.3	21.0	11.7	1.6	50.5
		13 and over	100.0	86.0	...	5.8	2.2	3.4	...	...	2.6
Brazil	1999	Total	100.0	3.9	2.2	2.1	4.8	13.6	0.1	8.9	64.4
		0 - 8	100.0	0.8	1.7	0.5	3.8	13.2	...	9.1	70.9
		9 - 11	100.0	17.8	4.2	9.4	10.9	18.2	0.4	8.6	30.4
		12 and over	100.0	38.9	10.9	22.2	7.0	4.0	1.2	6.2	9.6
Chile	2000	Total	100.0	4.1	2.3	4.8	4.9	19.2	5.5	9.8	49.4
		0 - 8	100.0	0.2	1.6	0.4	2.6	15.4	6.0	9.0	64.9
		9 - 12	100.0	3.4	2.7	7.8	7.2	24.6	5.4	10.9	38.0
		13 and over	100.0	32.8	3.9	16.0	7.0	15.5	2.6	9.3	12.9
Colombia	1999	Total	100.0	4.2	0.3	4.3	11.3	11.3	3.2	8.7	56.7
		0 - 8	100.0	0.2	0.1	1.2	7.7	11.7	3.5	7.7	67.8
		9 - 11	100.0	8.0	0.3	12.5	22.3	11.7	2.6	12.9	29.7
		12 and over	100.0	52.8	3.3	13.8	15.4	3.3	...	2.8	8.6
Costa Rica	1999	Total	100.0	5.4	1.7	6.7	9.4	34.9	6.6	7.1	28.1
		0 - 8	100.0	0.5	0.8	2.0	7.1	36.8	8.3	8.1	36.4
		9 - 11	100.0	3.9	1.6	17.9	18.9	40.3	3.4	5.6	8.3
		12 and over	100.0	40.1	8.0	20.0	9.1	13.7	0.7	3.5	5.0
El Salvador	1999	Total	100.0	2.1	0.2	1.9	11.5	31.5	6.7	8.3	37.8
		0 - 8	100.0	0.3	...	0.5	7.3	28.5	7.4	10.6	45.3
		9 - 12	100.0	0.3	0.4	5.5	23.9	43.9	4.7	2.3	19.0
		13 and over	100.0	56.0	2.8	5.5	14.0	7.3	5.7	...	8.8
Guatemala	1998	Total	100.0	3.3	7.6	1.9	4.1	17.7	43.4	2.5	19.4
		0 - 8	100.0	1.3	8.1	0.6	4.0	17.3	45.5	2.8	20.5
		9 - 12	100.0	18.5	2.5	17.6	6.5	23.6	23.0	0.2	8.1
		13 and over	100.0	100.0	...	...	...	...	...	...	...
Honduras	1999	Total	100.0	6.3	0.7	1.3	8.3	17.0	4.5	4.0	57.8
		0 - 8	100.0	1.1	0.3	0.6	7.9	17.6	5.0	4.3	63.1
		9 - 11	100.0	18.8	1.5	1.6	17.1	15.7	0.9	3.1	41.4
		12 and over	100.0	55.6	5.1	8.7	7.7	10.8	1.0	1.2	10.0
Mexico	2000	Total	100.0	4.3	0.4	5.5	11.7	25.4	10.9	8.0	33.8
		0 - 8	100.0	0.4	...	1.7	10.6	18.7	12.8	8.2	47.6
		9 - 12	100.0	4.9	0.7	8.9	12.8	35.9	9.1	8.7	19.1
		13 and over	100.0	41.3	2.8	18.1	13.1	6.8	5.1	0.3	12.6
Nicaragua	1998	Total	100.0	0.9	0.9	0.4	13.0	13.5	3.6	9.2	58.6
		0 - 8	100.0	0.3	1.0	0.3	7.9	13.0	2.7	9.3	65.5
		9 - 11	100.0	0.7	0.9	0.8	33.5	16.5	3.5	9.4	34.7
		12 and over	100.0	10.6	...	...	45.9	15.1	17.1	6.6	4.6
Panama	1999	Total	100.0	6.2	2.5	7.0	12.4	35.1	2.4	10.5	23.9
		0 - 8	100.0	0.5	0.5	0.7	10.3	33.5	1.9	13.1	39.5
		9 - 12	100.0	8.5	4.0	9.2	16.7	42.1	4.0	7.9	7.7
		13 and over	100.0	26.1	7.3	29.5	9.1	20.7	...	6.1	1.1
Paraguay	1999	Total	100.0	6.4	0.4	2.5	7.9	16.1	4.5	7.6	54.7
		0 - 8	100.0	0.4	0.3	0.6	6.0	16.1	4.3	8.0	64.3
		9 - 12	100.0	14.4	1.1	8.6	18.1	20.1	6.6	7.2	24.0
		13 and over	100.0	68.9	...	11.1	3.7	2.5	...	3.1	10.8

(Continued)

Table A.13 (concluded)

Country	Year	Educational level	Total	Occupation							
				Professionals and specialist workers	Managers	Administrative employees and accountants	Salespersons and shop assistants	Industrial, transport and warehouse labourers	Construction workers	Domestic employees, waiters and guards	Agricultural workers
Peru	1999	Total	100.0	2.0	...	0.3	6.6	14.6	2.9	2.1	71.5
		0 - 8	100.0	...	...	...	5.0	10.3	1.9	1.5	81.3
		9 - 11	100.0	0.7	...	1.2	8.8	23.5	5.7	3.5	56.6
		12 and over	100.0	29.3	...	...	12.5	18.5	...	1.6	38.1
Dominican Republic	1997	Total	100.0	2.5	0.2	2.7	13.3	48.6	3.2	5.3	24.2
		0 - 8	100.0	0.6	...	0.3	11.8	48.4	3.7	4.4	30.8
		9 - 12	100.0	0.9	...	7.0	19.9	53.9	2.1	8.1	8.1
		13 and over	100.0	39.7	4.9	19.6	5.2	25.6	...	4.9	...
Simple average for the countries	1999	Total	100.0	4.1	1.4	3.0	8.9	21.9	7.3	6.7	46.9
		0 - 8	100.0	0.5	1.0	0.7	6.8	20.4	7.5	7.0	56.1
		9 - 12	100.0	7.6	1.4	7.7	16.2	27.9	5.9	6.4	26.8
		13 and over	100.0	48.4	3.5	12.2	10.9	10.5	2.4	3.3	8.9

Source: ECLAC, based on special tabulations of household survey data from the countries concerned.

Table A.14
LATIN AMERICA (18 COUNTRIES): AVERAGE INCOME OF YOUNG PEOPLE BETWEEN 20 AND 29 YEARS OF AGE WHO WORK 20 OR MORE HOURS PER WEEK, BY OCCUPATIONAL CATEGORY AND EDUCATIONAL LEVEL, URBAN AREAS
(Multiples of the per capita poverty line)

Country	Year	Educational level	Total	Professionals and specialist workers	Managers	Administrative employees and accountants	Salespersons and shop assistants	Industrial, transport and warehouse labourers	Construction workers	Domestic employees, waiters and guards	Agricultural workers
Argentina	1999	Total	4.5	7.1	9.2	4.4	4.0	4.1	3.8	3.4	3.2
		0 - 8	3.4	...	4.5	3.5	3.2	3.6	3.6	2.9	2.6
		9 - 12	4.3	...	7.0	4.2	4.3	4.4	4.1	3.7	4.1
		13 and over	5.9	7.1	12.1	4.6	4.0	4.1	3.7	3.5	3.8
Bolivia	1999	Total	2.9	4.8	6.0	3.7	2.6	2.3	3.7	1.5	2.2
		0 - 8	2.3	...	5.8	1.5	2.0	2.1	3.8	1.4	2.2
		9 - 12	2.5	2.2	6.0	3.9	2.3	2.1	3.8	1.7	2.0
		13 and over	4.1	4.9	6.1	3.7	4.1	3.7	1.7	1.6	2.7
Brazil	1999	Total	3.4	5.9	7.7	3.6	2.9	2.9	5.5	2.3	1.6
		0 - 8	2.4	2.9	5.9	2.7	2.3	2.7	2.9	1.8	1.5
		9 - 11	3.4	3.3	6.8	3.2	3.1	3.3	5.7	3.0	2.3
		12 and over	7.2	8.1	10.8	5.2	5.1	5.2	7.2	7.3	5.5
Chile	2000	Total	4.9	9.2	10.8	4.1	3.7	3.9	3.9	3.0	3.0
		0 - 8	2.9	4.4	8.2	3.1	2.7	3.0	3.4	2.5	2.6
		9 - 12	3.9	5.8	8.6	3.9	3.7	3.8	4.0	3.0	3.0
		13 and over	7.5	10.2	12.9	4.6	4.2	5.1	5.4	3.8	6.8
Colombia	1999	Total	2.8	4.9	6.3	3.0	2.4	2.4	1.8	2.3	2.8
		0 - 8	2.0	2.5	2.0	2.3	1.7	2.1	1.8	1.9	2.7
		9 - 11	2.5	3.2	4.7	2.6	2.3	2.5	1.9	2.8	2.5
		12 and over	4.6	5.3	6.7	3.7	4.3	3.6	2.1	4.4	4.7
Costa Rica	1999	Total	5.1	7.5	9.5	5.0	4.6	4.5	4.4	2.7	4.3
		0 - 8	3.9	3.8	9.4	4.0	3.9	4.0	4.3	2.1	3.7
		9 - 11	4.7	5.3	6.1	4.5	4.2	5.0	5.6	3.5	6.5
		12 and over	7.1	7.8	10.4	5.6	7.2	5.8	...	3.6	...
Ecuador	1999	Total	2.3	3.6	5.4	3.2	2.0	2.0	1.7	1.4	1.5
		0 - 8	1.5	1.5	2.6	1.6	1.7	1.6	1.7	1.1	1.5
		9 - 12	2.1	2.0	2.8	2.6	1.9	2.3	1.8	1.7	1.4
		13 and over	3.9	4.0	6.4	4.3	3.0	2.5	2.0	2.4	1.0
El Salvador	1999	Total	3.6	5.9	12.4	4.2	3.2	3.1	2.9	2.1	1.6
		0 - 8	2.5	4.1	8.9	2.6	2.6	2.6	2.6	2.0	1.8
		9 - 12	3.5	3.1	10.9	4.0	3.4	3.4	3.4	2.2	1.1
		13 and over	5.7	6.1	13.0	4.8	3.0	4.0	2.9	2.4	...
Guatemala	1998	Total	2.5	3.5	4.7	2.8	2.0	2.1	1.6	0.6	1.8
		0 - 8	1.9	2.3	3.9	1.8	2.3	1.9	1.6	0.6	1.5
		9 - 12	2.6	3.0	4.0	2.8	1.9	2.3	0.8	0.5	1.1
		13 and over	4.6	4.9	7.3	3.5	1.6	4.2	3.4	2.3	4.6
Honduras	1999	Total	2.1	2.9	4.5	2.5	1.9	1.9	1.9	0.9	1.2
		0 - 8	1.5	1.6	2.2	1.5	1.4	1.6	1.8	0.8	0.9
		9 - 11	2.4	2.9	5.4	2.1	2.2	2.8	2.4	0.9	0.5
		12 and over	3.0	3.1	4.8	2.7	2.6	2.6	5.5	2.6	2.9
Mexico	2000	Total	3.0	4.0	14.1	3.3	2.9	2.3	2.4	1.8	2.0
		0 - 8	2.0	2.4	...	2.5	2.2	1.9	2.4	1.5	1.6
		9 - 12	2.7	3.6	26.5	2.8	2.4	2.4	2.5	1.9	2.7
		13 and over	4.7	4.2	10.5	4.5	5.4	2.9	...	3.1	...
Nicaragua	1998	Total	2.8	14.3	8.0	2.6	2.2	2.6	2.3	1.7	1.6
		0 - 8	2.1	...	2.0	2.4	1.9	2.4	2.2	1.6	1.5
		9 - 11	2.7	...	12.5	3.0	2.1	2.8	2.5	2.1	2.4
		12 and over	5.9	14.3	7.8	2.1	2.8	3.7	...	1.8	...

(Continued)

Table A.14 (concluded)

Country	Year	Educational level	Total	Professionals and specialist workers	Managers	Administrative employees and accountants	Salespersons and shop assistants	Industrial, transport and warehouse labourers	Construction workers	Domestic employees, waiters and guards	Agricultural workers
Panama	1999	Total	4.7	7.4	8.2	4.9	4.2	4.0	4.0	3.0	2.7
		0 - 8	3.0	4.9	4.2	3.5	3.0	3.3	3.1	2.1	2.5
		9 - 12	4.1	5.0	5.0	4.0	3.7	4.2	4.4	3.8	2.9
		13 and over	7.0	7.9	10.1	5.9	6.2	5.5	5.1	2.7	9.2
Paraguay	1999	Total	2.9	4.3	9.4	3.0	2.7	2.6	1.9	2.0	1.1
		0 - 8	2.0	2.0	3.5	2.4	2.2	2.2	1.8	1.9	1.3
		9 - 12	2.7	3.2	4.1	2.7	2.8	3.1	2.0	2.2	0.9
		13 and over	4.8	4.6	12.5	3.6	3.8	3.8	2.3	2.7	0.0
Peru	1999	Total	2.0	4.0	17.8	4.2	2.5	2.5	2.4	2.5	1.7
		0 - 8	2.0	...	...	0.9	2.2	1.8	2.5	2.9	1.4
		9 - 11	2.0	3.9	...	2.9	2.4	2.3	2.5	2.2	1.9
		12 and over	4.0	4.1	17.8	5.4	2.9	3.7	1.8	2.7	1.4
Dominican Republic	1997	Total	3.7	7.0	15.6	3.5	3.3	3.5	3.7	2.1	3.2
		0 - 8	3.0	2.8	...	3.8	3.0	3.3	3.2	1.8	3.4
		9 - 12	3.6	5.7	10.8	3.4	3.5	3.8	4.9	2.8	2.7
		13 and over	5.1	7.3	17.3	3.5	3.8	3.8	4.8	...	2.3
Uruguay	1999	Total	3.9	5.2	7.0	4.1	3.6	3.7	3.8	2.8	3.3
		0 - 8	3.2	3.1	4.5	3.6	2.9	3.5	3.6	2.5	3.0
		9 - 12	4.0	4.3	7.7	4.1	3.8	3.9	4.3	3.1	3.5
		13 and over	5.0	5.8	7.0	4.2	4.5	4.9	4.4	4.6	5.7
Venezuela [a]	1999	Total	3.0	4.2	7.1	2.9	1.8	2.8	3.2	2.4	2.8
		0 - 8	2.4	2.3	8.2	2.6	1.7	2.5	2.9	2.1	2.6
		9 - 11	3.0	2.6	7.4	2.9	2.0	2.9	3.5	2.5	3.1
		12 and over	4.1	4.7	6.9	3.3	3.5	3.4	5.4	3.7	5.2

Source: ECLAC, based on special tabulations of household survey data from the countries concerned.

[a] National total.

Table A.15

LATIN AMERICA (14 COUNTRIES): AVERAGE INCOME OF YOUNG PEOPLE BETWEEN 20 AND 29 YEARS OF AGE WHO WORK 20 OR MORE HOURS PER WEEK, BY OCCUPATIONAL CATEGORY AND EDUCATIONAL LEVEL, RURAL AREAS, 1999
(Multiples of the per capita poverty line)

Country	Year	Educational level	Total	Occupation							
				Professionals and specialist workers	Managers	Administrative employees and accountants	Salespersons and shop assistants	Industrial, transport and warehouse labourers	Construction workers	Domestic employees, waiters and guards	Agricultural workers
Bolivia	1999	Total	1.2	3.5	...	3.1	1.9	2.6	4.0	1.8	0.7
		0 - 8	0.9	...	...	4.6	1.9	2.9	2.8	2.1	0.6
		9 - 12	1.8	2.1	...	...	2.2	2.3	5.0	1.0	0.8
		13 and over	3.7	3.8	...	2.3	0.4	...	...	...	8.3
Brazil	1999	Total	1.9	4.0	7.7	3.3	2.5	3.1	4.3	2.0	1.2
		0 - 8	1.6	2.5	5.1	2.8	2.4	3.0	3.7	1.7	1.2
		9 - 11	2.7	2.8	8.5	3.1	2.5	3.4	2.4	2.7	1.5
		12 and over	7.8	8.3	21.0	4.1	4.2	7.7	8.0	8.3	1.2
Chile	2000	Total	4.4	10.9	13.3	5.1	4.2	4.7	4.6	3.3	3.5
		0 - 8	3.5	4.0	4.8	3.8	3.6	4.4	4.4	2.9	3.2
		9 - 12	4.5	5.1	13.8	4.7	4.2	4.6	4.6	3.4	3.9
		13 and over	10.0	14.3	33.5	6.2	5.8	6.7	6.4	4.6	7.2
Colombia	1999	Total	2.7	5.0	5.6	3.7	2.1	2.2	2.4	3.4	2.7
		0 - 8	2.4	2.1	1.8	3.1	1.9	2.0	2.6	1.8	2.6
		9 - 11	3.4	4.1	10.4	3.5	2.1	2.8	1.5	6.7	2.9
		12 and over	4.9	5.8	6.2	5.3	3.0	2.9	...	2.9	3.0
Costa Rica	1999	Total	5.7	9.9	10.5	6.5	5.3	5.8	5.7	3.7	4.8
		0 - 8	5.0	6.0	9.0	6.0	4.8	5.5	5.6	3.4	4.8
		9 - 11	6.3	7.4	7.3	6.1	5.6	7.0	7.3	4.2	4.7
		12 and over	9.1	10.7	12.6	7.6	7.3	6.9	7.0	6.8	8.3
El Salvador	1999	Total	3.3	7.7	5.2	4.6	4.5	3.7	3.6	2.9	2.3
		0 - 8	2.9	2.4	...	4.5	3.3	3.3	3.6	2.9	2.4
		9 - 12	4.2	11.2	5.3	4.3	5.5	4.4	3.8	3.0	2.0
		13 and over	6.4	8.1	5.0	6.4	5.0	5.4	1.8	...	1.5
Guatemala	1998	Total	2.2	3.8	3.9	3.9	1.9	2.1	1.5	0.8	3.0
		0 - 8	2.1	3.5	3.8	1.0	1.8	1.9	1.5	0.8	3.1
		9 - 12	3.2	4.2	6.3	5.0	2.7	3.6	1.0	3.9	1.8
		13 and over	3.2	3.2	...	...	...	...	...	...	...
Honduras	1999	Total	1.8	3.4	3.6	3.0	1.5	2.4	3.3	1.1	1.3
		0 - 8	1.6	2.4	3.0	2.5	1.4	2.3	3.2	1.1	1.3
		9 - 11	1.8	3.0	8.7	2.2	0.9	1.6	3.6	0.6	1.6
		12 and over	3.5	3.7	3.2	3.5	3.0	4.5	10.1	2.0	1.7
Mexico	2000	Total	2.4	4.6	4.6	3.7	2.7	2.8	3.0	2.0	1.5
		0 - 8	1.9	2.2	...	2.3	2.1	2.3	3.2	1.7	1.4
		9 - 12	2.7	3.1	4.2	3.2	2.9	3.0	2.8	2.3	1.9
		13 and over	5.7	6.4	5.2	7.0	6.0	6.4	1.0	5.0	3.2
Nicaragua	1998	Total	2.2	3.2	2.3	6.7	2.5	3.1	3.0	3.3	1.7
		0 - 8	2.1	2.3	2.1	8.1	2.9	2.7	2.6	2.8	1.8
		9 - 11	2.4	2.6	4.1	2.6	1.7	3.5	3.3	6.2	1.4
		12 and over	3.7	3.6	...	...	2.8	7.6	3.8	3.3	...
Panama	1999	Total	4.1	8.9	14.7	5.7	3.3	4.1	3.9	1.8	2.7
		0 - 8	3.0	1.9	4.7	6.3	2.5	4.0	3.3	1.6	2.7
		9 - 12	4.4	7.0	7.7	5.4	3.8	4.4	4.4	2.3	2.9
		13 and over	8.3	11.5	29.9	6.0	4.3	3.8	...	2.1	3.2
Paraguay	1999	Total	1.9	4.3	4.7	4.5	1.5	2.9	3.5	2.1	1.1
		0 - 8	1.6	3.6	4.6	2.0	1.6	2.7	3.4	2.1	1.1
		9 - 12	2.5	4.0	4.8	4.5	1.6	3.6	3.7	1.9	0.5
		13 and over	4.7	4.6	...	6.3	...	0.8	...	4.0	6.3

(Continued)

Table A.15 (concluded)

Country	Year	Educational level	Total	Occupation							
				Professionals and specialist workers	Managers	Administrative employees and accountants	Salespersons and shop assistants	Industrial, transport and warehouse labourers	Construction workers	Domestic employees, waiters and guards	Agricultural workers
Peru	1999	Total	1.0	5.5	...	1.8	2.1	2.8	2.5	2.0	0.9
		0 - 8	1.0	...	...	...	1.6	3.0	2.5	1.8	0.8
		9 - 11	1.0	3.7	...	1.8	3.0	2.8	2.5	2.3	1.2
		12 and over	2.0	5.7	...	...	1.5	1.9	...	0.4	0.7
Dominican Republic	1997	Total	4.1	9.2	11.1	5.6	3.6	4.1	5.3	2.6	3.8
		0 - 8	3.8	5.1	...	3.2	2.9	4.1	5.5	2.8	3.4
		9 - 12	4.6	11.7	...	5.4	5.0	4.2	3.9	2.2	7.9
		13 and over	7.3	9.9	11.1	6.5	2.1	5.0	...	3.1	...
Simple average for the countries	1999	Total	2.8	6.0	7.3	4.4	2.8	3.3	3.6	2.3	2.2
		0 - 8	2.4	3.2	4.3	3.9	2.5	3.2	3.4	2.1	2.2
		9 - 12	3.3	5.1	7.4	4.0	3.1	3.7	3.6	3.1	2.5
		13 and over	5.7	7.1	14.2	5.6	3.8	5.0	5.4	3.9	4.1

Source: ECLAC, based on special tabulations of household survey data from the countries concerned.

Table A.16
LATIN AMERICA (17 COUNTRIES): PER CAPITA PUBLIC SOCIAL EXPENDITURE,
1990-1999
(1997 dollars)

Country	1990-1991	1992-1993	1994-1995	1996-1997	1998-1999
Latin America [a]	360	419	466	499	540
Argentina	1 211	1 447	1 583	1 576	1 687
Bolivia	...	...	121	147	168
Brazil [b]	786	765	932	952	1 011
Chile	440	538	597	719	827
Colombia	158	195	297	403	381
Costa Rica	476	495	536	568	622
El Salvador	...	...	60	70	82
Guatemala	52	65	66	69	107
Honduras	60	67	59	56	57
Mexico	259	333	358	352	402
Nicaragua	48	44	52	47	57
Panama	497	582	606	653	642
Paraguay	56	114	131	149	132
Peru	69	100	140	158	192
Dominican Republic	64	92	100	108	135
Uruguay	888	1 095	1 248	1 358	1 539
Venezuela	337	355	287	318	313

Source: ECLAC, Social Development Division, social expenditure database. With regard to the estimate of consolidated social expenditure for Brazil, see ECLAC, *Social Panorama of Latin America, 2000-2001* (LC/G.2138-P), Santiago, Chile, March 2002. United Nations publication, Sales No. E.01.II.G.141, box IV.1.

[a] Simple average for the countries, excluding Bolivia and El Salvador. If these two countries are included, the average for Latin America is US$ 422 for the biennium 1994-1995, US$ 453 for 1996-1997 and US$ 491 for 1998-1999.
[b] Estimate of consolidated social expenditure.

Table A.17
LATIN AMERICA (17 COUNTRIES): PUBLIC SOCIAL EXPENDITURE AS A
PERCENTAGE OF GROSS DOMESTIC PRODUCT (GDP), 1990-1999

Country	1990-1991	1992-1993	1994-1995	1996-1997	1998-1999
Latin America [a]	10.4	11.4	12.1	12.5	13.1
Argentina	17.7	19.2	21.0	19.8	20.5
Bolivia	...	...	12.4	14.6	16.1
Brazil [b]	18.1	17.7	20.0	19.7	21.0
Chile	13.0	13.6	13.6	14.4	16.0
Colombia [c]	8.0	9.4	11.5	15.3	15.0
Costa Rica	15.7	15.3	16.0	17.0	16.8
El Salvador	...	...	3.3	3.8	4.3
Guatemala	3.4	4.1	4.1	4.2	6.2
Honduras	7.9	8.5	7.7	7.2	7.4
Mexico	6.5	8.1	8.8	8.5	9.1
Nicaragua	10.8	10.6	12.6	11.0	12.7
Panama	18.6	19.5	19.8	20.9	19.4
Paraguay	3.1	6.2	7.0	8.0	7.4
Peru	3.3	4.8	5.8	6.1	6.8
Dominican Republic	4.3	5.9	6.1	6.0	6.6
Uruguay	16.8	18.9	20.3	20.9	22.8
Venezuela	9.0	8.9	7.6	8.3	8.6

Source: ECLAC, Social Development Division, social expenditure database. With regard to the estimate of consolidated social expenditure for Brazil, see ECLAC, *Social Panorama of Latin America, 2000-2001* (LC/G.2138-P), Santiago, Chile, March 2002. United Nations publication, Sales No. E.01.II.G.141, box IV.1.

[a] Simple average for the countries, excluding Bolivia and El Salvador. If these two countries are included, the average for Latin America is 11.6% for the biennium 1994-1995, 12.1% for 1996-1997 and 12.7% for 1998-1999.
[b] Estimate of consolidated social expenditure.
[c] As of 1994, the figures were calculated using the new gross domestic product series at current prices.

Table A.18

LATIN AMERICA (8 COUNTRIES): DISTRIBUTION OF SOCIAL EXPENDITURE BY HOUSEHOLD INCOME QUINTILES [a]

	Distribution of social expenditure by quintile					Gini coefficient[b]	Index of progressiveness of social expenditure[c]
	I (poorest)	II	III	IV	V (richest)		
ARGENTINA 1991 [d]							
Education	32.5	18.7	21.1	15.4	12.4	-0.17	3.69
Primary	42.7	21.0	19.9	11.9	4.5	-0.34	4.60
Secondary	28.7	19.0	26.0	15.6	10.7	-0.16	3.45
Tertiary	8.3	11.1	16.0	25.8	38.8	0.30	1.40
Health and nutrition	38.7	16.6	25.5	14.8	4.5	-0.28	3.99
Housing and other	20.5	18.0	25.8	19.0	16.7	-0.03	2.77
Social security	11.0	17.2	20.9	22.5	28.4	0.16	2.04
Social expenditure excluding social security	33.1	17.9	23.0	15.6	10.3	-0.19	3.68
Social expenditure including social security	21.1	17.5	21.9	19.3	20.1	-0.001	2.79
Income distribution [e]	5.3	8.6	14.1	21.4	50.6	0.41	
BOLIVIA 1990							
Education	32.0	24.3	20.0	14.8	8.9	-0.22	4.66
Primary and secondary	36.6	26.3	19.3	12.3	5.5	-0.30	5.21
Tertiary	12.4	15.5	22.9	25.8	23.4	0.13	2.31
Health and nutrition	15.2	14.7	24.4	24.4	21.3	0.09	2.48
Housing and other	7.8	11.1	14.7	20.6	45.8	0.34	1.56
Social security	13.5	19.9	22.4	19.0	25.2	0.09	2.76
Social expenditure excluding social security	25.8	20.5	19.6	16.9	17.2	-0.08	3.83
Social expenditure including social security	23.5	20.4	20.2	17.3	18.7	-0.05	3.63
Income distribution [e]	3.4	8.7	13.1	20.5	54.3	0.45	
BRAZIL 1994 [f]							
Primary education	30.1	27.3	21.6	14.3	6.8	-0.24	4.34
Health and nutrition	31.5	26.5	19.5	14.2	8.3	-0.23	4.38
Housing and other	30.8	26.9	20.6	14.2	7.5	-0.24	4.36
Social security	42.0	10.1	13.5	15.1	19.4	-0.16	3.94
Social expenditure including social security	33.8	22.1	18.1	14.8	11.3	-0.21	4.22
Income distribution [e]	4.5	8.8	11.8	19.5	55.4	0.45	
CHILE 1996							
Education	34.0	26.1	19.4	14.0	6.5	-0.27	5.05
Primary	38.2	26.3	17.6	12.5	5.3	-0.32	5.42
Secondary	26.5	24.7	22.2	17.6	9.1	-0.17	4.30
Tertiary	6.3	16.3	37.9	20.5	19.0	0.12	1.90
Health and nutrition	30.9	23.2	22.2	16.5	7.2	-0.22	4.55
Housing and other	37.3	27.5	20.3	11.2	3.8	-0.33	5.45
Social security	4.0	9.0	15.0	25.0	47.0	0.41	1.09
Social expenditure excluding social security	33.3	25.0	20.5	14.4	6.8	-0.25	4.90
Social expenditure including social security	16.0	16.0	17.0	21.0	30.0	0.13	2.69
Income distribution [e]	3.9	8.0	11.8	19.2	57.1	0.47	
COLOMBIA 1997							
Education	21.4	21.2	21.5	18.1	17.6	-0.04	3.40
Primary	35.9	28.7	21.2	10.2	4.1	-0.33	5.15
Secondary	24.9	26.8	24.4	16.6	7.3	-0.18	4.12
Tertiary	3.4	8.0	19.1	27.6	41.6	0.39	0.91
Health and nutrition	17.5	19.7	22.2	20.7	19.7	0.02	2.97
Social expenditure excluding social security	27.0	25.0	21.0	17.0	10.0	-0.17	4.15
Social expenditure including social security	23.0	23.0	20.0	18.0	15.0	-0.07	3.67
Income distribution [e]	3.9	8.7	12.9	19.7	54.9	0.45	

(Continued)

Table A.18 (concluded)

	Distribution of social expenditure by quintile					Gini coefficient[b]	Index of progressiveness of social expenditure[c]
	I (poorest)	II	III	IV	V (richest)		
COSTA RICA 1986							
Education	15.7	18.4	19.6	23.8	22.5	0.08	2.04
Primary	30.0	27.0	22.0	13.0	8.0	-0.23	3.40
Secondary	17.8	21.4	23.1	21.2	16.5	-0.01	2.34
Tertiary	1.7	9.1	15.5	35.0	38.7	0.40	0.65
Health and nutrition	27.7	23.6	24.1	13.9	10.7	-0.17	3.06
Social security	7.1	13.2	12.0	23.1	44.6	0.34	1.21
Social expenditure excluding social security	22.1	21.2	22.0	18.5	16.2	-0.06	2.58
Social expenditure including social security	17.6	18.8	19.0	19.9	24.8	0.06	2.17
Income distribution[e]	5.1	11.6	16.7	24.5	42.0	0.35	
ECUADOR 1994							
Education	26.5	31.8	18.5	12.8	10.4	-0.20	3.74
Primary	37.5	25.6	18.2	10.8	7.9	-0.30	4.04
Secondary	26.7	34.5	17.3	15.6	5.9	-0.24	3.92
Tertiary	22.3	32.8	18.8	12.1	14.0	-0.15	3.53
Health and nutrition	18.8	41.9	16.0	16.3	7.0	-0.20	3.89
Social expenditure excluding social security	24.5	30.3	18.5	14.4	12.2	-0.16	3.51
Income distribution[e]	5.0	10.6	15.9	22.2	46.3	0.38	
URUGUAY 1993							
Total education	33.2	21.3	16.5	14.7	14.3	-0.18	3.03
Primary	51.6	22.2	12.7	9.9	3.7	-0.43	4.10
Secondary	30.3	28.9	17.6	14.2	9.0	-0.23	3.30
Tertiary	5.4	7.2	21.4	24.3	41.7	0.36	0.70
Health and nutrition	34.9	19.9	22.1	13.2	10.0	-0.23	3.05
Housing and other	14.1	17.2	13.6	25.3	29.8	0.16	1.74
Social security	12.4	16.2	20.5	20.1	30.8	0.16	1.59
Social expenditure excluding social security	31.8	20.1	19.1	15.2	13.9	-0.16	2.88
Social expenditure including social security	19.6	17.6	20.0	18.3	24.5	0.04	2.07
Income distribution[e]	7.3	10.7	13.3	23.8	44.9	0.35	
Unweighted average							
Total education						-0.14	3.66
Primary						-0.31	4.44
Secondary						-0.17	3.57
Tertiary						0.22	1.63
Health and nutrition						-0.15	3.54
Housing and other						-0.02	3.18
Social security						0.17	2.11
Social expenditure excluding social security						-0.15	3.65
Social expenditure including social security						-0.01	3.03

Source: ECLAC, on the basis of national studies. With regard to social expenditure including social security in Chile, and to social expenditure including and excluding social security in Colombia, see ECLAC, *Social Panorama of Latin America, 1994* (LC/G.1844), Santiago, Chile, November 1994, p. 65.

[a] Refers to quintiles of households ranked according to their per capita income.
[b] Special calculation based on five categories of expenditure.
[c] Refers to the quotient between the proportion of social expenditure items earmarked for households in the poorest 40% of the population and their share of primary income distribution.
[d] Greater Buenos Aires.
[e] Refers to the distribution of households ranked according to their autonomous per capita income. Autonomous income is the sum of income received by individuals after deduction of social security contributions, income tax and monetary subsidies provided by the State. For purposes of comparison, the Gini coefficient of autonomous income distribution was calculated on the basis of household quintiles.
[f] Refers to São Paulo. In Brazil, social security expenditure includes pensions only.

Table A.19

LATIN AMERICA (15 COUNTRIES):[a] LEVEL AND TRENDS OF SOCIAL EXPENDITURE, BY SECTOR, IN THE 1990s

Countries	Education		Health and nutrition		Social security		Housing, water, sanitation and other	
	Per capita social expenditure in 1998-1999 (in 1997 dollars)	Absolute variation in relation to 1990-1991	Per capita social expenditure in 1998-1999 (in 1997 dollars)	Absolute variation in relation to 1990-1991	Per capita social expenditure in 1998-1999 (in 1997 dollars)	Absolute variation in relation to 1990-1991	Per capita social expenditure in 1998-1999 (in 1997 dollars)	Absolute variation in relation to 1990-1991
Simple average	137	51	111	28	243	91	49	10
Argentina	383	157	380	109	719	150	206	62
Brazil [b]	187	26	163	8	554	203	107	-11
Chile	202	115	145	76	389	154	92	45
Colombia	120	58	104	81	132	72	26	14
Costa Rica	163	48	181	31	216	68	63	1
Guatemala	40	16	22	8	16	4	30	28
Honduras	32	-1	16	-4	0	-1	10	4
Mexico	167	63	93	-26	103	92	40	14
Nicaragua	26	4	20	0	0	0	12	6
Panama	198	73	223	60	179	24	42	-11
Paraguay	66	44	19	14	46	25	2	-6
Peru	62	34	38	23	80	57	14	11
Dominican Republic	57	40	31	16	16	10	31	11
Uruguay	218	88	187	34	1 101	511	33	17
Venezuela	140	11	49	-8	94	5	31	-31

Source: ECLAC, Social Development Division, social expenditure database. With regard to the estimate of consolidated social expenditure for Brazil, see ECLAC, *Social Panorama of Latin America, 2000-2001* (LC/G.2138-P), Santiago, Chile, March 2002. United Nations publication, Sales No. E.01.II.G.141, box IV.1.

[a] Excludes Bolivia and El Salvador. For these countries, information is available only from 1995 onward and from 1994 onward, respectively.
[b] Estimate of consolidated social expenditure. The average for the biennium 1998-1999 refers to the figure for 1998.

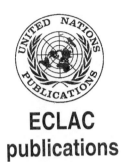

ECLAC
publications

ECONOMIC COMMISSION FOR LATIN AMERICA
AND THE CARIBBEAN
Casilla 179-D   Santiago, Chile

Publications may be accessed at: www.eclac.cl/publicaciones

CEPAL Review

CEPAL Review first appeared in 1976 as part of the Publications Programme of the Economic Commission for Latin America and the Caribbean, its aim being to make a contribution to the study of the economic and social development problems of the region. The views expressed in signed articles, including those by Secretariat staff members, are those of the authors and therefore do not necessarily reflect the point of view of the Organization.

CEPAL Review is published in Spanish and English versions three times a year.

Annual subscription costs for 2003 are US$ 30 for the Spanish version and US$ 35 for the English version. The price of single issues is US$ 15 in both cases.

The cost of a two-year subscription (2002-2003) is US$ 50 for Spanish-language version and US$ 60 for English.

Revista de la CEPAL, número extraordinario: CEPAL CINCUENTA AÑOS, reflexiones sobre América Latina y el Caribe, 1998, 376 p. (out of stock)

Annual reports
Issues for previous years also available

- *Panorama social de América Latina, 2001-2002,* 272 p.
  Social Panorama of Latin America, 2001-2002, 272 p.

- *Balance preliminar de las economías de América Latina y el Caribe, 2002,* 125 p.
  Preliminary Overview of the Economies of Latin America and the Caribbean, 2002, 125 p.

- *Estudio económico de América Latina y el Caribe 2002-2003,* forthcoming.
  Economic Survey of Latin America and the Caribbean 2001-2002, 295 p.

- *Situación y perspectivas, estudio económico de América Latina y el Caribe 2002-2003,* 46 p.
  Current conditions and outlook, Economic Survey of Latin America and the Caribbean 2002-2003, 46 p.

- Anuario estadístico de América Latina y el Caribe /
  Statistical Yearbook for Latin America and the Caribbean (bilingual). *2002, 762 p.*

- La inversión extranjera en América Latina y el Caribe, 2002, 170 p.
  Foreign investment of Latin America and the Caribbean, 2002, 158 p.

- Panorama de la inserción internacional de América Latina y el Caribe, 2001-2002, 240 p.
  Latin America and the Caribbean in the World Economy, 2001-2002, 238 p.

Libros de la CEPAL

76 *A decade of Light and Shadow. Latin America and the Caribbean in the 1990s*, 2003, 366 p.
76 *Une décennie d'ombres et de lumières. L'Amérique latine et les Caraibes dans les années 90,* 2003, 401 p.
74 Mercados de tierras agrícolas en América Latina y el Caribe: una realidad incompleta, Pedro Tejo (compilador), 2003, 416 p.
73 Contaminación atmosférica y conciencia ciudadana, 2003. Daniela Simioni (Compiladora), 260 p.
72 Los caminos hacia una sociedad de la información en América Latina y el Caribe, 2003, 139 p.
72 **Road maps towards an information society in Latin America and the Caribbean**, 2003, 130 p.
71 Capital social y reducción de la pobreza en América Latina y el Caribe. En busca de un nuevo paradigma, 2003, Raúl Atria y Marcelo Siles, Editors, CEPAL/Michigan State University, 590 p.
70 **Meeting the Millennium Poverty Reduction Targets in Latin America and the Caribbean**, 2002, ECLAC/IPEA/UNDP, 70 p.
69 El capital social campesino en la gestión del desarrollo rural. Díadas, equipos, puentes y escaleras, 2002, John Durston, 156 p.
68 La sostenibilidad del desarrollo en América Latina y el Caribe: desafíos y oportunidades, 2002, 251 p.
68 **The sustainability of development in Latin America and the Caribbean: challenges and opportunities**, 2002, 248 p.
67 **Growth with stability, financing for development in the new international context**, 2002, 178 p.
66 **Economic reforms, growth and employment. Labour markets in Latin America and the Caribbean**, 2001, Jürgen Weller, 205 p.
65 **The income distribution problem in Latin America and the Caribbean**, 2001, Samuel Morley, 169 p.
64 **Structural reforms, productivity and technological change in Latin America**, 2001, Jorge Katz, 143 p.
63 **Investment and economic reforms in Latin America**, 2001, Graciela Moguillansky y Ricardo Bielschowsky, 186 p.
62 **Equity, development and citizenship** (abridged edition), 2001, 86 p.
62 L'équité, le développement et la citoyenneté. Version condensée, 2001, 110 p.
61 Apertura económica y (des)encadenamientos productivos- Reflexiones sobre el complejo lácteo en América Latina, 2001, Martine Dirven (compiladora), 396 p.
60 **A territorial perspective: Towards the consolidation of human settlements in Latin America and the Caribbean**, 2001, 157 p.

59 *Juventud, población y desarrollo en América Latina y el Caribe. Problemas, oportunidades y desafíos,* 2001, 457 p.
58 *La dimensión ambiental en el desarrollo de América Latina,* 2001, 265 p.
57 *Las mujeres chilenas en los noventa. Hablan las cifras,* 2000, 213 p.
56 *Protagonismo juvenil en proyectos locales: lecciones del cono sur,* 2001, 170 p.
55 **Financial globalization and the emerging economies,** José Antonio Ocampo, Stefano Zamagni, Ricardo Ffrench-Davis y Carlo Pietrobelli, 2000, 328 p.
54 *La CEPAL en sus 50 años. Notas de un seminario conmemorativo,* 2000, 149 p.
53 *Transformaciones recientes en el sector agropecuario brasileño, lo que muestran los censos,* M. Beatriz de A. David, Philippe Waniez, Violette Brustlein, Enali M. De Biaggi, Paula de Andrade Rollo y Monica dos Santos Rodrigues, 1999, 127 p.
52 *Un examen de la migración internacional en la Comunidad Andina,* 1999, 114 p.
51 *Nuevas políticas comerciales en América Latina y Asia. Algunos casos nacionales,* 1999, 583 p.
50 *Privatización portuaria: bases, alternativas y consecuencias,* Larry Burkhalter, 1999, 248 p.
49 *Teorías y metáforas sobre el desarrollo territorial,* Sergio Boisier, 1999, 113 p.
48 *Las dimensiones sociales de la integración regional en América Latina,* Rolando Franco y Armando Di Filippo, compiladores, 1999, 223 p.
47 *El pacto fiscal. Fortalezas, debilidades, desafíos,* 1998, 280 p. (out of stock)
47 **The fiscal covenant. Strenghts, weaknesses, challenges,** 1998, 290 p.
46 *Agroindustria y pequeña agricultura: vínculos, potencialidades y oportunidades comerciales,* 1998, 166 p.
45 *La grieta de las drogas. Desintegración social y políticas públicas en América Latina,* 1997, 218 p.
44 *La brecha de la equidad. América Latina, el Caribe y la Cumbre Social,* 1997, 218 p.
44 **The equity Gap. Latin America, the Caribbean and the Social Summit,** 1997, 218 p.
43 *Quince años de desempeño económico. América Latina y el Caribe, 1980-1995,* 1996, 127 p.
43 **The economic experience of the last fifteen years. Latin America and the Caribbean, 1980-1995,** 1996, 125 p.
42 *Fortalecer el desarrollo. Interacciones entre macro y micro-economía,* 1996, 116 p.
42 **Strengthening development. The interplay of macro- and microeconomics,** 1996, 116 p.
41 *Las relaciones económicas entre América Latina y la Unión Europea: el papel de los servicios exteriores,* 1996, 395 p.
40 *América Latina y el Caribe: políticas para mejorar la inserción en la economía mundial, 1995,* 314 p. (out of stock)
40 **Latin America and the Caribbean: policies to improve linkages with the global economy,** 1995, 308 p.
39 *El regionalismo abierto en América Latina y el Caribe. La integración económica en servicio de la transformación tecnológica,* 1994, 120 p.
39 **Open regionalism in Latin America and the Caribbean. Economic integration as a contribution to changing productions patterns with social equity,** 1994, 103 p.
38 *Imágenes sociales de la modernización y la transformación tecnológica,* 1995, 198 p.
37 *Familia y futuro: un programa regional en América Latina y el Caribe,* 1994, 137 p.
37 **Family and future: a regional programme in Latin America and the Caribbean,** 1994, 123 p.
36 *Cambios en el perfil de las familias: la experiencia regional,* 1993, 434 p.
35 *Población, equidad y transformación productiva,* 1993, 2ª ed. 1993, 158 p. (out of stock)
35 **Population, social equity and changing production patterns,** 1993, 153 p.
34 *Ensayos sobre coordinación de políticas macroeconómicas,* 1992, 249 p.

Recent co-publications

On occasion ECLAC concludes agreements for the co-publication of texts that may be of special interest to other international organizations or to publishing houses. In the latter case, the publishing houses have exclusive sales and distribution rights.

El desarrollo de complejos forestales en América Latina, Néstor Bercovich y Jorge Katz (editores), CEPAL/Alfaomega, 2003

Territorio y competitividad en la agroindustria en México. Condiciones y propuestas de política para los clusters *del limón mexicano en Colima y la piña en Veracruz,* Enrique Dussel Peters, CEPALPlaza y Valdés, 2002

Capital social rural. Experiencias de México y Centroamérica, Margarita Flores y Fernando Rello, CEPAL/ Plaza y Valdés, 2002.

Eqüidade, desenvolvimento e cidadania, José Antonio Ocampo, CEPAL/Editor Campus, 2002.

Crescimento, emprego e eqüidade; O Impacto das Reformas Econômicas na América Latina e Caribe, Barbara Stallings e Wilson Peres, CEPAL/Editor Campus, 2002.

Crescer com Estabilidade, O financiamento do desenvolvimento no novo contexto internacional, José Antonio Ocampo, CEPAL/Editora Campus, 2002.

Pequeñas y medianas empresas industriales en América Latina y el Caribe, Wilson Peres y Giovanni Stumpo (coordinadores), CEPAL/Siglo XXI, México.

Aglomeraciones mineras y desarrollo local en América Latina, Rudolf M. Buitelaar (compilador), CEPAL/Alfaomega, Colombia, 2002.

Panorama de la agricultura en América Latina y el Caribe 1990-2000 / Survey of Agriculture in Latin America and the Caribbean 1990-2000, CEPAL/IICA, 2002.

Reformas, crecimiento y políticas sociales en Chile desde 1973, Ricardo Ffrench-Davis y Barbara Stallings (editores), CEPAL/LOM Ediciones, 2001.

Financial Crises in 'Successful' Emerging Economies, Ricardo Ffrench-Davis (editor), CEPAL/ Brookings Institution Press, 2001.

Crecer con estabilidad. El financiamiento del desarrollo en un nuevo contexto internacional, José Antonio Ocampo (coordinador), CEPAL/Alfaomega, Colombia, 2001.

CLAROSCUROS, integración exitosa de las pequeñas y medianas empresas en México, Enrique Dussel Peters (coordinador), CEPAL/JUS, México, 2001.

Sociología del desarrollo, políticas sociales y democracia, Rolando Franco (coordinador), CEPAL/Siglo XXI, México, 2001.

Crisis financieras en países exitosos, Ricardo Ffrench-Davis (compilador), CEPAL/McGraw Hill, Santiago, 2001.

Una década de luces y sombras. América Latina y el Caribe en los noventa, CEPAL/Alfaomega, Colombia, 2001.

Desarrollo Rural en América Latina y el Caribe, Beatriz David, CEPAL/Alfaomega, Colombia, 2001.

Equidad, desarrollo y ciudadanía, Tomos I, II y III, CEPAL/Alfaomega, Colombia, 2000.

La distribución del ingreso en América Latina y el Caribe, Samuel Morley, CEPAL/Fondo de Cultura Económica, Santiago, 2000.

Inversión y reformas económicas en América Latina, Graciela Moguillansky y Ricardo Bielschowsky, CEPAL/ Fondo de Cultura Económica, Santiago, 2000.

Reformas estructurales, productividad y conducta tecnológica en América Latina, Jorge Katz, CEPAL/ Fondo de Cultura Económica, Santiago, 2000.

Reformas económicas, crecimiento y empleo. Los mercados de trabajo en América Latina y el Caribe, Jürgen Weller, CEPAL/Fondo de Cultura Económica, Santiago, 2000.

Crecimiento, empleo y equidad. El impacto de las reformas económicas en América Latina y el Caribe, Barbara Stallings y Wilson Peres, CEPAL/Fondo de Cultura Económica, Santiago, 2000.

Growth, employment, and equity. The impact of the Economic Reforms in Latin America and the Caribbean, Barbara Stallings and Wilson Peres, CEPAL/Brookings Institution Press, Washington, D.C., 2000.

Cinqüenta anos de pensamento na CEPAL, Tomos I y II, Ricardo Bielschowsky, CEPAL /RECORD/ COFECOM, Brasil, 2000.

Integración regional, desarrollo y equidad, Armando Di Filippo y Rolando Franco, CEPAL/Siglo XXI, México, 2000.

Ensayo sobre el financiamiento de la seguridad social en salud, Tomos I y II, Daniel Titelman y Andras Uthoff, CEPAL/Fondo de Cultura Económica, Chile, 2000.

Brasil uma década em transição, Renato Baumann, CEPAL/ CAMPUS, Brasil, 2000.

El gran eslabón: educación y desarrollo en el umbral del siglo XXI, Martín Hopenhayn y Ernesto Ottone, CEPAL/Fondo de Cultura Económica, Argentina, 1999.

La modernidad problemática: cuatro ensayos sobre el desarrollo Latinoamericano, Ernesto Ottone, CEPAL/JUS, México, 2000.

La inversión en Chile ¿El fin de un ciclo de expansión?, Graciela Mouguillansky, CEPAL/Fondo de Cultura Económica, Santiago, 1999.

La reforma del sistema financiero internacional: un debate en marcha, José Antonio Ocampo, CEPAL/ Fondo de Cultura Económica, Santiago, 1999.

Macroeconomía, comercio y finanzas para reformar las reformas en América Latina, Ricardo Ffrench Davis, CEPAL/Mc Graw-Hill, Santiago, 1999.

Cincuenta años de pensamiento en la CEPAL: textos seleccionados, dos volúmenes, CEPAL/Fondo de Cultura Económica, Santiago, 1998.

Grandes empresas y grupos industriales latinoamericanos, Wilson Peres (coordinador), CEPAL/Siglo XXI, Buenos Aires, 1998.

Flujos de Capital e Inversión Productiva. Lecciones para América Latina, Ricardo Ffrench-Davis-Helmut Reisen (compiladores), CEPAL/Mc Graw Hill, Santiago, 1997.

Estrategias empresariales en tiempos de cambio, Bernardo Kosacoff (editor), CEPAL/Universidad Nacional de Quilmes, Argentina, 1998.

La Igualdad de los Modernos: reflexiones acerca de la realización de los derechos económicos, sociales y culturales en América Latina, CEPAL/IIDH, Costa Rica, 1997.

La Economía Cubana. Reformas estructurales y desempeño en los noventa, Comisión Económica para América Latina y el Caribe. CEPAL/Fondo de Cultura Económica, México, 1997.

Políticas para mejorar la inserción en la economía mundial. América Latina y El Caribe, CEPAL/Fondo de Cultura Económica, Santiago, 1997.

América Latina y el Caribe quince años después. De la década perdida a la transformación económica 1980-1995, CEPAL/Fondo de Cultura Económica, Santiago, 1996.

Tendências econômicas e sociais na América Latina e no Caribe/ Economic and social trends in Latin America and the Caribbean / Tendencias económicas y sociales en América Latina y el Caribe, CEPAL/IBGE/CARECON RIO, Brasil, 1996.

Hacia un nuevo modelo de organización mundial. El sector manufacturero argentino en los años noventa, Jorge Katz, Roberto Bisang, Gustavo Burachick (editores), CEPAL/IDRC/Alianza Editorial, Buenos Aires, 1996.

Las nuevas corrientes financieras hacia América Latina: Fuentes, efectos y políticas, Ricardo Ffrench-Davis y Stephany Griffith-Jones (compiladores), México, CEPAL/Fondo de Cultura Económica, primera edición, 1995.

Cuadernos de la CEPAL

87 Congestión de tránsito. El problema y cómo enfrentarlo, 2003, 194 p.

86 Industria, medio ambiente en México y Centroamérica. Un reto de supervivencia, 2001, 182 p.

85 Centroamérica, México y República Dominicana: maquila y transformación productiva, 1999, 190 p.

84 El régimen de contratación petrolera de América Latina en la década de los noventa, 1998, 134 p.

83 Temas y desafíos de las políticas de población en los años noventa en América Latina y el Caribe, 1998, 268 p.

82 **A dinámica do Setor Saúde no Brasil**, 1997, 220 p.

81 La apertura económica y el desarrollo agrícola en América Latina y el Caribe, 1997, 136 p.

80 Evolución del gasto público social en América Latina: 1980-1995, 1998, 200 p.

Cuadernos Estadísticos de la CEPAL

Estudios e Informes de la CEPAL

79 *La industria de bienes de capital en América Latina y el Caribe: su desarrollo en un marco de cooperación regional*, 1991, 235 p.
78 *La apertura financiera en Chile y el comportamiento de los bancos transnacionales*, 1990, 132 p.
77 *Los recursos hídricos de América Latina y del Caribe: planificación, desastres naturales y contaminación*, 1990, 266 p.
77 **The water resources of Latin America and the Caribbean–planning, hazards and pollution**, 1990, 252 p.

Serie INFOPLAN: Temas Especiales del Desarrollo

13 *Políticas sociales: resúmenes de documentos II*, 1997, 80 p.
12 *Gestión de la información: reseñas de documentos*, 1996, 152 p.
11 *Modernización del Estado: resúmenes de documentos*, 1995, 75 p.
10 *Políticas sociales: resúmenes de documentos*, 1995, 95 p.
 9 *MERCOSUR: resúmenes de documentos*, 1993, 219 p.
 8 *Reseñas de documentos sobre desarrollo ambientalmente sustentable*, 1992, 217 p. (out of stock)
 7 *Documentos sobre privatización con énfasis en América Latina*, 1991, 82 p.

Boletín demográfico/Demographic Bulletin (bilingual)

Bilingual publication (Spanish and English) proving up–to–date estimates and projections of the populations of the Latin American and Caribbean countries. Also includes various demographic indicators of interest such as fertility and mortality rates, life expectancy, measures of population distribution, etc.

Published since 1968, the Bulletin appears twice a year in January and July.

Annual Subscription: US$ 20.00 Per issue: US$ 15.00

Notas de población

Specialized journal which publishes articles and reports on recent studies of demographic dynamics in the region, in Spanish with abstracts in Spanish and English. Also includes information on scientific and professional activities in the field of population.

Published since 1973, the journal appears twice a year in June and December.

Annual Subscription: US$ 20.00 Per issue: US$ 12.00

Series de la CEPAL

Comercio internacional
Desarrollo productivo
Estudios estadísticos y prospectivos
Financiamiento del desarrollo
Gestión pública
Información y desarrollo
Manuales
Medio ambiente y desarrollo
Población y desarrollo
Política fiscal
Políticas sociales
Recursos naturales e infraestructura
Seminarios y conferencias
Temas de coyuntura
Macroeconomía del desarrollo
Estudios y perspectivas regionales
Informes y estudios especiales

A complete listing is available at: www.eclac.cl/publicaciones

Las publicaciones de la Comisión Económica para América Latina y el Caribe (CEPAL) y las
del Instituto Latinoamericano y del Caribe de Planificación Económica y Social (ILPES) se pueden
adquirir a los distribuidores locales o directamente a través de:

Publicaciones de las Naciones Unidas
Sección de Ventas – DC-2-0853
Fax (212)963-3489
E-mail: publications@un.org
Nueva York, NY, 10017
Estados Unidos de América

Publicaciones de las Naciones Unidas
Sección de Ventas, Fax (22)917-0027
Palais des Nations
1211 Ginebra 10, Suiza

Unidad de Distribución
CEPAL – Casilla 179-D
Fax (562)208-1946
E-mail: publications@eclac.cl
Santiago de Chile

Publications of the Economic Commission for Latin America and the Caribbean (ECLAC) and those
of the Latin American and the Caribbean Institute for Economic and Social Planning (ILPES) can be
ordered from your local distributor or directly through:

United Nations Publications
Sales Sections, DC-2-0853
Fax (212)963-3489
E-mail: publications@un.org
New York, NY, 10017
USA

United Nations Publications
Sales Sections, Fax (22)917-0027
Palais des Nations
1211 Geneve 10, Switzerland

Distribution Unit
CEPAL – Casilla 179-D
Fax (562)208-1946
E-mail: publications@eclac.cl
Santiago, Chile